W9-CHK-593

"This book has three things I'm very interested in: eighteenth-century Scottish church history, doctrinal clarity on the gospel, and learning from Sinclair Ferguson. As fascinating as this work is as a piece of historical analysis, it is even more important as a careful biblical and theological guide to the always-relevant controversies surrounding legalism, antinomianism, and assurance. I'm thankful Ferguson has put his scholarly mind and pastoral heart to work on such an important topic."

Kevin DeYoung, Senior Pastor, University Reformed Church, East Lansing, Michigan

"This book could not come at a better time or from a better source. Sinclair Ferguson brings to life a very important controversy from the past to shed light on contemporary debates. But *The Whole Christ* is more than a deeply informed survey of the Marrow Controversy. It is the highest-quality pastoral wisdom and doctrinal reflection on the most central issue in any age."

Michael Horton, J. Gresham Machen Professor of Systematic Theology and Apologetics, Westminster Seminary California; author, *Calvin on the Christian Life*

"I know of no one other than Sinclair Ferguson who has the capacity, patience, and skill to unearth an ancient debate, set in a Scottish village with an unpronounceable name, and show its compelling relevance to gospel preaching and Christian living. This may be Sinclair's best and most important book. Take up and read!"

Alistair Begg, Senior Pastor, Parkside Church, Chagrin Falls, Ohio

"Sinclair Ferguson scratches through the surface definitions of legalism and antinomianism to reveal the marrow, the whole Christ. When we are offered the whole Christ in the gospel, we do not want to settle for anything that undermines the greatness and power of God's grace. Both pastors and lay people will benefit from reading this historical, theological, and practical book."

Aimee Byrd, author, *Housewife Theologian* and *Theological Fitness*

"I marvel at Sinclair Ferguson's grasp of historical detail, but I praise God more for Sinclair's love of and zeal for gospel clarity. The grace that saves our souls and enables our obedience is defined, distinguished, and treasured in this discussion about keeping the proclamation of the gospel free from human error."

Bryan Chapell, President Emeritus, Covenant Theological Seminary; Senior Pastor, Grace Presbyterian Church, Peoria, Illinois

"It is no exaggeration to insist that the issue dealt with in this book is more important than any other that one might suggest. For, as Ferguson makes all too clear, the issue is the very definition of the gospel itself. The errors of antinomianism and legalism lie ready to allure unwary hucksters content with mere slogans and rhetoric. I can think of no one I trust more to explore and examine this vital subject than Sinclair Ferguson. For my part, this is one of the most important and definitive books I have read in over four decades."

Derek W. H. Thomas, Senior Minister, First Presbyterian Church, Columbia, South Carolina; Robert Strong Professor of Systematic and Pastoral Theology, Reformed Theological Seminary, Atlanta, Georgia

"In a day when there is so much confusion about sanctification, Sinclair Ferguson cuts through all the noise and provides us with beautiful clarity on this glorious doctrine of the Christian faith. Without hesitation, this will be the first book I recommend to those who want to understand the history and theology of this most precious doctrine."

Burk Parsons, Copastor, Saint Andrew's Chapel, Sanford, Florida; Editor, *Tabletalk* magazine

"This great book takes up the perennial issue of how grace and works relate to each other in our salvation. Ferguson begins with an old debate that took place in Scotland. He writes with deep knowledge and acute judgment, bringing clarity and insight to this issue and showing us the way out of our contemporary muddle."

David F. Wells, Distinguished Senior Research Professor, Gordon-Conwell Theological Seminary

"Writing with a pastoral heart and scholarly mind, Sinclair Ferguson provides a biblical understanding of grace that sets a solid foundation for life, ministry, and worship. Using the backdrop of the Marrow Controversy, Ferguson exposes the subtle hues of legalism and antinomianism that continue to permeate the church today. I found *The Whole Christ* personally convicting, theologically challenging, and Christ exalting."

Melissa B. Kruger, Women's Ministry Coordinator, Uptown Church, Charlotte, North Carolina; author, *The Envy of Eve* and *Walking with God in the Season of Motherhood*

"Ours is a day when we again hear charges of 'antinomianism' and 'legalism' thrown back and forth, often between folks who share the same confessional background. During such times of tension, more light and less heat is generally needed. I believe Sinclair Ferguson's *The Whole Christ* offers us timely perspective, helping us better understand grace, human agency, and gospel assurance. By taking us back to historical debates Ferguson also helps us better understand our own moment, even our own confusions."

Kelly M. Kapic, Professor of Theological Studies, Covenant College

"It's easy to cry "legalist" or "antinomian," but the realities are far subtler than we admit. Sinclair Ferguson takes an old Scottish controversy and uses it as a spotlight to illuminate our spiritual struggles today. This outstanding book untangles many a knot about God's law and grace and powerfully reminds us that legalism and antinomianism are not opposites, but evil allies in Satan's bitter war to dishonor the great name of Jesus Christ."

Joel R. Beeke, President, Puritan Reformed Theological Seminary

"It's hard to imagine a more important book written by a more dependable guide. From a seemingly obscure theological controversy, Sinclair Ferguson brings to light issues of fundamental and perennial significance for twenty-first century evangelicals. With deep learning, theological discernment, and pastoral wisdom, he not only exposes distortions of the gospel but also helps us savor the substance of the gospel, which is Christ himself."

Jeff Purswell, Dean, Sovereign Grace Ministries Pastors College

THE WHOLE CHRIST

Legalism, Antinomianism, and Gospel Assurance—Why the Marrow Controversy Still Matters

SINCLAIR B. FERGUSON

Foreword by Tim Keller

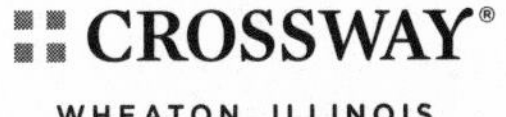

WHEATON, ILLINOIS

The Whole Christ: Legalism, Antinomianism, and Gospel Assurance—
Why the Marrow Controversy Still Matters

Published by Crossway
1300 Crescent Street
Wheaton, Illinois 60187

Cover design: Studio Gearbox

First printing 2016

Printed in the United States of America

All emphases in Scripture quotations have been added by the author.

Hardcover ISBN: 978-1-4335-4800-0
ePub ISBN: 978-1-4335-4803-1
PDF ISBN: 978-1-4335-4801-7
Mobipocket ISBN: 978-1-4335-4802-4

Library of Congress Cataloging-in-Publication Data

Ferguson, Sinclair B.
The whole Christ : legalism, antinomianism, and gospel assurance : why the Marrow controversy still matters / Sinclair B. Ferguson ; foreword by Tim Keller.
pages cm
Includes bibliographical references and index.
ISBN 978-1-4335-4800-0 (hc)
1. Law and gospel—History of doctrines. 2. Law (Theology) 3. Grace (Theology) 4. Fisher, Edward, active 1627-1655. Marrow of modern divinity. 5. Antinomianism. 6. Assurance (Theology) 7. Church of Scotland—Doctrines—History. 8. Reformed Church—Scotland—Doctrines—History. I. Title.
BT79.F47 2015
234—dc23 2015019712

Crossway is a publishing ministry of Good News Publishers.

LB 26 25 24 23 22 21 20 19 18 17 16
15 14 13 12 11 10 9 8 7 6 5 4 3 2

For
Walt and Joie
Chantry
with
gratitude and affection

CONTENTS

FOREWORD BY TIM KELLER

The volume in your hands is not just a helpful historical reflection; it is also a tract for the times.

The Marrow Controversy was a debate within the Church of Scotland in the early eighteenth century. The occasion, though not the main cause, was the reprint and subsequent division over Edward Fisher's *The Marrow of Modern Divinity.* The root of the dispute was the perennial difficulty of properly relating works and grace, law and gospel, not merely in our systematic theology but in our preaching and pastoral ministry and, ultimately, within our own hearts. Sinclair does a good job of recounting the Marrow Controversy in an accessible and interesting way. However, his real aim is not merely to do that. Against the background and features of that older dispute, he wants to help us understand the character of this perpetual problem—one that bedevils the church today. He does so in the most illuminating and compelling way I know of in recent evangelical literature.

One of the striking features of the Marrow Dispute is that supporters of the *Marrow* were accused of defending antinomianism, and at least some of its critics were, in turn, suspected of legalism—even though all parties had subscribed to what the Westminster Confession says about justification and works. The Confession's presentation of the doctrine is remarkably precise and clear. It teaches that faith in Christ leads to justification on the basis of

Christ's "obedience and satisfaction" being imputed to us, not on the basis of anything wrought in us or done by us.[1] Nevertheless, while good works are in no way the reason for our justification, they are absolutely necessary evidences that we have justifying faith.[2] Nevertheless (again!) such "evangelical obedience"—good works out of "thankfulness and assurance" for our gracious salvation[3]—never in any way become part of our standing as justified before God,[4] a standing that cannot be lost, even when we fall through sin under "God's fatherly displeasure."[5]

That is an extraordinarily nuanced exposition of the Protestant understanding of justification by faith alone through Christ alone. All those involved in the Marrow Controversy had subscribed to this precisely worded theological statement. How then could charges and countercharges of antinomianism and legalism arise that would expose a fault line in the church and eventually lead to a split in the denomination? While such theological precision is crucial, evidently it does not finally solve this ongoing problem of the role of the law and of obedience in the Christian life.

From the Marrow Controversy as a case in point, Sinclair draws several conclusions but expands and looks at each one so that we can apply them to our own time. Here are some of his theses and arguments that I found so very helpful, convicting, and wise.

The first and inarguable conclusion is that *legalism and antinomianism are much more than doctrinal positions*. Neither side in the Marrow Controversy was saying, "You can save yourself through works," or, "Once you are saved, you don't have to obey the law of God." Neither side subscribed to overt, explicit legalistic or antinomian doctrine. Nonetheless, legalism and antinomianism can be strongly present in a ministry. Each is a web of attitudes of

[1] Westminster Confession of Faith, 11.1.
[2] Ibid., 16.2.
[3] Ibid.
[4] Ibid., 11.1.
[5] Ibid., 11.5.

heart, practices, character, and ways of reading Scripture. At one point Sinclair even says, rightly, that a legal spirit consists in part in how you *feel* toward God.

The legal spirit is marked by jealousy, oversensitivity to slights, "metallic" harshness toward mistakes, and an ungenerous default mode in decision making. Both the author of *The Marrow of Modern Divinity* and Thomas Boston, the leading "Marrow Man" and supporter of the work, shared moving and convicting accounts of how they spent years in ministry, subscribing to the correct doctrine of justification, but at a practical level still functioned as if the law of God was a "covenant of works" rather than a "rule of life."[6] At the same time, practical antinomianism can develop even when doctrinal antinomianism is denied. It can take the form of a secular gospel of self-acceptance masquerading as Christianity. Even more often, it is present when the minister's preaching and pastoring is characterized by a subtle divorce of duty and delight. Any failure to present full, eager, complete obedience and submission to God as ultimately a great joy—as a way to resemble, know, and bring delight to God—is a tendency toward the antinomian spirit.

The second thing I learned was that *the root of both legalism and antinomianism is the same.* My guess is that most readers will find this the best new insight for them, one that could even trigger a proverbial paradigm shift. It is a fatal pastoral mistake to think of legalism and antinomianism as complete opposites. Sinclair says that, rather, they are "nonidentical twins from the same womb." He traces both of them back to the "lie of Satan" in the garden of Eden, namely, that you can't trust the goodness of God or his commitment to our happiness and well-being and that, therefore, if we obey God fully, we'll miss out and be miserable.

Because both mind-sets refuse to believe in the love and graciousness of God, they assume that any commands given to us are evidence that he is unwilling to bless us. They both fail to see

[6] Ibid., 19.6.

obedience as the way to give the gracious God delight as well as the way to become our true selves, the people we were created to be. They participate in the same incomprehension of the joy of obedience—they see obedience as something imposed on us by a God whose love is conditional and who is unwilling to give us blessing unless we do quite a lot of work. The only difference is that the legalist wearily assumes the burden, while the antinomian refuses it and casts it off by insisting that if God is really loving, he wouldn't ask for it. In order to salvage an idea of a gracious God, antinomians find ways to argue that God doesn't require obedience.

Therefore, the third thing I learned was that *to think the main problem out there is one particular error is to virtually put one foot into the other error.* If you fail to see what Sinclair is saying—that both legalism and antinomianism stem from a failure to grasp the goodness and graciousness of God's character—it will lead you to think that what each mind-set really needs for a remedy is a little dose of the other. In this view, it would mean that the remedy for legalism is just less emphasis on the law and obedience, and the remedy for antinomianism is more.

This is dangerous. If you tell those tending toward legalism that they shouldn't talk so much about obedience and the law, you are pushing them toward the antinomian spirit that cannot see the law as a wonderful gift of God. If you tell those tending toward antinomianism that they should point people more to divine threats and talk more about the dangers of disobedience, you are pushing them toward the legal spirit that sees the law as a covenant of works rather than as a way to honor and give pleasure to the one who saved them by grace.

Finally, this book showed me that *the cure for both legalism and antinomianism is the gospel.* Sinclair writes:

> The gospel is designed to deliver us from this lie [of the Serpent], for it reveals that behind and manifested in the coming of Christ

> and his death for us is the love of a Father who gives us everything he has: first his Son to die for us, and then his Spirit to live within us. . . . There is only one genuine cure for legalism. It is the same medicine the gospel prescribes for antinomianism: understanding and tasting union with Jesus Christ himself. This leads to a new love for and obedience to the law of God.

Since the root of both errors is the same, the cure is the same—to lift up the essential goodness and love of God by recounting the gospel, thereby making obedience a joy. The remedy for both is a fuller, biblical, and profound understanding of grace and of the character of God.

There are plenty of other helpful veins of inquiry and argument in this book. Just to name two examples, Sinclair shows how the New Perspective on Paul can, in some instances, encourage a more legalistic way of reading the Bible, while those who criticize the traditional threefold nature of the Old Testament law—moral, ceremonial, and civil—can support an antinomian mind-set. However, here are the main inferences I draw from this fine book for our current discussions around these issues.

Calvin called justification the "chief axis" or "main hinge on which religion turns." He proceeded to say that "unless you first of all grasp what your relationship to God is, and the nature of his judgment concerning you, you have [no] foundation . . . on which to build piety toward God."[7] That is certainly right, namely, that our justified standing with God cannot be "one motive among many." It must be the foundation of all our thinking, feeling, and doing; otherwise our default mode—our belief that God is not *for* us—will pull us back into a covenant of works.

But if it is true that our main problem is a disbelief in the love and goodness of God, then to say, "All you need for sanctification is to believe in your justification," is too simplistic. That may lead

[7] John Calvin, *Institutes of the Christian Religion*, trans. F. L. Battles, ed. J. T. McNeill (Philadelphia: Westminster Press, 1960), 3:11:1.

you to try to cure a legalistic spirit with just less emphasis on law. You need more than just an abstract belief in your legal exemption from punishment; you need a renovation of your view of God. However, John Owen, in his work on mortification, shows that the answer is not, on the other hand, just to say, "What you need for sanctification is to work hard to become holy." Owen argues that the root of our sinful behavior is an inability to hate sin for itself, and this stems from a tendency to see obedience as simply a way to avoid danger and have a good life—not as a way to love and know Jesus for who he is.

So to grow in grace comes not simply from believing more in our justification, though we should meditate on that reality daily. Understood more comprehensively, it flows from using the gospel of grace on the root of our sin—the mistrust of God's goodness and the inordinate love of other things. When we behold the glory of Christ in the gospel, it reorders the loves of our hearts, so we delight in him supremely, and the other things that have ruled our lives lose their enslaving power over us. This *is* sanctification by going deeper into the gospel, but it is not merely telling yourself that you are accepted and forgiven, as foundational as that is. In this book, Sinclair Ferguson shows us how important it is for preaching and pastoral effectiveness to get this straight.

INTRODUCTION

The Whole Christ: Legalism, Antinomianism, and Gospel Assurance—Why the Marrow Controversy Still Matters sounds like a book title with a history. And so it is. The story itself begins in early eighteenth-century Scotland. It then moves briefly backwards some seventy years to England and to the writing of an obscure and unusual book set in the form of a Socratic dialog. There are four participants: a young Christian, a legalist, an antinomian, and a minister of the gospel. It is a patchwork quilt of quotations from the good and godly of the Reformation and Puritan periods.

Were it not for a Scottish pastor spotting the book in a home in his obscure parish in the Scottish Borders, it would have remained the relatively unread work it already was. His discovery of it led, two decades later, to a theological controversy that has permanently engraved the book's title into the history of the church.

Fast-forward 260 years, and we arrive at the origin of this book.

In the spring of 1980 a letter arrived at our home in Glasgow, Scotland. It contained an invitation to speak later in the year at a ministers' conference in Indianapolis on this subject: "Pastoral Lessons from the Marrow Controversy."

The topic struck me in probably much the same way it may strike you: "Really?" Were it not for the adventure of visiting the United States (I had been only once before), my respect for the minister who had invited me, and the privilege of addressing fellow ministers when I was still a very young one myself, the invitation would perhaps have been declined. A contemporary minister might be excused for thinking that "Pastoral Lessons from the Marrow Controversy" sounds unnervingly like a "Veggie Tale for Ministers"! Perhaps every self-respecting Scottish theological student had heard of this controversy and the book that lay behind it, but had anybody else?

Now, more than three decades later, one memory still stands out vividly in my mind's eye. A few days before I was scheduled to leave for the conference, my wife, Dorothy, brought coffee into the study. I recall looking up from the notes I was preparing and saying, slightly despondently, "I don't know why I am spending time on this. I can't imagine there is anyone in the United States who has the slightest interest in the Marrow Controversy!"

The conference came and went. I was soon grateful that I had gone. I enjoyed the conference; the addresses seemed to strike a chord; and during the event I made a number of lifelong friendships.

I came home, and life went on.

Three years later, in 1983, our family moved to Philadelphia where I was to join the faculty of Westminster Theological Seminary and begin a long season of ministry in the United States. Between then and now, almost everywhere I have gone to preach, speak, or lecture, *someone* has said to me, "I have listened to your Marrow tapes [yes, "tapes"!]." The Christian life, and certainly Christian ministry, is full of surprises. William Cowper was right: "God moves in a mysterious way, His wonders to perform."[1]

There are reasons for interest in this apparently recondite topic. On the surface the Marrow Controversy was about how we preach the gospel; what role, if any, God's law and our obedience play in the Christian life; and what it means to have assurance of salvation. But those issues are always, at bottom, about the gospel itself.

[1] William Cowper, "Light Shining Out of Darkness," better known by its first line, "God Moves in a Mysterious Way" (1774).

While these themes have taken center stage at particular periods in the church's history, that is only the tip of the iceberg. They are perennially relevant because underneath them lies the most fundamental question of all: Who is the God whom we come to know in Jesus Christ (John 17:3)? What is he really like, truly like—deep down, through and through? The atmosphere that characterizes my Christian life will reflect my answer to these questions.

That was the issue that lay deeply embedded in the Marrow Controversy. To that extent, reflecting on it can never be merely an antiquarian hobby or an academic exercise.

Over the years people have asked if the material behind those conference addresses would ever be put into print. Others who speak (especially if they have seen transcripts of what they actually said!) know that the metamorphosis of material prepared for an ad hoc occasion into book form usually requires more time and energy than the original preparation. In the intervening decades time and energy have, of necessity, been employed in other tasks. But at the back of my mind the thought has lingered, *Perhaps one day?*

That day has now come.

What is *The Whole Christ*? It is not a study of *The Marrow of Modern Divinity* as such, although reference will be made to it. It is not an historical analysis of the often heated Marrow Controversy, although that serves as the background to it. Nor is it a study of the theology of Thomas Boston, although his name regularly appears in it.

Perhaps the best way to describe it is by borrowing from the world of classical music: *The Whole Christ* might well be subtitled, "Variations on themes from *The Marrow Controversy*." It is an extended reflection on theological and pastoral issues that arose in the early eighteenth century, viewed from the framework of the present day.

One particular consideration has motivated me to put this material into print. Thomas Boston, who perhaps more than any other wrestled with the issues raised by the *Marrow*, said that his ministry was transformed as a result of his reading and reflection:

> These things, in these days, while I was in the Merse,[2] gave my sermons a certain tincture, which was discerned; though the Marrow, from whence it sprang, continued in utter obscurity.[3]

I hope it will become clear throughout these pages what this tincture was. There is a perennial need for it in the ministry of the gospel. It is not linked to a particular personality type or a way of preaching. It is both more profound and more atmospheric than that. But God's discerning people recognize it when they see it, even if they cannot articulate what exactly it is.

It seems to me that anyone who wrestles theologically and personally with the great themes of gospel grace, legalism, antinomianism, and assurance, and is redirected to the Scriptures, should emerge with something of this "tincture." I hope that these pages will do something to encourage the desire for, the expression of, and then the recognition of this tincture. Whether or not people discern its source is immaterial.

Every book is a debt repayment, and this one is no exception.

I am grateful to Justin Taylor and the staff at Crossway for being willing to publish *The Whole Christ*. The final stimulus to forge this material into book form I owe to a conversation with Tim Keller. Once colleagues at Westminster Seminary in Philadelphia and therefore often in each other's company, our paths now cross only on rare occasions. They did so in January 2014 when we were both speaking at a conference in Texas. During a coffee break he mentioned the Marrow addresses. In half jest I responded that if I

---

[2] "The Merse" is the low-lying area of Berwickshire in the Scottish Borders between the River Tweed and the Lammermuir Hills. Boston's first pastoral charge of Simprin lay within this area.

[3] *The Memoirs of Thomas Boston*, in *The Whole Works of the Late Reverend Thomas Boston*, ed. S. M'Millan, 12 vols. (Edinburgh, 1848–1852), 12:157. The nineteenth-century edition, *Memoirs of the Life, Time, and Writings of Thomas Boston*, with introduction and notes by G. H. Morrison (Edinburgh: Oliphant, Anderson & Ferrier, 1899), was reprinted by Banner of Truth in 1988. On the assumption that more readers may have access to this edition, it will be the one cited in subsequent references to *Memoirs*. The quote here can be found on p. 171 of the 1988 edition.

wrote the book, then he could write the foreword! I am indebted to him for following through with the latter and grateful to him for the final stimulus to do the former.

In addition I owe a lasting debt to Walt Chantry. He was the minister who, in the spring of 1980, sent the invitation to give addresses on the Marrow Controversy. (There was at least one person in the United States who was interested in the Marrow Controversy after all!). Behind the invitation lay his keen discernment that if a group of ministers thought together about the issues in this debate of yesteryear, it would at the same time help them wrestle with some of the biggest pastoral issues in ministry in any day. To Walt and his wife, Joie, who have been friends and encouragers ever since, these pages are affectionately dedicated.

My wife, Dorothy, has once more been the encourager, patient observer, and prayer helper who has meant that the solitary and sometimes intense activity of writing a book has not been a lonely one. Her ongoing love and lasting friendship have long made me seem more efficient than I actually am, and for that and a host of other blessings I am grateful to her and to God.

Since the message of this book has a special relevance to those who are pastors and teachers, it goes now with my prayer that the same fresh tincture that marked Thomas Boston's ministry will be seen again in our own day.

Sinclair B. Ferguson
October 2014

"MARROW"

II. In figurative and other extended senses.

3.

a. Nourishing richness; the most rich, succulent, or nourishing part of something.
b. The innermost or central part of something.
c. (The seat of) a person's vitality and strength.

4.

a. The vital or essential part of something, the essence.
b. In the titles of books: the key points or sum of knowledge *of* a particular subject, field, etc.; a compendium or digest *of* writings in a subject. Chiefly in 16th-and 17th-cent. titles.
c. *Church Hist.* Short for or in allusion to *The Marrow of Modern Divinity,* the title of a book by Edward Fisher (1645, republished with notes by the Revd. James Hog in 1718).

The Oxford English Dictionary, 3rd edition (updated December 2000): *sub* "Marrow," http://www.oed.com.

1

HOW A *MARROW* GREW

This story begins some three hundred years ago in a small Scottish town, at a meeting attended by perhaps a few dozen men. It records the progress of a theological conflict that grew out of a single question asked of a young man hoping to become a Presbyterian minister.

The question, however, had a sting in its tail.

Nobody knows who first thought up the question or who formulated its precise wording. Nobody knows who was first to ask the question or how many times it had been asked before. But it was intended to tell the questioner much more than the person who answered it might want to reveal.

Nobody at the meeting could have imagined what would happen as a result of the answer that was given. Nor could any of them have suspected that three hundred years later people would still be discussing it. If you had suggested to them that they were setting in motion the "Marrow Controversy," they would have said (as people still do!), "The *what* controversy?"

So, where and when and why did all this take place? And what was the question?

Auchterarder

Some forty-five miles or so to the northwest of Edinburgh, the Scottish capital, lies Auchterarder, population less than five thousand. Until a few decades ago the main road from Stirling to Perth ran through the long main street, from which the town was popularly known as "The Lang Toun." The slow one-and-a-half-mile drive regulated by a thirty-mile-an-hour speed limit caused many a frustrated driver to be caught in a speed trap at its far end. Better by far to have taken a break in town and enjoyed a fine coffee accompanied by some excellent home baking!

To the outsider little seems to happen in Auchterarder.

Someone knowledgeable in Scottish family history might just know that much of the land in the area was once owned by John Haldane of Gleneagles, who had sat in the last Scottish Parliament and also, from 1707, in the first British Parliament.[1]

A few Christians might recognize the Haldane name. It was from this family line that the remarkable brothers Robert Haldane (1764–1842) and James Haldane (1768–1851) were descended. Robert would become the more famous in the annals of the church because of a remarkable awakening that took place among theological students in Geneva through a Bible study that he led while visiting the city. The Enlightenment-influenced theological faculty was so hostile to the informal gatherings at which he expounded Paul's letter to the Romans that the professors took it in turns to stand sentry outside the Haldanes' rented apartment. They noted and reported the names of students who attended, later threatening them with being barred from ordination![2]

Haldane of *Gleneagles*. Gleneagles? This is the great estate that is now the famous Gleneagles Hotel and golf courses. If today the

[1] While the crowns of Scotland and England had been united in 1603, when James VI (of Scotland) had also become James I (of England), the Parliaments were not united until 1707.

[2] The whole story makes for thrilling reading. See Alexander Haldane, *The Lives of Robert Haldane of Airthrey and His Brother James Alexander Haldane* (1852; repr. Edinburgh: Banner of Truth, 1990), 413–62.

tranquility of Auchterarder is disturbed, it is likely to be because the hotel is hosting an occasion of international interest. It was here that the July 6–8, 2005, G8 Summit took place, when Auchterarder played host to world leaders and a veritable army of media and security experts. A report to the Scottish executive on the economic impact of this weekend gathering put the price tag at around one hundred million dollars.

September 2014 saw a similar invasion for the playing of the Ryder Cup, the biennial golf match between the United States and Europe, which now captures the third-largest television viewing audience for a sporting event, with spectators present from as many as seventy-five countries. Simply hosting the event had the potential to boost the value of the Scottish tourist industry by an annual figure well in excess of one hundred million dollars.

But three hundred years ago, Auchterarder and its people presented a very different picture. It was then a small mill town where most of its residents squeezed out a subsistence living as weavers, tenant farmers, and, for the women, as domestic servants. An extant set of accounts for the household of a local farm laborer indicates an annual income of $40.00 for the year, with expenditures of around $39.90. The wealth and publicity of a G8 Summit or a Ryder Cup would have been far beyond the wildest dreams of those who passed their days here.

In a rural Scottish village like Auchterarder in the early eighteenth century, nothing was expected to happen that would excite the interest of the wider world or be recorded in the annals of church history.

That is, until the regular meeting of the Auchterarder Presbytery of the Church of Scotland in February 1717.

Presbyterianism

Scottish church life has been dominated by Presbyterianism since the days of John Knox and the Reformation in the sixteenth century. In Presbyterian churches each congregation is led, or "governed," by elders, usually one *teaching* elder (the minister) and a number of *ruling* elders,[3] at best men of spiritual integrity and some measure of discernment and pastoral ability. The teaching elder was normally a university-educated, theologically trained man. The ruling elders had no formal theological education. They learned to be elders by years of receiving biblical instruction, by themselves being led by elders, and by a kind of osmosis as in due course they took their place in the company of longer-standing elders in what was known as the "Kirk Session."

In addition to the life of the local congregation, the minister and an elder would regularly gather with representatives of other local congregations at the presbytery to hear reports and discuss matters of common interest and concern.

Beyond this simple structure lay a less frequent gathering of several presbyteries, known as the "Synod," and also the annual national gathering of congregational representatives at the General Assembly. While each congregation was basically self-sufficient, and was led by its own elders, these "courts of the church" provided a sense of unity and a kind of ascending hierarchy of authority in matters of common concern or dispute.

The selection, examination, and ordination of ministers were all the responsibility of the local presbytery. With this in view candidates for the ministry were taken under supervision. Throughout the period of their training they completed prescribed exercises. These culminated in a final oral examination administered in the presence of the whole presbytery—any member of which might ask a question, and all of whom would eventually vote on the candidate. Daunting indeed!

A Narrative of Surprising Presbytery Meetings

Imagine then, that you have traveled back in time. It is Friday, February 12, 1717. The presbytery of Auchterarder is holding its

[3] The distinction was usually based on Rom. 12:7–8 and 1 Tim. 5:17.

monthly gathering. The agenda has now moved to the case of a young candidate for the ministry. He has already preached, presented the requisite church exercises, and completed his dissertation on a doctrinal point put to him in Latin. The trials can be rigorous. But this particular young candidate has completed all of the stages. Indeed at the previous presbytery meeting he had been licensed as a preacher of the gospel.

But now there is a problem.

Two meetings before this, on December 11, 1716, the presbytery had given the candidate his examination in theology. It had, however, postponed further consideration of him until the next meeting. And so, on January 15, 1717, he came before the presbytery again. He was now asked to sign his name to his answers to the questions the presbytery had put to him.

In the nature of the case in most presbyteries, patterns of questioning become somewhat stereotyped. In addition there are sometimes individuals who will ask their personal "litmus test" question. These are rarely straightforward. At best they challenge the candidate to take biblical teaching with which he is familiar and apply it to a question or situation with which he is unfamiliar. At worst they set theological traps. These need to be carefully negotiated.

The candidate before the presbytery of Auchterarder is William Craig. He has been caught in such a trap.

"The Creed"

As a candidate in the presbytery of Auchterarder, William Craig had been asked to agree to a statement that had become a unique hallmark of its examinations. Were it not for his response, it might well have remained hidden in the dust-gathering volumes of the presbytery's handwritten minutes. The question itself came to be known as the "Auchterarder Creed." He was asked to agree to the following statement:

> I believe that it is not sound and orthodox to teach that we forsake sin in order to our coming to Christ, and instating us in covenant with God.[4]

Perhaps Craig was well enough known to the members of the presbytery that they already suspected he would be in some difficulty.

Turn the question over in your own mind. How would you respond? Do you agree that "it is not sound and orthodox to teach that we forsake sin in order to our coming to Christ?" Perhaps you can hear the echo of the words beloved by TV lawyers: "Mr. Craig, just answer the question yes or no."

Craig had some scruples about the precise wording of the test question. Nonetheless, at the January meeting he had been willing to subscribe his name on the presbytery copy of the [Westminster] Confession of Faith, and had been duly licensed.

In the event, however—perhaps you have some sympathy with him?—Craig's conscience was troubled, and he returned to the following presbytery meeting. He explained that he had subscribed his signature in haste and now wished for an opportunity to explain his position.

The presbytery of Auchterarder heard him out, and at its stated meeting on February 12, 1717, proceeded to declare William Craig's license to preach the gospel null and void.

Perhaps the presbytery assumed the matter would rest there. If so they were to be disappointed.

In the months that followed, through a process of appeal against the presbytery decision, the issue of the Auchterarder Creed came before the next meeting of the General Assembly of the Church of Scotland. The fathers and brethren of the Kirk condemned the creed and declared "their abhorrence of the foresaid proposition as un-

---

[4] Cited here from the Minutes of the thirteenth session of the General Assembly, on May 14, 1717, recording the "Act discharging Presbyteries to use any Formula in licensing Probationers, and ordaining or admitting Ministers, but such as is or shall be agreed unto by the General Assembly, with a Reference to the Commission of the Presbytery of Auchterarder's carriage in that matter."

sound and most detestable doctrine, as it stands, and was offered by the said Presbytery to the said Mr. William Craig."[5] The presbytery of Auchterarder was ordered to restore his license.

That might have been the end of the matter were it not for a private discussion that took place immediately afterward between two ministers who "happened" to fall into conversation when the session concluded.

Who Is My (Assembly) Neighbor?

Present at the 1717 Assembly was the Reverend John Drummond, a minister from the town of Crieff and a member of the presbytery of Auchterarder. Beside him at the critical session sat one of the most remarkable ministers in the entire history of the Church of Scotland.

The Assembly neighbor was at that time forty-one years old. He had written his first book some two decades earlier while still a young probationer minister. Its quaintly worded title, *Soliloquie on the Art of Man Fishing*, expressed his evangelistic zeal as well as his pastoral heart. He soon hoped to publish what would become his best-known book, *Human Nature in Its Fourfold State*.[6]

His own congregation lay deep in the border country between Scotland and England in the valley of the River Ettrick, set within what has been described as a "sea of hills." He had been called to this widespread parish in 1711. It had had no minister for four years.

When he had arrived in his new parish, he found the people were far more concerned about this world than the world to come. ✓

[5] In keeping with the procedural rules of the Church of Scotland, during the debate on "The Auchterarder Creed" members of the Presbytery of Auchterarder were "removed," that is, they were not able to take part. They were later called to appear before a Commission of the Assembly in August of the same year, which was given power of final decision making.

[6] *The Fourfold State*, as it became known, was first published (in an imperfect edition) in 1720. It began life in a series of sermons preached in Simprin, which were then reworked for the congregation in Ettrick. In due course the book became virtually synonymous with the evangelical tradition in Scotland and could be found in many homes along with a family Bible, the Shorter Catechism, and a copy of John Bunyan's *Pilgrim's Progress*.

They were conceited and censorious. A shy man by natural disposition, although a preacher of unusual ability, he suffered the indignity of members of the congregation making noises while he was preaching, walking out, and even wandering around the churchyard outside talking deliberately loudly. Fathers who conducted family prayers when at home could be heard cursing in the streets. While a minister in the congregation he had previously served in Simprin, Sundays had been the best day of the week. But now he wrote: "The approaching Sabbath, that sometimes was my delight, is now a terror to me."[7] In addition, another, more exclusive, church fellowship had gathered in the same area, and its members were not slow to criticize the parish minister of such a spiritually indifferent congregation.

By God's grace, now in 1717, things had begun to change wonderfully under his rich ministry of the gospel.

The name of John Drummond's Assembly neighbor was Thomas Boston.[8] But we can let him tell the story of their conversation in his own words:

> The "Auchterarder Creed," was all at once at that diet [i.e., of the General Assembly] judged and condemned; though some small struggle was made in defence thereof. And poor I was not able to open a mouth before them in that cause; although I believed the proposition to be truth, howbeit not well worded. . . .
>
> And here, namely, in the condemnation of that proposition, was the beginning of the torrent, that for several years after ran, in the public actings of this church, against the doctrine of grace, under the name of Antinomianism. . . . Meanwhile, at the same time sitting in the assembly house, and conversing with Mr. John Drummond, minister of Crief, one of the brethren of that presbytery above mentioned, I happened to give him my

[7] Thomas Boston, *Memoirs of Thomas Boston* (Edinburgh: Banner of Truth, 1988), 220.
[8] 1676–1732.

> sense of the gospel offer; Isa. lv. 1, Matt. xi: 28, with the reason thereof; and withal to tell him of *The Marrow of Modern Divinity*.[9]

Treasure Hidden on a Window Head

In his earlier ministry in Simprin, at that time one of the smallest parish churches in Scotland,[10] Boston had long struggled with issues of the law and the gospel. But around the year 1700,[11] while on a pastoral visit, he spotted on a window head a book entitled *The Marrow of Modern Divinity*. He took it down, read it, and discovered that it spoke to both his heart and his mind and to a wide variety of pastoral issues in his ministry. He imbibed the insights it stimulated into biblical and pastoral theology. His own preaching and teaching began to reflect what he saw as a new, Christ-centered, gospel-rooted emphasis.

Boston had in fact noticed *two* books lying on the window head of his parishioner's house. His reaction to the second book, *Christ's Blood Flowing Freely to Sinners*,[12] was very different. His comments are significant in light of the controversy that would later arise, and particularly the accusation of antinomianism that was leveled against the teaching he espoused:

> These [the two books] I reckon, had been brought home from England by the master of the house, a soldier in the time of the civil wars. Finding them to point to the subject I was in particular concern about, I brought them both away. The latter, a book of Saltmarsh's, I relished not; and I think I returned it without reading it quite through. The other, being the first part only of the Marrow, I relished greatly; and purchased it, at length from

[9] Boston, *Memoirs*, 317. I have retained Boston's spelling and punctuation throughout.

[10] The ruins of the church building suggest it was no more than 50 feet long and 18 feet wide.

[11] It is worth noting that the influence of the theology of the *Marrow* had already been percolating into the fiber of Boston's thinking and preaching for almost two decades before the book itself became a matter of public controversy. He was a very *mature* Marrow Man long before the time of the controversy.

[12] John Saltmarsh, *Free Grace; or the Flowings of Christ's Blood Freely to Sinners* (London: for Giles Calvert, 1645).

> the owner . . . and it is still to be found among my books. I found it to come close to the points that I was in quest of and to shew the consistency of these, which I could not reconcile before; so that I rejoiced in it, as a light which the Lord had seasonably struck up to me in my darkness.[13]

Saltmarsh—that is, John Saltmarsh—was one of the most notable antinomians of the seventeenth century.[14] Boston had so little taste for his teaching that he returned the book—unfinished.

John Drummond immediately acted on this "chance" conversation:

> Hereupon he [Drummond], having inquired in the shops for the said book, at length got it; and from him Mr. James Webster[15] getting it, was taken therewith; and afterward, Mr. Drummond himself being hardly allowed time to read it through it came into the hands of Mr. James Hog, minister of Carnock;[16] and in end was reprinted in the year 1718, with a preface by the said Mr. Hog, dated at Carnock, Dec. 3, 1717.[17]

So deeply opposed was the General Assembly of the Church of Scotland to the teaching and influence of the *Marrow* that it passed an act in 1720 prohibiting ministers from recommending the book either in preaching or writing and from saying anything in its favor. In addition, if they discovered any of their members reading it, they

[13] Boston, *Memoirs*, 169.

[14] John Saltmarsh (d. 1647) was a gifted Cambridge graduate with a mystical disposition that seems to have unhinged him from the stability of the more balanced members of the "Puritan Brotherhood." Described by William Haller as "a mystic, an enthusiast, [and] a metaphysical poet," he was not without the kind of insight that is possessed by those on the margins, but at the end of the day seems to have been "strange genius, part poet and part whirling dervish." William Haller, *The Rise of Puritanism* (Philadelphia: University of Pennsylvania Press, 1938), 79, 214. Saltmarsh, who had been an army chaplain, rose from his deathbed in November 1647 and rode almost 40 miles from Ilford to the headquarters of the New Model Army to tell General Fairfax that "the Lord had forsaken them and would not prosper them." C. Hill, *The World Turned Upside Down* (1972; repr. London: Penguin, 1991), 70.

[15] James Webster (1659–1720) was minister of the Tolbooth church in Edinburgh and a leading opponent of John Simson, professor of divinity in the University of Glasgow who was accused of Arian theology (denying the full deity of Jesus Christ).

[16] The village of Carnock is in Fife, some 3 miles from the outskirts of Dunfermline and 20 miles northwest of Edinburgh.

[17] Boston, *Memoirs*, 317. Boston comments that he later had no memory of the conversation.

were to warn them of its dangers and urge them neither to use it nor to read it.[18]

In reaction, in 1721 Boston's friends, impressed by the sense of the grace of Christ in his ministry, urged him to write his own explanatory notes on the *Marrow*. These he duly published in a new edition of the book in 1726. Given the ban that had been placed on the book, he did so under the name of Philalethes Irenaeus.[19]

A book placed on an *Index Librorum Prohibitorum*[20] of a Presbyterian and Reformed Church? We may well ask, What was so extraordinary about this book?

The Marrow of Modern Divinity

The *Marrow* had been published in two parts under the initials "E. F.": part 1 in 1645, part 2 in 1648. The author's identity has been disputed, but the consensus view is that he was Edward Fisher, a barber surgeon in London and the author of several other minor works in the Puritan period.[21]

The book itself is a series of dialogues. The participants at various points are: *Neophytus*, a young Christian who is troubled about basic elements of gospel truth; *Evangelista*, the pastor who counsels him; and two others, *Nomista*, a legalist; and *Antinomista*, an antinomian. Part 1 deals with theological issues in the relationship between law and gospel. Part 2 contains an exposition of the Ten Commandments.

---

[18] To the best of my knowledge the act has never been rescinded. As a minister in a denomination (Associate Reformed Presbyterian Church) whose roots lie in part in this controversy, it is a pleasure to recommend the edition with Boston's notes!

[19] Boston, *Memoirs*, 379. The suggestion was made to him on July 10, 1721 (ibid., 361), and his notes were completed in July of the following year (ibid., 366). Poignantly, the month in which Boston agreed to the publication of his notes along with a new edition of the *Marrow*—April 1725—was also the month in which he recorded the last occasion on which his wife was able to be present at public worship when he was preaching. For the last six years of his ministry she experienced debilitating sickness and paralyzing mental distress.

[20] The allusion is to the *Index* of the Roman Catholic Church whose original version was promulgated by Pope Paul IV in 1559—as it happens, the same year as the publication of the final Latin edition of Calvin's *Institutes*.

[21] See the discussion by D. M. McIntyre, "First Strictures on *The Marrow of Modern Divinity*," *Evangelical Quarterly* 10 (1938): 61–70. Fisher favored the dialog as the vehicle of his writing. His other works—*A Touchstone for a Communicant* (London, 1647); *London's Gate to the Lord's Table* (London, 1648); and *Faith in Five Fundamental Principles* (London, 1650)—all have this format.

The General Assembly accused the *Marrow* (and suspected its supporters) of encouraging antinomianism and a subtle form of universal redemption. The group of ministers who were publicly identified as its chief supporters came to be known as "the Brethren" and sometimes as "the Twelve Apostles" (since there were twelve of them). They included James Hog, James Wardlaw, the brothers Ralph and Ebenezer Erskine (under whose father's ministry Thomas Boston had been converted), and, of course, Boston himself.

These ministers responded to the Assembly's action by publishing a "Protest and Representation"[22] against the condemnation of the book. In response, an assembly commission[23] presented them with twelve questions related to the teaching of the *Marrow*. The "Marrow Men" (as they have come to be known) replied that while they would not subscribe to every jot and tittle in the book, they believed that its overall doctrinal thrust was both biblical and wholesome.[24] Their case, they believed, was never really answered.

The Big Issue

What was it about the preaching of the church in the early eighteenth century that led to the existence of the Auchterarder Creed and such emotional tensions over *The Marrow of Modern Divinity*? And what was it that chiefly concerned the Marrow Men? Boston, we remember, said that he agreed with the *tenor* of the Auchterarder Creed, although he felt its *wording* left something to be desired. But what did the creed reveal? And what were Boston's burdens?

[22] Hence they were known by their contemporaries not as "Marrow Men" but as "Representers" or simply as "the Brethren."

[23] That is, a group appointed for specific purposes to represent the Assembly.

[24] These are conveniently printed as an appendix to *The Marrow of Modern Divinity with Notes by the Late Rev. Thomas Boston*, in *Whole Works*, 7:465–89. Boston's edition of the *Marrow* was reprinted (Swengel, PA: Reiner, 1978), and there the appendix is on pp. 344–70. In 2009 Christian Focus produced a new edition of the *Marrow* with Boston's notes in a new arrangement under their Christian Heritage imprint. In this edition the appendix is on pp. 345–76. Hereinafter all references to the *Marrow* are to the last of these, the Christian Focus edition.

The Marrow Men were suspected of antinomianism. What they most deeply feared was that many of the condemners of the Marrow doctrine were themselves guilty of a subtle form of legalism.[25] At the root of the matter lay the nature of the grace of God in the gospel and how it should be preached. Boston's concern about the "moderation" that had begun to grip his denomination was exacerbated by the fact that the same General Assembly that had dealt so harshly with the Marrow doctrine passed over what he regarded as a grave case of incipient Arminianism and Arianism.[26] This acted as a catalyst for the somewhat reserved and diffident Boston to engage in public controversy and to take up arms against what he saw as false doctrine.[27] For him the issue was not the merits or demerits of a human publication, or the expressions of a local presbytery's test question, but the gospel itself. Here is how he saw it:

> As matters now stand, the gospel-doctrine has got a root-stroke by the condemning of that book.[28]

And so the Marrow Men objected to the way in which the Assembly's focus on *The Marrow of Modern Divinity* was liable to

> turn the matter off its proper hinge, by giving a wrong colour to our Representation, as if the chief design of it was to plead, not for the precious truths of the gospel which we conceived to be wounded by the condemnatory act, but for *The Marrow of Modern Divinity*, the which though we value for a good and useful book, and doubt not but the Church of God may be much edified by it as we ourselves have been, yet came it

[25] It should be noted that there was a spectrum of opinion in the context of this controversy. Not all who refrained from siding with the Marrow Men were by any stretch of the imagination legalists. Many were fellow evangelicals, John Willison of Dundee being perhaps the most notable.

[26] In the case of Professor Simson mentioned above (n15).

[27] On one occasion, when a commissioner, he stood entirely alone in the Assembly in protest against the demeaning of Christ in the face of the Arianism of John Simson (1668–1740). Simson was eventually suspended in 1729, but his salary was continued until his death, even though it was thought "not fit or safe" for him to teach. For Boston's intervention, see *Memoirs*, 414–19.

[28] Ibid., 361.

> never into our minds to hold it, or any other private writing, faultless, nor to put it on a level with our approved standards of doctrine.[29]

To the heart of these matters we can now turn.

[29] Fisher, *Marrow*, 346. Boston's own differences with the *Marrow* range from his rejection of the view that Melchizedek (Gen. 14:18; Heb. 7:1–4) should be identified as Christ: "This seems to be to me a more than groundless opinion" (ibid., 73), to scrupling at a reference to *Saint* John: "This word might well have been spared here" (*Marrow*, 69), to matters of substance such as whether the Sinaitic covenant was the covenant of works, which evokes a short essay-length comment (ibid., 76–77).

2

GRACE IN THE GOSPEL

Thomas Boston and his friends believed that "the gospel-doctrine" had been attacked in the Marrow Controversy.[1]

Several doctrinal and pastoral issues emerged within this context. In the chapters that follow we will focus on four of them:

1) The gospel of the grace of God and its offer to all.
2) The gospel and legalism.
3) The gospel and antinomianism.
4) The gospel and assurance of salvation.

Grace

The Marrow Controversy raised a major question about how the gospel is to be preached. But the answer to that question depends on our answer to a more fundamental one: What *is* the gospel? Contemporary discussion simply underlines how central this question is and the extent to which the answer we give determines how we preach and communicate the gospel.

Ostensibly—as becomes clear from the criticisms leveled against the *Marrow*—the controversy was about *the offer of the gospel.*

[1] Thomas Boston, *Memoirs of Thomas Boston* (Edinburgh: Banner of Truth, 1988), 361.

But much more than the semantics of gospel presentation was at stake. The issue was the heart of the gospel itself. The Marrow Men were concerned to stress the importance, and true nature, of God's grace. This they saw is rooted in a yet deeper issue: the nature and character of God himself revealed in the gospel.

The tenth in the series of questions the Assembly commission put to the Marrow Brethren brings us to the heart of the matter:

> Whether the revelation of the Divine will in the word, affording a warrant to offer Christ unto all, and a warrant to all to receive him, can be said to be the Father's making a deed of gift and grant of Christ unto all mankind? Is this grant to all mankind by sovereign grace? And whether it is absolute or conditional?[2]

To reduce the issue to simple terms: what do you say when you call people to come to Christ? On what grounds are they entitled to come? Several statements in *The Marrow of Modern Divinity* gave rise to this question. Two are particularly significant.

At one point, Evangelista, the pastor, says:

> I beseech you, consider, that God the Father, as he is in his Son Jesus Christ, moved with nothing but with his free love to mankind lost, hath made a deed of gift and grant unto them all, that whosoever shall believe in this his Son, shall not perish, but have eternal life.[3]

These words are quoted from the Puritan writer Ezekiel Culverwell.[4] What do they stress? Boston understood the point in this way:

[2] Edward Fisher, *The Marrow of Modern Divinity* (Ross-shire, UK: Christian Focus, 2009), 371.

[3] Ibid., 144. Intriguingly, although probably unknown to him, the language used here by Culverwell has deep roots in the covenant idea. While the language of "deed of gift and grant" may sound alien even to those familiar with the historical formulations of covenant theology, some Old Testament scholars have seen deep parallels between the divine covenant with Abraham and similar arrangements made within the culture of the ancient Near East, which "were in effect, a *deed of gift signifying a royal grant*." W. J. Dumbrell, *Covenant and Creation* (Nashville: Thomas Nelson, 1984), 48n2; emphasis added.

[4] From *A Treatise of Faith* (London, 1623), 15. Culverwell (1554–1631) was a close friend of the leading Puritan Richard Rogers. In 1587 he was suspended for a period from his ministry in the Church of England "for the surplice," i.e., for refusing to wear it. John Winthrop, later governor of Massachusetts, credited him with pointing him to faith in Christ. He was deprived of his ministry in

> This deed of gift and grant, or authentic gospel offer . . . is expressed in so many words, John iii.16. . . . Where the gospel comes, this grant is published, and the ministerial offer made; and there is no exception of any of all mankind in the grant. . . . This is the good old way of discovering to sinners their warrant to believe in Christ; and it doth indeed bear the sufficiency of the sacrifice of Christ for all,[5] and that Christ crucified is the ordinance of God for salvation unto all mankind, in the use-making of which only they can be saved; but not an universal atonement or redemption.[6]

Notice what Boston is saying. There is no question, as far as he is concerned, of the church's confessional standards being compromised.[7] Few have loved the Westminster Assembly documents as steadfastly as Boston and his fellow Marrow Men did. But against the background of the emphasis on particular redemption or "limited atonement"[8] found in these documents, Boston is stressing that Christ is to be offered to all men everywhere without exception or qualification.

1609 and spent the rest of his life in London. His work was criticized and accused of Arminianism the year following its publication by Alexander Leighton in *A Friendly Triall of The Treatise of Faith* (London, 1624). Culverwell replied in *A Briefe Answere to Certain Objections Against The Treatise of Faith* (London, 1626). He was the grandfather of William Gouge, a distinguished member of the Westminster Assembly.

[5] Here Boston alludes to a distinction that went back to medieval theologians, that while Christ's death is *sufficient* for all, it is *efficient* only for the elect. Calvin also adhered to this view although he did not think it was the appropriate hermeneutical and exegetical principle to interpret every universal statement in relation to the atonement. See, e.g., his comments on 1 John 2:2 where, noting the sufficient/efficient distinction, he states, "This solution has commonly prevailed in the schools. Although *I allow the truth of this* I deny that it fits this passage. For John's purpose was only to make this blessing common to the whole Church. Therefore under the word 'all' he does not include the reprobate, but refers to all who would believe and those who were scattered through various regions of the earth." John Calvin, *The Gospel according to St John 11–21 and The First Epistle of John*, trans. T. H. L. Parker, ed. D. W. Torrance and T. F. Torrance (Edinburgh: Oliver & Boyd, 1961), 244; emphasis added.

[6] Fisher, *Marrow*, 152. By "atonement or redemption" here, Boston implies the accomplishing of salvation by Christ and the application of it in our faith union with Christ.

[7] That is, the Confession of Faith composed at the Westminster Assembly and authorized by the Church of Scotland in 1648 and by the Scottish Parliament in 1649. Along with the Larger Catechism and especially the Shorter Catechism, the Confession was the working document of biblical and doctrinal instruction in the church, and expositions based on the Shorter Catechism were often the substance of the exposition in the second service of the Lord's Day.

[8] While it may be redundant to say so, it bears repeating that unless one is a universalist, one's doctrine of the atonement is "limited" either in intention (Christ died to save his people) or in application (Christ died for all, yet all are not saved).

Why?

Because Jesus Christ *is* the gospel.

Hard on the heels of these statements in the *Marrow* comes a quotation that would raise the stakes in the controversy even higher. The words are those of the Puritan John Preston:[9]

> And hence it was, that Jesus Christ himself said unto his disciples, Mark xvi. 15, "Go and preach the gospel to every creature under heaven:" that is, Go and tell every man, without exception, that here is good news for him! Christ is dead for him! and if he will take him, and accept of his righteousness, he shall have him.[10]

Recent critical scholarship has argued that Preston held to a form of hypothetical universalism, which is reflected in the words

[9] John Preston (1587–1628) is widely regarded as one of the most significant figures among Church of England Puritans. Hugh Trevor-Roper described him as "this sinister character," but in fact this says more about Trevor-Roper's consistent bias against Puritan theology than about Preston. Hugh Trevor-Roper, *Archbishop Laud* (1940; repr. London: Phoenix Press, 1962), 61. The story of his conversion in Cambridge is one of many encouraging personal narratives to emerge from this period. He was awakened from a life of spiritual indifference through hearing a sermon of John Cotton in Great St. Mary's, Cambridge (Cotton himself had earlier rejoiced when he heard the bell toll the death of William Perkins but had been later brought to faith through the preaching of Richard Sibbes). The sermon itself was despised by most of its hearers, but when Cotton returned to his rooms (he was a fellow of Emmanuel College), Preston knocked on his door to tell him that it had brought him to Christ. Cotton was to become a major Puritan influence and ministered in Boston, Lincolnshire, and later in Boston, Massachusetts. Thomas Shephard, who would also become a major figure in the New World, was converted through Preston's ministry. A man of outstanding gifts, Preston became a chaplain to Charles I in 1621 and a lecturer at Trinity Church in Cambridge. His works were officially edited posthumously by Richard Sibbes, John Davenport, Thomas Goodwin, and John Ball and unofficially by others. Goodwin had been converted under Preston's ministry. The interconnectedness of "The Puritan Brotherhood" is notable. Richard Sibbes had been converted under the ministry of Paul Baynes, who succeeded the great William Perkins. Sibbes in turn was instrumental in the conversion of Cotton, who was instrumental in the conversion of Preston, who in turn was instrumental in the conversion of Goodwin. The closeness of the bonds of affection and esteem among members of this brotherhood, reminiscent of the "Luther circle" and the "Calvin circle" of the previous century, gives credence to the notion that when God begins a new work, he characteristically gathers groups of younger men into such brotherhoods. Something similar took place in eighteenth-century Scotland with the Marrow Brethren, and in England with the Eclectic Society and with William Wilberforce and "the Clapham Sect," and in the nineteenth century with the M'Cheyne-Bonar group. Perhaps the most fascinating link in the chain of conversion that bound these men together in the Puritan "brotherhood" is the fact that Perkins himself was awakened spiritually by overhearing a mother warning her misbehaving child that if he did not behave better, she would "hand him over to drunken Perkins yonder." Perkins saw himself as he really was, a needy drunkard, and was brought to faith in Christ. Surely a striking illustration of the principle that where sin abounds grace super-abounds! How much followed the words of the unknown mother and, later, of something Thomas Boston forgot he had mentioned in a conversation.

[10] Fisher, *Marrow*, 144. The quotation itself is from John Preston, *The Breastplate of Faith and Love* (London, 1630, facsimile repr. Edinburgh: Banner of Truth, 1979), 8.

cited from the *Marrow*. But the Marrow Brethren did not read him thus, nor did Boston understand Preston's statement quoted in the *Marrow* to be an expression of hypothetical universalism (or of Amyraldianism in particular). Indeed he categorically states, "It appears that universal atonement, or redemption, is not taught here, neither by our author [i.e., of the *Marrow*]."[11] Even if critics of the *Marrow* proved to be correct in interpreting Preston's theology, in this context the relevant issue is *Boston's understanding and use* of the statement.[12]

In his own edition of the *Marrow*, Boston adds a lengthy note stating why he believes that it is not here teaching either Arminianism (that Christ died in order to make salvation possible for all) or Amyraldianism (that Christ died conditionally for all, should they actually believe). Rather, Boston held that these words stress what

[11] Jonathan D. Moore, *English Hypothetical Universalism: John Preston and the Softening of Reformed Theology* (Grand Rapids, MI: Eerdmans, 2007), 116ff. For his discussion of Boston's use of Preston, see pp. 117–21. In relation to the use of the phrase "is dead for you," Moore argues that in Preston's mind this is the functional equivalent of "died for you." His argument hinges on the way the *Geneva Bible* translates Romans 8:34: "'Who shall condemne? It is *Christ* that *is dead*; yea, or rather, which is risen againe.': Which words are quoted 'almost *verbatim*' at the head of Preston's sermon on the text.'" The King James Version had translated Paul's words as "It is Christ that died." Moore's argument over against David Lachman, who had defended the possibility of Boston's interpretation of Preston, in his *The Marrow Controversy, 1718–1723, An Historical and Theological Analysis* (Edinburgh: Rutherford, 1988), is that in the light of this, "died" and "is dead" must be treated as equivalents. He continues, "The words 'Christ which is dead' in the Geneva version are a translation of 'Χριστὸς Ἰησοῦς ὁ ἀποθανών.' This is an aorist active participle (that is to say, not a complex past participle but a simple participle standing for a completed action.)" Moore goes on to note that the phrase "is dead for" also appears in 1 Thess. 4:14 in the *Geneva Bible* where the KJV has "died," and that this interchangeability is found in other theological literature, and, in addition, that Preston's hypothetical universalism becomes "increasingly clear as his sermons are further examined." For Moore, *tertium non datur* with respect to *identifying* these two translations as equivalents. But to prove this, one would need to provide evidence that elsewhere the *Geneva Bible* translates ἀποθανών as "died for." Otherwise there remains the possibility that the reason the *Geneva Bible* translates "is dead for" rather than "died for" is that the translators thought that is what the text actually intended to say and that these two translations are not in fact equivalents. While further discussion of these points would take us far beyond the theme of these pages, what is clear is that Boston believed there was a difference between the expressions and that they were not equivalents. His own conviction was that Preston had seen something significant in the translation and expression "Christ is dead for you." In a note on the semantics of the text, C. L. Rogers Jr. and C. L. Rogers III comment, in some distinction from Moore, "ἀποθανών aor(ist) pass(ive) part(iciple) ἀποθνῄσκω . . . to die. Part(iciple) used as a noun to emphasize a defining trait. Aor(ist) indicates logically antecedent action." C. L. Rogers Jr. and C. L. Rogers III, *The New Linguistic and Exegetical Key to the Greek New Testament* (Grand Rapids, MI: Zondervan, 1998), 332. It is this notion of "defining trait" that was so significant for Boston, as we shall see. For him Preston's language allows one to offer Christ defined by reason of his death as able to save those who come to God through him and to offer him to all in that capacity. It would require a larger reassessment to explore Preston's thinking in this connection, which is not the burden of the present study.

[12] A further indication why it was that the Marrow Brethren were less concerned about the book and more concerned about the fate of the gospel itself.

was being obscured in a moribund confessional "orthodoxy," in which evangelistic rigor mortis had already set. By way of contrast he wanted to stress that the gospel's center is found in *Jesus Christ himself*, who has been crucified for sin and raised for justification, with the inbuilt implication that *Christ himself thus defined and described* should be proclaimed as able to save all who come to him.

Vital Emphases

While affirming his church's Calvinism, Boston stressed that this emphasis of the *Marrow* preserved two of the great keynotes of the New Testament's message.

First, that in Jesus Christ there is a fullness of grace for all who will come to him. This was Boston's interpretation of the notion that God has made "a deed of gift and grant" to all men because of his free love to lost humanity. This is genuinely good news for every man. There are no exceptions. "Christ is dead for him."

Second, it preserved the New Testament's emphasis not only on the *fullness* of the grace of Christ but also on the *freeness* of that grace in Christ. To this extent Boston was in agreement with the intention of the Auchterarder Creed, that it is not sound to say that a man must *first* quit sin in order to be qualified for the offer of Christ. The offer of the gospel is to be made not to the righteous or even the repentant, but to all. There are no conditions that need to be met in order for the gospel offer to be made. The warrant for faith does not rest in anything in ourselves. Indeed it cannot. After all, the "natural man . . . is not able, by his own strength, to convert himself, *or to prepare himself thereunto*."[13]

The significance of these statements of Culverwell and Preston is obvious, even if some thought they were pointedly, even dangerously, worded. Boston felt the sheer graciousness of the Christ of the gospel was being stifled by a Calvinism that had developed a

[13] The [Westminster] Confession of Faith (London, 1647), 9.3, emphasis added.

preaching logic of its own and had become insensitive to the style and atmosphere of the New Testament. In his view God's particular election had too easily been distorted into preaching a doctrine of conditional and conditioned grace. That often goes hand in glove with a form of gospel preaching that is in danger of severing the elements in the *ordo salutis* from "Jesus Christ and him crucified"[14]—that is, from Christ *himself*.

It may clarify this if the thinking that the Marrow Men *opposed* is put in the form of a syllogism:

> *Major premise*: The saving grace of God in Christ is given to the elect alone.
> *Minor premise*: The elect are known by the forsaking of sin.
> *Conclusion*: Therefore forsaking sin is a prerequisite for saving grace.

If that were your logic, even if present in your mind subliminally rather than self-consciously, you would certainly be suspicious of the Auchterarder Creed and with it of the Marrow Men themselves. And many were.

The fallacy here? The subtle movement from seeing forsaking sin as the fruit of grace that is rooted in election, to making the forsaking of sin the necessary precursor for experiencing that grace. Repentance, which is the fruit of grace, thus becomes a qualification for grace.

This puts the cart before the horse. It stands the gospel on its head so that the proclamation of the gospel, with the call to faith in Christ, becomes conditional on something in the hearer. The gospel thus became a message of grace for the credentialed, not an offer of Christ to all with the promise of justification to the ungodly who believes. This "credentialing" carried disastrous implications evangelistically. Further, it sowed the seeds of deep pastoral problems in the lives of those who were nevertheless genuinely brought to faith

[14] 1 Cor. 2:2.

under such a system of preaching. Enter the kingdom from this matrix and it is likely to shape one's entire Christian life.

Nor was this warping of the gospel the idiosyncrasy of one unique time span in the history of Scottish Presbyterianism exclusively. It is perennial and universal. The central elements in the Marrow Controversy remain some of the most important pastoral issues of today.

Several errors that distort healthy Reformed theology were present in the positions the Marrow Men opposed. They are alien growths in our theological garden and require constant weeding.

What was happening in this distorted preaching?

Perhaps the most significant underlying issue was that the gospel was being preached in a way that implied a separation between Christ and the benefits of the gospel. It is possible in stating the biblical truth "Christ died for you" to separate the person (now risen) from the work (he "died" sometime in the past). But for Boston part of the appeal of Preston's language is the way in which it encapsulated the unity of person and work in Christ: " '*he is dead*'—and it is as such that I offer him to you as a risen and all-sufficient Savior."

False Separation

This point might be clarified by expressing it the other way around. The benefits of the gospel (justification, reconciliation, redemption, adoption) were being separated from Christ, who is himself the gospel. The benefits of the gospel are *in Christ. They do not exist apart from him.* They are *ours* only *in him.* They cannot be abstracted from him as if we ourselves could possess them independently of him.

This separation rarely takes place deliberately as a conscious decision in either doctrinal exposition or gospel preaching; nevertheless it does frequently take place. It is a subtle change from the preaching and teaching of the New Testament, with potentially far-reaching effects. By no means has it been limited to the history of *Reformed* preaching, but that is the focus of our interest here.

A major indication that such a separation has taken place is that one of the most prominent emphases in the New Testament becomes marginalized, namely, union with Christ.

We can think of the significance of this in the following way: what is my default way of describing a believer? Perhaps it is exactly that: "believer." Or perhaps "disciple," "born-again person," or "saint" (more biblical but less common in Protestantism!). Most likely it is the term "Christian."

Yet these descriptors, while true enough, occur relatively rarely in the pages of the New Testament. Indeed the most common of them today ("Christian") is virtually nonexistent in the New Testament, and the contexts in which it occurs might suggest that it was a pejorative term used of (rather than by) the early church.[15]

New Testament Christians did not think of themselves as "Christians"! But if not, how did they think of themselves?

Contrast these descriptors with the overwhelmingly dominant way the New Testament describes believers. It is that we are "in Christ." The expression, in one form or another, occurs well over one hundred times in Paul's thirteen letters.[16]

Then draw the obvious conclusion: If this is not the overwhelmingly dominant way in which we think about ourselves, we are not thinking with the renewed mind of the gospel. But in addition, without this perspective it is highly likely that we will have a tendency to separate Christ from his benefits and abstract those benefits from him (in whom alone they are to be found) *as though we possessed them in ourselves*.[17]

---

[15] On the few occasions the term "Christian" appears in the New Testament, this may well be the implication: Acts 11:26; 26:28; 1 Pet. 4:16.

[16] It is reckoned that in the Pauline corpus, *en Christō* occurs eighty-three times and *en kuriō* another forty-seven times—and this does not include the frequent occurrence of "in him," etc. J. D. G. Dunn, *The Theology of Paul the Apostle* (Grand Rapids, MI: Eerdmans, 1998), 396–97. Given these statistics and the fact that they serve as an index to the centrality of this perspective, the neglect of the theme is as staggering as the evidence for it—and alarming to boot.

[17] The recovery of the role of covenant in biblical theology, followed closely by discussions of the role of the law and its place within the context of the gospel, leads by a kind of necessity to a resurgence of interest in union with Christ—since it answers the question of how, following the New Testament, we are to think about the Christian life. It is, therefore, striking (not to say encouraging) that a shelf of literature on union with Christ has been published since the turn of the millennium.

If the benefits of Christ's work (justification, reconciliation, adoption, and so on) are abstracted from Christ himself, and the proclamation of the gospel is made in terms of what it offers rather than in terms of Christ himself, the question naturally arises: To whom can I offer these benefits?

Against the background of a confessional particularism (a belief in distinguishing election and particular redemption), this separation led to the answer: since the benefits of the work of Christ belong to the elect (alone), it is to the elect alone that they should be offered. Hence—

> *Question:* But how do we know who the elect are?
> *Answer:* The elect according to grace repent of sin.
> *Conclusion:* Therefore the benefits of the gospel are to be offered to those who repent.

Thus in a subtle way we become insensitive to the difference between offering the benefits of Christ and offering Christ himself. When the Marrow Men's free offer of Christ without qualification was read from within this paradigm, friction was inevitable.

This was a tragically different approach to the gospel and its proclamation from the one found in the New Testament, the teaching of the Reformation, and the mainstream Puritans.

What was at the heart of their gospel message? Calvin has a beautiful expression that summarizes it: the gospel is Christ "clothed with his gospel."[18] This, to use an Augustinian term, is *totus Christus*, the whole Christ, the person in whom incarnation has been accomplished and in whom atonement, resurrection, ascension, and heavenly reign are now realized.

While we can distinguish Christ's person and his work in analytical theological categories, they are inseparable from each other. Since there is no "work of Christ" that takes place *abstracted from,*

[18] John Calvin, *Institutes of the Christian Religion*, trans. F. L. Battles, ed. J. T. McNeill (Philadelphia: Westminster Press, 1960), 3.2.6.

and in that sense outside of, his person, the blessings of his work cannot be appropriated apart from receiving Christ himself with all his benefits. What God has joined together, we must not put asunder.

Yet this was precisely what had happened—and continues to happen. The result was that the benefits of Christ's work were being offered only to those who saw signs in themselves that they belonged to the elect. In stark contrast—as the Marrow Brethren understood, and none more clearly than Boston—the gospel offer is Christ *himself* in whom the blessings are found.

The annotations Boston prepared for his own edition of *The Marrow of Modern Divinity* provide us with a transcript of the reading and reflection pilgrimage that it prompted. Edward Fisher led him to John Preston and to some words that may well have provided the clue he needed to resolve the issues that troubled him in preaching the gospel:

> You must first have Christ himself, before you can partake of those benefits by him.[19]

This was perfectly in keeping with Calvin's emphasis that salvation becomes ours *in* Christ and not merely *through* Christ.[20] Indeed it had been deeply embedded in the Scottish theological tradition by the *Confessio Scotticana* of 1560: "By this faith we grasp Christ

---

[19] Boston notes these words from his own reading of Preston in Fisher, *Marrow*, 154. In keeping with this perspective, Boston impressively expounds union with Christ as the context for the application of redemption and also as the context for sanctification. *The Whole Works of the Late Reverend Thomas Boston*, ed. S. M'Millan, 12 vols. (Edinburgh, 1848–1852), 1:544–56; 2:5–14.

[20] These are almost "throwaway comments" (although such are few and far between in Calvin's writings!). Calvin states on more than one occasion that he prefers to use the phrase "in Christ" rather than "through Christ." Whereas the latter communicates that Christ is source and mediator of salvation, the former stresses that the salvation is to be found only *in* him and is ours only through union with him: "I prefer, however, to retain Paul's words *in Christ Jesus*, rather than to render with Erasmus *by Christ Jesus*, because this conveys more clearly the ingrafting by which we are made one with Christ." John Calvin, *The Epistles of Paul the Apostle to the Romans and to the Thessalonians*, trans. Ross Mackenzie, ed. D. W. Torrance and T. F. Torrance (Edinburgh, Oliver & Boyd, 1965), 128. "I preferred to keep the phrase 'in Him' rather than change it to 'by Him' because in my opinion it is more vivid and forceful. For we are enriched in Christ, because we are members of His body, and we have been ingrafted into Him; and, furthermore, since we have been made one with Him, He shares with us all that He has received from the Father." *The First Epistle of Paul the Apostle to the Corinthians*, trans. J. W. Fraser, ed. D. W. Torrance and T. F. Torrance (Edinburgh, Oliver & Boyd, 1965), 21.

with the graces and blessings promised in him." But this truth had been lost sight of and badly needed to be recovered.

What was true then may still be true now. It is not only that until very recently an emphasis on union with Christ was tellingly absent from the evangelical subculture, but with it the corollary that the reason we need to grasp this emphasis is that everything we need for salvation is *in him* and not in us.

This point is arrestingly made by Professor John Murray at the conclusion of an extended exposition of Romans 3:24. He comments on the expression "the redemption that is in Christ Jesus" in words loaded with significance for gospel preaching:

> It should be noted in addition that the apostle conceives of this redemption as something that has its permanent and abiding tenancy in Christ; it is "the redemption that is in Christ Jesus." The redemption is not simply that which we have in Christ (Ephesians 1:7) but it is the redemption of which Christ is the embodiment. Redemption has not only been wrought by Christ but in the Redeemer this redemption resides in its unabbreviated virtue and efficacy. And it is redemption thus conceived that provides the mediacy through which justification by God's free grace is applied.[21]

Notice the difference in emphasis here. When the benefits are seen as abstractable from the Benefactor the issue becomes:

1) For the preacher: "How can I offer these benefits?" and
2) For the hearer: "How can I get these benefits into my life?"

But when it is seen that Christ and his benefits are inseparable and that the latter are not abstractable commodities, the primary question becomes:

[21] John Murray, *The Epistle to the Romans*, vol. 1 (Grand Rapids, MI: Eerdmans), 116. While it would be rash to go to the stake for Boston's interpretation of Preston's expression "Christ is dead for you," it is precisely the point Professor Murray is here emphasizing that lends to the expression the value Boston found in it.

1) For the preacher: "How do I preach Christ himself?" and
2) For the hearer: "How do I get into Christ?"[22]

The difference in orientation of thought, and subsequently in our preaching, may seem incidental—after all, do we not get the same salvation at the end of the day? But this focus on benefits has a profound impact on how we understand and preach the gospel, and, almost imperceptibly, Christ *himself* ceases to be central and becomes a means to an end. This is why it is even possible to preach through one of the Gospels with a focus on *how we share the experience of the various characters in the narratives*. While this is proper in its place, it can easily divert us from the central question: *Who is the Christ who IS the gospel, and how is he equipped to save us?*[23]

If we are slow to grasp the distinction, its significance can be illustrated by reflecting on contemporary evangelical preaching and writing. Wherever the benefits of Christ are seen as abstractable from Christ himself, there is a decreasing stress on his person and work in preaching and in the books that are published to feed that

[22] In this context, note that the vast preponderance of New Testament passages speak of our getting "into Christ" and not of "getting Christ into us." There is a massively greater stress on being "in Christ" than there is on how Christ indwells us, important though this latter emphasis is. This gives rise to the suggestion that the undergirding theological emphasis is that our need is to "get out of ourselves and into Christ" rather than "get Christ into ourselves." While there is a proper duality to be maintained (we are "in Christ," and, by the Spirit, Christ dwells "in us") the fundamental dynamic is centrifugal rather than centripetal. In the light of this, it is probably a fair criticism of post-seventeenth-century evangelicalism that the "Christ in us" motif played a greater role than the "we are in Christ" perspective and thereby contributed to an imbalance of the subjective orientation over the objective orientation and the indwelling over the fundamental union. Paradoxically, therefore, evangelicalism, on its pietistic side (the adjective is used here in a technical rather than an emotive sense), became fertile soil for elements reminiscent of Schleiermacher's emphasis on the importance of the subjective "feeling" of the Christian, in distinction from the rational and intellectual aspects of the gospel. What was sometimes (often?) lost sight of was the biblical (not merely "academic" or "intellectual") principle that *spiritual* transformation takes place through the renewal of the *mind* (Rom. 12:1–2). This is simply a further aspect of the story traced by Mark A. Noll in *The Scandal of the Evangelical Mind* (Grand Rapids, MI: Eerdmans, 1995), which opens with the chilling sentence, "The scandal of the evangelical mind is that there is not so much of an evangelical mind" (3).

[23] As a codicil to this comment, we should also notice that knowing how to "preach Christ from the Old Testament," or understanding biblical theology, or seeing the flow of redemptive history, or knowing how to get to Christ from any part of the Scriptures does not necessarily result in actually preaching *the person of Jesus Christ himself*. Seeing Christ as the solution to a series of clues embedded in the Old Testament is not actually the same as proclaiming Jesus *himself*, in our flesh, bearing our sins, dying our death, and rising for our justification. A formula for preaching Christ is not identical to the *persona* of Christ, and we must never confuse hermeneutical principles with Christ himself. The former did not die for us on the cross; the latter did.

preaching. This is accompanied by an increased stress on our experience of salvation rather than on the grace, majesty, and glory of the Lord Jesus Christ.[24]

Is it possible that most preachers reading these pages own more books on preaching (and even on *preaching Christ*!) than they own on Christ himself?

If that is true (a survey would certainly be illuminating), we should probably ask a further question: Is it obvious to me, and of engrossing concern, that the chief focus, the dominant note in the sermons I preach (or hear), is "Jesus Christ and him crucified"? Or is the dominant emphasis (and perhaps the greatest energies of the preacher?) focused somewhere else, perhaps on how to overcome sin, or how to live the Christian life, or on the benefits to be received from the gospel? All are legitimate emphases in their place, but that place is never center stage. The same question can be asked more starkly in our techno-sermon age when many Christians listen not only to preaching in their own church but to their "favorite" preachers in the contemporary galaxy. Is the dominant theme, the lasting impression, the most natural word association, in relation to the preaching I hear "Jesus Christ and him crucified"—or something else?[25]

There was no doubt about the focus of the Marrow Brethren.

---

[24] This might be illustrated by the way in which, for example, John Owen's work *Of the Mortification of Sin* has undoubtedly been read by many more younger ministers than either his *Glory of Christ* or *Communion with God*. That may be understandable because of the deep pastoral insight in Owen's short work; but it may also put the practical cart before the theological horse. Owen himself would not have been satisfied with hearers who learned mortification without learning Christ. A larger paradigmatic shift needs to take place than only exchanging a superficial subjectivism for Owen's rigorous subjectivism. What is required is a radical recentering in a richer and deeper knowledge of Christ, understood in terms of his person and work. There can be little doubt that Owen himself viewed things this way.

[25] Without wanting to denigrate the value many experience from listening to sermons on the World Wide Web, two words of caution are surely in order here, namely: (1) Am I fully aware of the emphases to which I am allowing myself to be exposed? (For often people listen to more sermons on the Web than they do to those preached in their own church fellowship). Is it a "Christ-full" emphasis? (2) What effect is this having on our affection for and appreciation of the preaching and the preacher in the church to which we belong? Are we engaged in an activity that, without placing a guard on our hearts and lips, may lead us to demean the servant(s) of the Word God has given to our churches and our families? By the same token, those who preach and whose preaching is then available virtually anywhere on earth need to retain a proper focus on feeding the local flock and more broadly to encourage a concern to honor the local ministry of the Word.

They wanted their preaching to be full of Christ himself. This to them was the attraction of the two expressions in the *Marrow* that caused most controversy, namely, that Christ is "the Father's deed of gift and grant to all mankind" and that it was possible to go to anyone and say to him or her, "Christ is dead for you"; that is to say, "There is a living Savior who, because he died and rose again, is sufficient to save you and indeed each and every person who comes to him in faith. There is fullness of grace in Christ crucified. And you, too, may find salvation in his name."

Sadly, just at this point Calvinists and Arminians (in historical terms, deformed Calvinists in their theology) fell into the same error of abstracting the blessings of the gospel from the person of Christ.

Arminians believe in a universal atonement that makes salvation possible for everyone (although guaranteed for none) because Christ died for everyone without exception. Thus a characteristic Arminian response to particular redemption (or "limited atonement") is to say, "If I believed this I could no longer preach the gospel to everyone, because I could no longer say to them 'Christ died for you.' So this cannot possibly be biblical teaching, since we are to preach the gospel to everyone."[26]

In a sense, the deformed Calvinism of the early eighteenth century agreed with the same underlying logic. But operating against the background of particular redemption, it reasoned that since the benefits of Christ's death do not belong to all, they should not be offered to all.

We have seen that the false step here is the separation of benefits and Benefactor. What, then, is the biblical response? It is simply that at no point do the apostles preach the gospel in these terms: "Believe because Christ died for you." No, the warrant for faith in Christ is neither knowledge of election nor a conviction of universal redemption. Nor is it a sense of our sinfulness. It is that

[26] In this connection, J. I. Packer, *Evangelism and the Sovereignty of God* (London: Inter-Varsity Press, 1961), remains a valuable guide. See esp. pp. 65ff.

Jesus Christ is able to save all those who come to God through him, since his is the only name given under heaven whereby we may be saved.[27]

Christ himself is the gospel.

Back to Jesus

Pastorally it is always helpful to go back to Jesus and his teaching to ask: How did Jesus himself preach his own gospel? Here, in the context of a prayer reflecting his belief in distinguishing election, is an example of how he engaged in evangelistic preaching:

> *Prayer*: I thank you, Father, Lord of heaven and earth, that you have hidden these things from the wise and understanding and revealed them to little children; yes, Father, for such was your gracious will.

That is, surely, unconditional election. But then Jesus says:

> *Preaching*: Come to me, all who labor and are heavy laden, and I will give you rest. Take my yoke upon you, and learn from me. For I am gentle and lowly in heart, and you will find rest for your souls. For my yoke is easy, and my burden is light.[28]

Here, to "labor" and to be "heavy laden" are not *qualifications* for coming to Christ. They are reassurances that none is disqualified from coming to him by weakness and unworthiness. Yes, even the "disqualified" who are weak and helpless are invited to come to him! The Gospels make clear that it was to the "disqualified" that he delighted to offer himself.

This separation of the benefits of the gospel from Christ, who is the gospel, is also the mother of the many varieties of "multiple stage" Christianity in which a person can enjoy some, but not nec-

[27] Heb. 7:23–25; Acts 4:12.

[28] Matt. 11:25–26, 29–30. Boston preached a series of sermons on this text in January and February 1711; *Works* 9:169–219.

essarily all, of the discrete blessings. Thus one may experience an abstractable "second blessing"; or alternatively enjoy the blessings of salvation without obedience, having Christ as Savior but not (at least not yet) as Lord. But this, as Calvin noted, is to "rend asunder" the Savior.[29] What Marrow theology grasped was the New Testament's stress on the fact that when we are "in him," we possess Christ himself; all spiritual blessings are ours immediately and simultaneously "in him." Yes, this is true eschatologically—in the sense that their full realization awaits glorification. But, nevertheless, if we are in Christ, all blessings are ours really.

This Pauline emphasis on union with Christ had been a dominant motif in Calvin's exposition of the gospel and the Christian life. He had expounded it extensively in the *Institutes*, weaving together the forensic and the dynamic aspects of the union in his stress on justification and sanctification as distinct dimensions but inseparable realities.[30] He had also provided a rich exposition of the way this union with Christ works its way out into the Christian life in a mortification (*mortificatio*) and vivification (*vivificatio*) that are both internal (in relation to sin and self) and external in the sense that the life of the individual believer and of the community of the congregation are pressed into a death-and-resurrection pattern.[31]

In this context a review of Boston's own record of his divinity studies,[32] and of the tradition of theological education in Scotland throughout the seventeenth century,[33] leaves the distinct impression that Calvin's *Institutes* had been deposed in favor of later summaries of the Christian faith. Boston himself tells us that he studied three texts:

---

[29] Cf. his comments on Rom. 8:13: "Let believers, therefore, learn to embrace Him, not only for justification, but also for sanctification, as He has been given to us for both these purposes, that they may not rend him asunder by their own mutilated faith." *Epistles of Paul the Apostle to the Romans and to the Thessalonians*, 166. He makes similar comments on 1 Cor. 1:30 and elsewhere.

[30] Most eloquently expressed by Paul in Eph. 1:3–14.

[31] Calvin, *Institutes*, 3.5.10.

[32] Boston, *Memoirs*, 20–21.

[33] For an informative survey see Jack Whytock, *"An Educated Clergy": Scottish Theological Education and Training in the Kirk and Secession, 1560–1850* (Milton Keynes, UK: Paternoster, 2007).

> I entered on the study of theology; Mr. James Ramsey . . . having put the book in my hand, viz. Paraeus[34] on Ursin's Catechism; the which I read over three or four times ere I went to the school of divinity. . . .
>
> About 20th January 1695 I went to Edinburgh to the school of divinity, then taught by the great Mr. George Campbell. . . . A few of us, newly entered to the school of divinity, were taught for a time Riissenius's compend,[35] in the professor's chamber. Publicly in the hall he taught Essenius's compend.[36]

In a sense these three works lent themselves to coherent theological preparation: the scholastic methodology with its question-and-answer format and the compendium of theology provide the shortest route for a student to grasp the architecture of systematic theology. But one cannot help feeling that there was a loss of the genius of Calvin's life project of producing commentaries on the text of Scripture and developing and perfecting the *Institutes* as a companion to Scripture.[37] His deeply expository approach to theology had led him to write a *summa pietatis*[38] as distinct from a *summa theologiae*. This afforded him the opportunity to reflect at length on the person and work of Christ and the significance of union with him. Indeed he had stressed in the opening paragraph to *Institutes* III:

> First, we must understand that as long as Christ remains outside of us, and we are separated from him, all that he has suffered

[34] David Paraeus (1548–1622) was a student of Zacharias Ursinus (1534–1583) at the Collegium Sapientiae in Heidelberg and became its director in 1591. From 1598 to 1622 he taught Old and New Testaments in the theological faculty of the university. The reference to the "catechism" is to the Heidelberg Catechism of which Ursinus was principal author and on which he wrote an extensive commentary.

[35] Leonardus Rijssenius (Leonard van Rijssen, 1636–1700) was a Dutch Reformed theologian whose entire ministry was set in pastoral context. He authored his own *summa theologiae* (1671) and also a compendium based on the work of Francis Turretin.

[36] Boston, *Memoirs*, 20–21. Andreas Essenius (1618–1677) was professor of theology at the University of Utrecht from 1653 to 1677 and served as *rector magnificus* of the university in 1673–1674. Essenius published a three-volume systematic theology (1659–1665) and in 1669 a shorter summary of it entitled *Compendium theologiae dogmaticum*.

[37] See "John Calvin to the Reader," *Institutes*, 1.4–5.

[38] These words formed part of the subtitle to the *Institutes* from its original edition in 1536 and contrast with (although do not contradict) the concept of *summa theologiae*.

> and done for the salvation of the human race remains useless and is of no value to us.

The reality of this union is effected, he continues, through

> the secret energy of the Spirit, by which we come to enjoy Christ and all his benefits.[39]

To which he later adds,

> This, then, is the true knowledge of Christ, if we receive him as he is offered by the Father: namely, clothed with his gospel.[40]

It was perhaps another decade before Boston, stimulated by the *Marrow* and grasping the "big idea" in Preston, came right through to see that what we receive in the gospel is not benefits but Christ and that therefore the focus of public preaching and private pastoral ministry must be to set forth Christ.

This eventually brought him to hold and to share the perspective expressed by Calvin in lyrical fashion as he expounds Christ in terms of the clauses of the Apostles' Creed:

> When we see salvation whole—its every single part
> is found in Christ,
> we must beware lest we derive the smallest drop
> from somewhere else.
>
> If we seek salvation,
> the very name of Jesus
> teaches us
> that he possesses it.
>
> If other Spirit-given gifts are sought—in his anointing they are
> found;
> strength—in his reign; and purity—in his conception;

[39] Calvin, *Institutes*, 3.1.1.
[40] Ibid., 3.2.6.

tenderness—expressed in his nativity,
in which he was made like us in all respects, that he might feel
our pain:

Redemption when we seek it, is in his passion found;
acquittal—in his condemnation lies;
and freedom from the curse—in his cross is known.
If satisfaction for our sins we seek—we'll find it in his
sacrifice.

There's cleansing in his blood.
And if it's reconciliation that we need, for it he entered Hades;
if mortification of our flesh—then in his tomb it's laid.
And newness of our life—his resurrection brings and
immortality as well come also with that gift.

And if we long to find that heaven's kingdom's our
inheritance,
His entry there secures it now
with our protection, safety too, and blessings that abound
—all flowing from his kingly reign.

The sum of all for those who seek such treasure-trove of
blessings,
These blessings of all kinds, is this:
from nowhere else than him can they be drawn;
For they are ours in Christ alone.[41]

---

[41] John Calvin, *Institutes of the Christian Religion*, 2.16.19, 1559 Latin ed., translation and versification mine.

3

PREPARATION, DISTORTION, POISON

What is the gospel, and how are we to preach it? The Marrow Controversy raised these vital questions. That is why it is of more than antiquarian interest. Nor was it an ethnic, distinctively Scottish controversy. It was a gospel one. It highlighted the error of separating the benefits of Christ's work from the Savior himself.

False Preparationism

There was an additional danger in the paradigm that separated Christ and his benefits and tended to make the subjective work of the Spirit in the elect the condition of the offer of the gospel. It encouraged a preparationism that in effect became an obstacle to the free offer of the gospel:

> You may know these benefits—if you are among the elect.
>
> You may receive forgiveness—if you have sufficiently forsaken sin.
>
> You may know the message of grace—if you have experienced a sufficient degree of conviction of sin.

But this was to put the cart before the horse and turn the message of the gospel on its head. Again it tended (and tends) to happen subtly and imperceptibly.[1] For whenever we make the warrant to believe in Christ to any degree dependent upon our subjective condition, we distort it. Repentance, turning from sin, and degrees of conviction of sin do not constitute the grounds on which Christ is offered to us. They may constitute ways in which the Spirit works as the gospel makes its impact on us. But they never form the warrant for repentance and faith.

This point is made in a sermon by C. H. Spurgeon entitled "Christ Crucified," preached in 1858. In a characteristically good-spirited aside he makes a critical comment on one of his favorite books by one of his favorite authors, John Bunyan's *Pilgrim's Progress*:

> By the way, let me tell you a little story about Bunyan's *Pilgrim's Progress*. I am a great lover of John Bunyan, but I do not believe him infallible. And the other day I met with a story about him which I think a very good one. There was young man in Edinburgh who wished to be a missionary. He was a wise young man so he thought, "If I am to be a missionary, there is no need for me to transport myself far away from home. I may as well be a missionary in Edinburgh."
>
> Well, this young man started and determined to speak to the first person he met. He met one of those old fish wives with her basket of fish on her back. Those of us who have seen them can never forget them. They are extraordinary women indeed.
>
> So stepping up to her, he said, "Here you are coming along with your burden on your back, let me ask you, have you got another burden, a spiritual burden?"
>
> "What," she asked, "you mean that burden in John Bunyan's *Pilgrim's Progress*? Because if you do, young man, I got

[1] As in everything else, there was, and is, a spectrum and a gradient in the impact a person's theology makes on his preaching of the gospel.

rid of that burden many years ago, probably before you were born. But I went a way better than the Pilgrim did. The Evangelist that John Bunyan talks about was one of your parsons that do not preach the gospel, for he said, 'keep that light in thine eye and run to the wicket gate.' Why, man alive, that was not the place to run to! He should have said, 'Do you see that Cross, run there at once.' But instead of that he sent the poor pilgrim to the wicket gate first and much good he got by going there, he got tumbling into the slough and was like to have been killed by it."

> The young man was rather abashed. "But did you not," the young man asked, "go through any Slough of Despond?"
>
> "Yes, I did, but I found it a great deal easier going through it with my burden off than with it on!"
>
> The old woman [continued Spurgeon] was quite right. John Bunyan put the putting off of the burden too far off from the commencing of the pilgrimage. If he meant to describe what usually happens, he was right. But if he meant to show what ought to have happened, he was wrong. The cross should be right in front of the wicket gate and we should say to the sinner, "Throw thyself down there and thou art safe, but thou art not safe 'til thou canst cast the burden and lie at the foot of the Cross and find peace in Jesus."[2]

In the interests of integrity it should be said that commentators on *Pilgrim's Progress* have debated Bunyan's exact intention at this point in the narrative. Is he depicting conversion or assurance? Clearly both Spurgeon and his fishwife believed the narrative was intended to describe conversion. If so, then the point is well taken.[3] It is not a denial of the work of the Spirit of God in bringing men to a sense of the conviction of their sin. But neither conviction nor the forsaking of sin constitutes the warrant for the gospel offer. Christ

[2] Charles Spurgeon, sermon, in *Metropolitan Tabernacle Pulpit*, vol. 44: 211–12.

[3] Even if, as some think, Bunyan is representing assurance, Spurgeon's comment nevertheless underscores the point that is being made here.

himself is the warrant, since he is able to save all who come to him.[4] He is offered without conditions. We are to go straight to him! It is not necessary to have any money in order to be able to buy Christ.[5]

The Gospel Spine

The subtle nature of the issue pointed up here emerges in a rather puzzling difference between two works produced at opposite ends of the Puritan era. Both William Perkins (1558–1602) and John Bunyan (1628–1688) produced what Perkins described as an "ocular catechism"—in his case a diagram of "The Golden Chaine of Salvation" and in Bunyan's "A Map Shewing the Order and Causes of Salvation and Damnation."[6]

Both "charts" appear to have the same goal—to give a pictorial representation of how God works in relation to salvation and damnation. They are single-page, visual representations of truths that would take an entire volume to expound; their diagrammatic form made them helpful for those with poor reading skills and perhaps even for some with none. In essence they were Puritan PowerPoint presentations!

The same elements are present in each chart as they trace salvation from eternity to eternity. There is, however, one major, striking, albeit puzzling, difference.

In Perkins's chart, every aspect of the application of salvation is tied in to a central spine representing Christ in terms of the various clauses of the Apostles' Creed. One might surmise that Calvin's words quoted earlier had made a profound impact on him.[7]

---

[4] Heb. 7:25.

[5] Isa. 55:1–2.

[6] Both charts can be readily accessed (and in some instances purchased) from a variety of websites by searching for Perkins Chart and Bunyan Map of Salvation.

[7] John Calvin, *Institutes of the Christian Religion*, trans. F. L. Battles, ed. J. T. McNeill (Philadelphia: Westminster Press, 1960), 2.16.19. This is stated in full consciousness that some scholars have taken the opposite view, namely, that Perkins's theology is one of the major influences on a later federal theology that moved away from Calvin and to that extent was less Christ centered. But the high Calvinism of Perkins's chart should not blind us to the central role of Christ in it. A better perspective is represented by Richard A. Muller, *Christ and the Decree: Christology and Predestination in Reformed Theology from Calvin to Perkins* (1986; repr. Grand Rapids, MI: Baker Academic, 2008).

In Bunyan's chart, however, the Father, the Son, and the Holy Spirit are portrayed as the fountainhead of salvation. Everything flows from them. But Bunyan's map has no Christ-spine.[8] Certainly the Trinity is seen as the original source and cause of salvation. But the various aspects of salvation applied are related *to each other*, not directly to Christ. To use Perkins's metaphor, it is as if the links in the chain are joined one to another but are remotely connected *to Christ himself* only as their original link and first cause.

It would doubtless require a doctoral dissertation to explore all the issues involved in these differences and to what extent they were played out in the preaching of the gospel.[9] But to whatever extent this impacted Bunyan's preaching, these charts represent two different configurations of how the gospel works. In the case of Perkins's *Golden Chaine* the central significance of Christ and union with him is obvious; in Bunyan's chart this is not so. In Perkins every spiritual blessing is related to Christ; benefits are never separated or abstracted from the Benefactor. In Bunyan's map, in fact they are.

If this mode of thinking permeates our approach to gospel preaching, the focus inevitably shifts to abstracted and discrete blessings, and then to the question of how we receive them, and thus ultimately to the issue: "Under or through what conditions can these blessings become mine?" The tendency is to turn me inward. But the warrant for justifying faith in Christ does not lie within. To think this was precisely the mistake of the young Luther. For this reason Staupitz's famous instruction to seek his predestination "in the wounds of Christ" was a telling exhortation that would lead him to discover that the warrant for the gospel is without, not within.

---

[8] I stress that whether Bunyan followed through to the logical implications of this diagram is not the question at issue here. My real concern is that de facto as *models*, these two portrayals represent important differences in configuring the *ordo salutis* in relationship to the person and work of Christ.

[9] See Pieter de Vries, *John Bunyan on the Order of Salvation*, trans. C. Van Haaften (Bern: Peter Lang, 1995).

Slowly this way of thinking about the *ordo salutis* may drift into what is sometimes referred to as "the steps of salvation" in which a quasi-chronological order of experience precedes actual faith. This can become an eerie echo of the medieval *ordo salutis.* In due course, since these steps follow one another, the completion of one step must precede the commencement of the next one.[10] And precisely there the question arises, How much conviction of sin, or sorrow for sin, or turning away from sin is required before the next step or phase can begin?

In this connection, in line with the wisest Reformed theologians and pastors, John Owen writes:

> No certain rule or measure of them can be prescribed as necessary in or antecedaneously unto conversion . . . perturbations, sorrows, dejections, dreads, fears, are no duty unto any; . . . God is pleased to exercise a prerogative and sovereignty in this whole matter, and deals with the souls of men in unspeakable variety. Some he leads by the gates of death and hell unto rest in his love . . . and the paths of others he makes plain and easy unto them. Some walk or wander long in darkness; in the souls of others Christ is formed in the first gracious visitation.[11]

Peter's preaching on the day of Pentecost furnishes us with a model. He does not make conviction of sin in his hearers the condition for the offer of Christ to them. Christ himself is the warrant for faith, and so his sermon is profoundly Christocentric. Christ

[10] This becomes especially dominant where the "chain" metaphor is made a hermeneutical and not merely a heuristic key, since each link *closes around* the preceding one.

[11] John Owen, *Pneumatologia* or *A Discourse Concerning the Holy Spirit* (London, 1674); *The Works of John Owen,* 24 vols., ed. W. H. Goold (Edinburgh: Johnstone & Hunter, 1850–1855), 3:360–61. The last two sentences in the quotation might readily be taken as a transcript of Bunyan's own experience and also, poignantly, of Owen's. Bunyan records his pilgrimage in detail in his autobiographical work, *Grace Abounding to the Chief of Sinners* (London, 1666). Owen's experience, while rarely, and much more guardedly, described by him in his writings, was also a painful pilgrimage, to which he makes veiled allusions in terms of the gospel pericope that brought him to a settled peace, namely, Christ's stilling of the storm. But the vivid and sometimes excruciating experience of individuals must not be allowed to dislodge Christ alone as the warrant for saving faith. Sadly, sometimes it has, and coming to Christ has been made more difficult than the Savior ever intended. Spurgeon himself has some wise pastoral observations in relationship to conviction of sin in *The Full Harvest* (Edinburgh: Banner of Truth, 1973), 235.

as the benefactor in whom the forgiveness of sins is to be found is proclaimed.

The response?

> When they heard this they were cut to the heart, and said to Peter and the rest of the apostles, "Brothers, what shall we do?" And Peter said to them, "Repent and be baptized every one of you in the name of Jesus Christ for the forgiveness of your sins, and you will receive the gift of the Holy Spirit."[12]

The "order" is:

> Christ is proclaimed in the fullness of his person and work as the crucified Savior raised as Lord (vindicated and able to save).
>
> Conviction of sin is wrought by the Spirit.
>
> Believing (implicit in what Peter says) and repenting (two aspects of one and the same reality in the New Testament) and experiencing the blessings that are found in Christ (given emblematic form in baptism).

We have noted that the shift from a "Perkins style" way of thinking to a "Bunyan style" ordinarily takes place imperceptibly, subconsciously. But precisely because that is so, *the reversal of it* may prove difficult and require a certain self-conscious awareness and even criticism. For some this may happen only if the biblical teaching causes a eureka moment when they see things in a different light. At least so it was for Boston.

If we were able to ask Bunyan, "Why did you make such a drastic change from William Perkins's 'Ocular Catechism' when you drew your 'Map'?" he might well reply, "Did I?" For such a difference in paradigm is usually crafted into the spectacle lenses through which we view the gospel. Without our realizing it, these

[12] Acts 2:37–38. Luke thus records the Father's answer to Jesus's prayer on the cross (Luke 23:34) for the forgiveness of those present who do not know what they are doing.

lenses are in measure determining what we see. It is for this reason a much more subtle and subliminal influence than we may appreciate.

The younger Boston did not seem to have understood the undergirding structure of his own preaching until he was stimulated by his reading of the *Marrow* and found fresh insight into how to preach the gospel biblically. When that did take place, a new freedom and joy seems to have broken out in his preaching. There was, he realized (and others recognized), a new "tincture" in it.[13]

"Tincture" was a particularly apt term to use. It is derived from the Latin *tinctura*, which refers to the process of dyeing—in which a piece of cloth is recolored by dipping it into liquid dye. The cloth remains the same but is now entirely of a different color or shade. Both to himself and others, Boston's preaching "felt" like that. Extending the metaphor, one might say that now the garment of the gospel in which Christ was dressed in Boston's preaching was dyed a shade of "Christ-in-whom-every-spiritual-blessing-is-found" rather than merely "I am offering you spiritual blessings."

But there was a yet deeper issue that lay behind the Marrow Controversy.

Distorting God

The whole point of the Auchterarder Creed was to test whether a ministerial candidate believed in and would stress the unfettered grace of God and the freeness and fullness of the gospel offer in his preaching and pastoral ministry. The same motivation energized the Marrow Brethren. They saw that to make the offer of grace dependent upon anything, not least upon graces, was to distort the true nature of grace.[14]

This was so in *the accomplishing of salvation in Christ*. The

[13] Thomas Boston, *Memoirs of Thomas Boston* (Edinburgh: Banner of Truth, 1988), 171.

[14] Doing so transforms an evangelical *ordo salutis* regressively into a medieval form in which what was accomplished in the individual "by grace" then became the ground for further operations of grace and ultimately actual justification.

Marrow theology emphasized that salvation is accomplished through grace. Passages such as Romans 5:6–8 underlined this. For when and how did God show his grace to us? Were there conditions to be met in us prior to Christ's grace? Clearly not, since it was:

> *While we were still weak*, at the right time Christ died for the *ungodly*.
> *While we were still sinners*, Christ died for us.
> *While we were enemies* we were reconciled to God by the death of his Son.[15]

What conditions were met in us in order for God to send his only Son into the world to die for sinners? None. Indeed there can be none. This is what Boston found valuable in the expression "Christ is dead for you." For Boston this meant: "I do not offer Christ to you on the grounds that you have repented. Indeed I offer him to men and women who are dead in their trespasses and sins. This gospel offer of Jesus Christ himself is for you, whoever and whatever you are."

One of the dangers Boston recognized was that conditionalism feeds back into how we view God himself. It introduces a layer of distortion into his character. For it is possible to see that no conditions for grace can be met by us yet still to hold to a subtle conditionality in God's grace in itself.

This comes to expression when the gospel is preached in these terms:

> God loves you because Christ died for you!

How do those words distort the gospel? They imply that the death of Christ is the reason for the love of God for me.

By contrast the Scriptures affirm that the love of God for us is

[15] See Rom. 5:6–8, 10.

the reason for the death of Christ. That is the emphasis of John 3:16. God (i.e., the Father, since here "God" is the antecedent of "his . . . Son") *so loved* the world that he gave his Son for us. The Son does not need to do anything to persuade the Father to love us; he already loves us!

The subtle danger here should be obvious: if we speak of the cross of Christ as *the cause* of the love of the Father, we imply that behind the cross and apart from it he may not actually love us at all. He needs to be "paid" a ransom price in order to love us.[16] But if it has required the death of Christ to persuade him to love us ("Father, if I die, will you begin to love them?"), how can we ever be sure the Father himself loves us—"deep down" with an everlasting love? True, the Father does not love us *because* we are sinners; but he does love us *even though* we are sinners. He loved us *before* Christ died for us. It is *because* he loves us that Christ died for us!

We must not confuse the truth that our sins are forgiven only because of the death and resurrection of Christ with the very different notion that God loves us only because of the death and resurrection of Christ. No, "he loved us from the first of time"[17] and *therefore* sent his Son, who came willingly, to die for us. In this way a right understanding of the work of Christ leads to a true understanding of the matchless love the Father has for us. There is no dysfunction in the fellowship of the Trinity.

Boston's reflections in this connection are illuminating. In his *Memoirs* he comments on the fact that in earlier life his preaching had been marred by legalism in his own spirit: "I had several convictions of legality in my own practice," he wrote in 1704 look-

[16]It is, alas, this distorted teaching that in part has exposed the doctrine of penal substitutionary atonement to abuse. But the ensuing caricature of the gospel is itself open to criticism. Critics of well-established doctrinal views should (1) be accurate in their representations of the views they oppose, and (2) choose the strongest version of the view they seek to critique. Otherwise all that is accomplished is the knocking down of a straw man and with it a certain lack of intellectual integrity in the critic. Unfortunately the *distortion* of the atonement is too often in the thinking of the critic, and he (or she) ends up criticizing his (or her) own misunderstanding and purveying it as insight, instead of realizing that he (or she) is exposing a personal lack of understanding of the gospel and setting on fire only a straw man.

[17]From the Scottish Paraphrase of Rom. 8:31–39: "Let Christian faith and hope dispel."

ing back on his earlier ministry.[18] Later, however, he was of a very different mind: "I had no great fondness for the doctrine of the conditionality of the covenant of grace."[19]

Interestingly Boston also had reservations about what is known as the "covenant of redemption" or the "covenant of peace [*pactum salutis*]," the idea of a supra-temporal covenant made between the Father and the Son with a view to our redemption. It was in connection with this that Jonathan Edwards commented that he did not "understand the scheme of thought" of Boston's work *The Covenant of Grace*, although of his *Human Nature in Its Fourfold State* he wrote, "I . . . liked it exceeding well. I think, in that, he shows himself to be a truly great divine."[20]

Boston's view was that the covenant of grace was made with Christ as the second man and last Adam, and in him for his people. The likely impetus for his rejecting the idea of the covenant of redemption was that it might suggest that the loving commitment of the Father toward sinners was conditional upon the obedience of the Son, instead of the context for that obedience. This in turn suggests a "love-gap" between the Father and the Son in their disposition toward sinners. Not only would such a doctrine imply a dysfunction within the life of the Trinity, but it especially distorts the character of the Father in the mind of the Christian believer.

[18] Boston, *Memoirs*, 168.

[19] Ibid., 170.

[20] A compliment indeed to have Edwards say in the same breath that he cannot understand Boston but considers him a "truly great divine." Edwards's comments are in a remarkable letter written on September 4, 1747, to his (Scottish) correspondent Thomas Gillespie. See *The Works of Jonathan Edwards*, 2 vols. (1834; repr. Edinburgh: Banner of Truth, 1974), 1:*xci*. At this time Edwards maintained a correspondence with a number of Scottish ministers who from time to time supplied him with books published in the United Kingdom. It was these brethren who originally proposed to him the idea of a "Concert for Prayer." At the time of Edwards's dismissal from his Northampton congregation, Ralph Erskine (a leading Marrow Man) raised with him the possibility of immigrating to Scotland to serve in the Presbyterian ministry. Edwards was—given his dates—a British subject, but interestingly described North America as "my own country." In declining the suggestion Edwards provides us with an illuminating insight into his thinking: "As to my subscribing to the substance of the Westminster Confession, there would be no difficulty; and as to the Presbyterian government, I have long been perfectly out of conceit of our unsettled, independent, confused way of church government in this land; and the Presbyterian way has ever appeared to me most agreeable to the word of God, and the reason and nature of things." Lest any Scot be carried away with this encomium, however, Edwards adds: "though I cannot say that I think, that the Presbyterian government of the church of Scotland is so perfect, that it cannot, in some respects, be mended." Ibid., 1:*cxxi*.

We can be sure that Jesus's disposition toward us is through and through love; but we fear that the Father's disposition is the result of persuasion, not personal devotion. Indeed it may be he is reluctantly gracious, since it took the death of Christ to make him so.

If this is the atmosphere in which we preach the gospel and people respond to it, a suspicion of the Father may linger long and prove to be a serious hindrance in the course of the Christian life. While often dormant in our souls, from time to time the thought will erupt that perhaps the Father himself, in himself, does not love us as the Son does. Such a disposition leads to a spirit of suspicion, and even of bondage, not one of freedom and joy. Then, when we ask the question, "Who is this Father God with whom we have to do and what manner of Father is he?" we may never fully escape the suspicion that he is not a Father of infinite love after all.[21]

Believing the Lie

In effect, this is the lie by which Eve was deceived.[22] She "exchanged the truth about God for a lie."[23]

The truth was that the Lord had given Adam and Eve an entire cosmos of good gifts to enjoy. In turn he provided them with a single "positive" law.[24] They were to show their love for him by refusing to eat the fruit of only one tree, on the basis that their loving Father said so, and that whatever he commanded must be for their good.

The lie by which the Serpent deceived Eve was enshrined in the double suggestion that

[21] The import of this is deeply harmful in the lives of many Christians with respect to their fellowship with the Father. This well illustrates the ramifications of a false view of the relationship between the Trinity and the atonement.

[22] While it is often with Paul that this observation is associated (2 Cor. 11:3; 1 Tim. 2:14), he makes it only by way of exegesis and exposition of Eve's own words in Gen. 3:13 ("The serpent deceived me").

[23] Rom. 1:25.

[24] "Positive" here in the technical sense that refraining from eating the fruit of the Tree of the Knowledge of Good and Evil was a command added to the instinctive obedience that was written into their constitution as the image of God.

> 1) this Father was in fact restrictive, self-absorbed, and selfish since he would not let them eat from any of the trees,[25] and 2) his promise of death if they were disobedient was simply false.[26]

Thus the lie was an assault on both God's generosity and his integrity. Neither his character nor his words were to be trusted. This, in fact, is the lie that sinners have believed ever since—the lie of the not-to-be-trusted-because-he-does-not-love-me-false-Father.

The gospel is designed to deliver us from this lie. For it reveals that behind and manifested in the coming of Christ and his death for us is the love of a Father who gives us everything he has: first his Son to die for us and then his Spirit to live within us.[27]

If one can reduce the concern of the Marrow Brethren to its starkest terms, it is this: the issue that arose was similar to the issue between our Lord Jesus Christ and the Pharisees. The reason our Lord's severest words were addressed to them was that they shared the theology of the Serpent:

> You are of your father the devil, and your will is to do your father's desires. He . . . does not stand in the truth, because there is no truth in him. When he lies, he speaks out of his own character, for he is a liar and the father of lies.[28]

The Pharisees were men who believed in the holiness of God, and in his law, in supernatural reality, and in predestination and election. "Grace" was a big idea to them.[29] But the Pharisees believed in conditional grace (it was at the end of the day because of something in them that God was gracious to them). Their God was

[25] Gen. 3:1.
[26] Gen. 3:4.
[27] Gal. 4:4–7.
[28] John 8:44. It is in this light that John's words in John 1:17 should be read. The truth that reverses the lies of the Devil is fully revealed in the incarnation.
[29] With narrative genius, Jesus portrays the Pharisee (in the parable of the Pharisee and the tax collector) as specifically thanking God for the sovereign distinction between himself and the tax collector—a subtle abuse of grace that dis-graces it!

a conditional God. Here there was no "Come, everyone who thirsts, come to the waters; and he who has no money, come, buy and eat! Come, buy wine and milk without money and without price."[30] No, for such unconditional grace can come only from a Father whose love is conditioned by nothing outside of his own heart.

And so Jesus brought down upon them his sevenfold dominical anathema.[31]

The pastoral implications of this malformed view of the Father are powerfully expressed in a telling passage from the pen of John Owen:

> Unacquaintedness with our mercies, our privileges, is our sin as well as our trouble. We hearken not to the voice of the Spirit which is given unto us, "that we may know the things that are freely bestowed upon us of God" (1 Cor. 2:2). This makes us go heavily, when we might rejoice; and to be weak, where we might be strong in the Lord.

He continues with such a perceptive diagnosis that we might be forgiven for thinking that some members of Owen's congregation in London had moved north of the Border to Simprin or Ettrick:

> How few of the saints are experimentally acquainted with this privilege of holding immediate communion with the Father in

---

[30] Isa. 55:1. A favorite text of Thomas Boston's.

[31] Matt. 23:13, 15, 16, 23, 25, 27, 29. This point is made in full awareness of the recent scholarship that argues: (1) Old Testament religion was a religion of grace, and (2) statements such as those above suggesting a deep-seated legalism in the Pharisees represent a false view of them. As to the first—of course the religion of the Pharisees was a religion of grace in terms of the *teaching* of the Old Testament. But one reason why so much of the Old Testament is dominated by the prophetic ministry is precisely that the people of God did not live in that grace and often turned it into either presumption, license, or legalism. As to the second, it is not necessary to deny that there were Pharisees who appreciated the grace of God, but it is clear that *the Pharisees Jesus typically encountered* had *disgraced* rather than magnified the grace of God. It is surely not for nothing that Luke tells us: "He . . . told this parable *to some who trusted in themselves that they were righteous*" (Luke 18:9). Furthermore, to be able to say, "The Pharisees, who were lovers of money" (Luke 16:14), is tantamount to saying that they lived in opposition to the grace of God (see the same phrase to describe the ungodly in 2 Tim. 3:2). Our Lord makes this clear when he says to them, "You are those who justify yourselves before men, but God knows your hearts" (Luke 16:15). Certainly Saul the Pharisee (Phil. 3:5) had lived in "a righteousness of my own that comes from the law" and not in "the righteousness from God that depends on faith" (Phil. 3:9). It may be true that not all Pharisees were tarred with the same brush. But Jesus described the ones he encountered as a "brood of vipers" (Matt. 12:34; 23:33). They were, he claimed, children of the Devil (John 8:44).

> love! With what anxious, doubtful thoughts do they look upon Him! What fears, what questionings are there, of his good will and kindness! At the best, many think that there is no sweetness at all in God towards us, but what is purchased at the high price of the blood of Jesus. *It is true, that that alone is the way of communication; but the free fountain and spring of all is in the bosom of the Father* (1 John 1:2).[32]

The *Marrow* became a catalyst for Boston's theology of grace. He could not now believe in an unconditional election that was not an expression of the inexpressible love of the Father as its "fountain and spring." There could be no such reality therefore as "conditional grace." At the end of the day, what was at stake for him in the Marrow Controversy was nothing less than the very character of God the Father. That was an issue large enough to call forth whatever sacrifice of reputation might be required of him. After all, it was to demonstrate the love of the Father that the Son had made himself "of no reputation."

Poisoning the Pastors?

These considerations lead to an important application to Christian ministry. A misshapen understanding of the gospel impacts the spirit of a minister and affects the style and atmosphere of his preaching and of all his pastoral ministry. What the Marrow Controversy actually unveiled was the possibility of acknowledging the truth of each discrete chapter of the Confession of Faith without those truths being animated by a grasp of the grace of God in the gospel. The metallic spirit this inevitably produced would then in turn run through one's preaching and pastoral ministry. There is a kind of orthodoxy in which the several loci of systematic theology, or stages of redemptive history, are all in place, but that lacks the

[32] John Owen, *On Communion with God* (1657), *Works* 2:32; emphasis added. Intriguingly, Owen's older colleague in Oxford, Thomas Goodwin, in a sermon entitled *Encouragements to Faith*, published in 1650, recognized the same heart problem. Thomas Goodwin, *The Works of Thomas Goodwin*, 12 vols. (Edinburgh: James Nicoll, 1861–1866), 4:208.

life of the whole, just as arms, legs, torso, head, feet, eyes, ears, nose, and mouth may all be present—while the body as a whole lacks energy and perhaps life itself. The form of godliness is not the same as its power.

Confessional orthodoxy coupled with a view of a heavenly Father whose love is conditioned on his Son's suffering, and further conditioned by our repentance, leads inevitably to a restriction in the preaching of the gospel. Why? Because it leads to a restriction in the heart of the preacher that matches the restriction he sees in the heart of God! Such a heart may have undergone the process that Alexander Whyte described as "sanctification by vinegar." If so, it tends to be unyielding and sharp edged. A ministry rooted in conditional grace has that effect; it produces orthodoxy without love for sinners and a conditional and conditioned love for the righteous.

In the nature of the case there is a kind of psychological tendency for Christians to associate the character of God with the character of the preaching they hear—not only the substance and content of it but the spirit and atmosphere it conveys. After all, preaching is the way in which they publicly and frequently "hear the Word of God." But what if there is a distortion in the understanding and heart of the preacher that subtly distorts his exposition of God's character? What if his narrow heart pollutes the atmosphere in which he explains the heart of the Father? When people are broken by sin, full of shame, feeling weak, conscious of failure, ashamed of themselves, and in need of counsel, they do not want to listen to preaching that expounds the truth of the discrete doctrines of their church's confession of faith but fails to connect them with the marrow of gospel grace and the Father of infinite love for sinners. It is a gracious and loving Father they need to know.

Such, alas, were precisely the kind of pastors who gathered round poor Job and assaulted him with their doctrine that God was against him. From their mouths issue some of the most sublime discrete theological statements anywhere to be found in the pages of the Bible. But they had disconnected them from the life-giving love of God for his needy and broken child Job. And so they too "exchanged the truth about God for the lie."[33]

This will not do in gospel ministry. Rather, pastors need themselves to have been mastered by the unconditional grace of God. From them the vestiges of a self-defensive pharisaism and conditionalism need to be torn. Like the Savior they need to handle bruised reeds without breaking them and dimly burning wicks without quenching them.[34]

What is a godly pastor, after all, but one who is like God, with a heart of grace; someone who sees God bringing prodigals home and runs to embrace them, weeps for joy that they have been brought home, and kisses them—asking no questions—no qualifications or conditions required?

In these respects the Marrow Controversy has a perennial relevance to all Christians. But it has a special relevance to gospel preachers and pastors.

It raises the question: What kind of pastor am I to my people?

Am I like the father?

Or am I, perhaps, like the elder brother who would not, does not, will not, and ultimately cannot join the party?

After all, how can an elder brother be comfortable at a party when he still wonders if his once-prodigal brother has been sorry enough for his sin and sufficiently ashamed of his faults?[35]

---

[33] See Rom. 1:25.

[34] Isa. 42:3.

[35] One of my own saddest recollections in pastoral ministry is of being told that during a new members' welcome that included a young husband with "a past," two "pillars of the church," esteemed for the model way in which they fulfilled all church membership responsibilities, were overheard to say, "What's he doing joining the church?" How easy it is to fall into a *spirit* of conditional grace toward prodigals even when the right doctrinal notes are struck!

4

DANGER! LEGALISM

What is *legalism*? The generic answer of evangelical Christians would probably be something like, "Trying to earn your salvation by doing good works." But around and underneath that, there gathers a web that extends more widely, which is woven intricately and invisibly to trap the unwary. And the web is always much stronger than we imagine, for legalism is a much more subtle reality than we tend to assume.

No minister in the Church of Scotland in the eighteenth century would have openly denied that salvation is by grace. What troubled the Marrow Brethren, however, was their sense that the web of legalism had been woven into the hearts and ministries of many of their fellow Presbyterians, including—and sometimes especially—into the souls of ministers. Some of them, like Thomas Boston, spoke from personal experience and knew that it had taken them years to find deliverance.

But we need to go further back than the eighteenth century if we are to think through this issue.

Biblical Theology, Covenant, and Law

Whenever there is a revival of biblical theology, there will be a rediscovery of the significance of the *covenantal* structure of God's redemptive activity from Noah through Moses to the new covenant in Christ. In this context questions about the role of the law of God in the life of the new-covenant people inevitably arise. When Paul realized that every covenant pointed to and was fulfilled in Christ, he found himself faced with the question, "Why then the law?"[1] Throughout his ministry he regularly encountered two wrong answers. One led to legalism by smuggling law into gospel; the other led to antinomianism with its implication that the gospel abolished law altogether.

This pattern of things resurfaced at the time of the Reformation,[2] and in the following century in the Puritan period. By the 1630s–1640s the role of the law was being hotly debated in both Old and New England.[3] The Westminster Divines gave as close attention to their chapter *Of the Law of God* as to any section of the Confession of Faith.

Thus it was in the context of rumors and fears of both legalism and antinomianism that *The Marrow of Modern Divinity* first saw the light of day in 1645.

"Isms" (such as *legalism* and *antinomianism*) can be dangerous, not only for those who espouse them but also for those who employ the categories. They too easily become "one size fits all" pigeonholes. Individuals are not categories, and treating them as such can be quite misleading and often ignores their context.

In particular we need to be cautious in using language in a pejorative way. Words ending in *-ism* and *-ist* seem to lend themselves to emotive rather than descriptive use.[4] In the era of the

---

[1] Gal. 3:19.

[2] Martin Luther's earlier emphasis on the law as an enemy that condemns us sometimes appeared to lose sight of the fact that it is *God's* law. Faced with disciples who took his teaching to its logical conclusion, he would later find himself defending the law against antinomianism.

[3] The controversy in New England had a kind of epicenter between 1636 and 1638 and a focus on the role of Anne Hutchinson, a member of John Cotton's congregation who responded enthusiastically to his emphasis on grace and the ministry of the Spirit but lost the measure of balance that Cotton maintained, and was excommunicated after being tried and found guilty, inter alia, of antinomianism. The Hutchinsons had an extensive family and therefore many descendants, including apparently the two presidents George Bush, senior and junior.

[4] I have, for example, in mentioning the name of a friend in conversation with a stranger "seen" the word *Calvinist* ejected from the mouth of a lady of years, carried on spittle traveling at a velocity

Marrow itself, "legalist" was a convenient put-down for a Puritan. Think here of Shakespeare's caricature in his portrayal of the legalistic killjoy Malvolio (Latin *malum* + *voleo* = "I will ill"!). On the other hand, in eighteenth-century Scotland it was the Marrow Brethren who feared "legalism" and were in turn suspected of incipient antinomianism by those who were fearful that the *Marrow* promoted it, for the General Assembly's condemnatory act had listed a whole series of its expressions deemed to be antinomian in nature.

A Creed Abolished but a Chair Preserved

The Auchterarder Creed had been condemned at the 1717 General Assembly. Yet at the morning session on the same day, the fathers and brethren had for all practical purposes glossed over charges of false teaching made against John Simson, professor of divinity at the University of Glasgow. His case had dragged on since 1715 and would continue for years to come. Simson had, the Assembly minutes stated,

> adopted some hypotheses different from what are commonly used among orthodox divines, that are not evidently founded on Scripture, and tend to attribute too much to natural reason and the power of corrupt nature,—which undue advancement of reason and nature is always to the disparagement of revelation and efficacious free grace.[5]

But in effect, he received little more than a rap over the knuckles. By contrast the Assembly's treatment of the Auchterarder Creed went to the opposite extreme. It was condemned as "unsound and

---

that suggested the word itself was infected with the bubonic plague! Although not personally the object of the disdain, what struck me was that the person expressing such hostility to "Calvinism" would probably have protested a love and tolerance for all the followers of the Lord. Yet she seemed so emotionally indifferent to the fact that the Presbyterian minister sitting next to her was supposed to be one of the hated species. Doubtless the word *Arminianism* has traveled at similar speeds! So too, have the words that will occupy much of our attention, namely *legalism* and *antinomianism*.

[5] *Acts of the General Assembly of the Church of Scotland 1638–1842*, ed. Church Law Society (Edinburgh: Edinburgh Printing & Publishing, 1843), session 12, May 14, 1717.

most detestable doctrine." Apparently antinomianism was seen as a more disturbing deviation than Arminianism.

The Marrow of Modern Divinity would later be given similar treatment. On May 20, 1720, the General Assembly passed its "Act concerning a book, entitled, The Marrow of Modern Divinity," condemning its teaching in five doctrinal areas and its "harsh and offensive" expressions:

> And therefore, the General Assembly do hereby strictly prohibit and discharge all ministers of this Church, either by preaching, writing, or printing, to recommend the said book, or, in discourse, to say anything in favor of it; but, on the contrary, they are hereby enjoined and required to warn and exhort their people, in whose hands the said book is, or may come, not to read or use the same.[6]

Doubtless many who voted at the Assembly knew of the *Marrow* only by reading a few quotations set within polemical statements against it or from the extended critique of it brought forward by a Committee for the Preserving the Purity of the Doctrine of the Church.

Expressions taken out of context can easily be abused—and some of the statements in the *Marrow* were relatively easily abused. It is not altogether surprising that men who were sympathetic to the Marrow Men's evangelical zeal were nevertheless troubled by what was presented to them as a lurch toward antinomianism. Yet the Marrow Brethren believed the criticisms were unfounded and that statements from the *Marrow* had been ripped out of their context. The feisty James Hog, who had been introduced to the *Marrow* by Thomas Boston and had been instrumental in its republication in 1718, acidly wrote that if books were to be treated the way the *Marrow* had been, then no book was safe, not even the Bible!

What deeply troubled Boston as a symptom of a deep malaise

[6] Ibid., session 5, May 20, 1720.

was the marked discrepancy between the superficial and, he felt, compromising treatment shown to Professor Simson's doctrinal aberrations while there was such wholesale condemnation of the *Marrow*. It was, he felt, a symptom of a deep malaise permeating the Kirk he loved.

This is not to deny that some who held evangelical convictions felt that the *Marrow* contained disturbing material. But in its own way this disturbance was itself proving to be a litmus test: reactions to it indicated the mind-and-heart condition of many preachers and pastors. Certainly en masse at the Assembly they had shown greater leniency to Simson's deviations than they did to the Auchterarder Creed's attempt to express the freeness of God's grace (albeit, in Boston's words "not well worded."). The Arminianism of which Professor Simson was also accused made room for a contributory role in the application of salvation. It was this that the Auchterarder Creed, in its somewhat tortuous wording, was designed to deny.[7] Thus while the General Assembly gave verbal assent to the Confession's emphasis on free grace, it tolerated its denial and also the heart of legalism that the Marrow Brethren so opposed.

What, then, were the nature and the dangers of such legalism?

L'Ancien Régime

For the Marrow Brethren, legalism was not a recondite doctrinal locus for leisurely theological discussion. Boston in particular viewed it as a major pastoral concern. He knew from experience that a "legal frame" or spirit can pervade the whole of an indi-

[7] Boston later wrote that the case against Simson "was ended, with great softness to the professor" who would later "overthrow the foundations of Christianity." He also believed, probably rightly, that the Auchterarder Creed had been deliberately formulated "for opposing the erroneous doctrine of Professor Simson." Thomas Boston, *Memoirs of Thomas Boston* (Edinburgh: Banner of Truth, 1988), 317. Simson's teaching had a baneful effect especially on students from Ulster and led to the rise of Arianism in the Presbyterian Church in Ireland. Eventually, in 1729, the General Assembly deposed Simson from his chair but continued his salary. On that occasion, Boston rose alone in the Assembly to protest at length that this was "no just testimony of this church's indignation against the dishonour done by the said Mr. Simson to our glorious Redeemer." Ibid., 416.

vidual's life. It can twist the soul in such a way that it comes near to and yet veers away from the grace of God in the gospel. Particularly if it is present in someone engaged in a preaching and pastoral ministry, it can multiply and become an epidemic in the congregation he serves.

The root of legalism is almost as old as Eden, which explains why it is a primary, if not the ultimate, pastoral problem. In seeking to bring freedom from legalism, we are engaged in undoing the ancient work of Satan.

In Eden the Serpent persuaded Eve and Adam that God was possessed of a narrow and restrictive spirit bordering on the malign. After all, the Serpent whispered, "Isn't it true that he placed you in this garden full of delights and has now denied them all to you?"

The implication was twofold.

It was intended to dislodge Eve from the clarity of God's word ("Did God actually say . . . ?"). Later the attack focused on the authority of God's word ("You will not surely die"). But it was more. It was an attack on God's character. For the Serpent's question carried a deeply sinister innuendo: "What kind of God would deny you pleasure and joy if he really loved you? He allows you nothing, and yet he demands that you obey him."[8]

Despite an initial struggle, Eve's ears were soon closed off to God's word. The Serpent's tactic was to lead her into seeing and interpreting the world through her eyes (*what she saw* when she looked at the tree) rather than through her ears (*what God had said* about it). So her gaze was diverted from the superabundant plenty God had *commanded* our first parents to enjoy. The use of the verb[9] is surely significant in this context: the enjoyment of plenty is the first element in the command; the prohibition of one

[8] Gen. 3:1–4.

[9] Gen. 2:16: "The LORD God *commanded* the man, saying, 'You may surely eat of every tree of the garden.'" The positive statement is as much part of the command as the negative.

tree is the second. The Serpent's tactic was to cause a fixation on the one negative command: "Do not eat the fruit of the Tree of the Knowledge of Good and Evil, lest you die."

Now all Eve saw was a negative command. One small object near the eye can make all larger objects invisible. Now it was the sight of the forbidden tree blocking her vision of a garden abounding in trees. Now she could not see the forest for the tree. Now her eyes were on God the negative lawgiver and judge. In both mind and affections God's law was now divorced from God's gracious person. Now she thought God wanted nothing for her. Everything was a myopic, distorted "now."

The entail of that theology is that if you are to receive anything from this misanthrope deity, then it must now be paid for and earned. By contrast the Father had actually said:

> I am giving you everything in this garden. Go and enjoy yourselves. But just before you head off, I have given you all of this because I love you. I want you to grow and develop in your understanding and in your love for me. So this is the plan:
>
> There is a tree here, "The Tree of the Knowledge of Good and Evil." Don't eat its fruit.
>
> I know—you want to know *why*, don't you?
>
> Well, I have made you as my image. I have given you instincts to enjoy what I enjoy. So in one sense you naturally do what pleases me and simultaneously gives you pleasure too.
>
> But I want you to grow in trusting and loving me just for myself, because I am who I am.[10]
>
> You can only really do that if you are willing to obey me, not because you are wired to, but because you want to show me that you trust and love me.
>
> If you do that you will find that you grow stronger and that your love for me deepens.
>
> Trust me, I know.

[10] The significance of the covenant name YHWH (Ex. 3:13–14).

That's why I have put that tree there. I so want you to be blessed that I am commanding you to eat and enjoy the fruit of all these trees. That's a *command*! But I have another command. What I want you to do is one simple thing: don't eat the fruit of that one tree.

I am not asking you to do that because the tree is ugly—actually it is just as attractive as the other trees. I don't create ugly, ever![11] You won't be able to look at the fruit and think, *That must taste horrible*. It is a fine-looking tree. So it's simple. Trust me, obey me, and love me because of who I am and because you are enjoying what I have given to you. Trust me, obey me, and you will grow.

A Surprising Root

What was injected into Eve's mind and affections during the conversation with the Serpent was a deep-seated suspicion of God that was soon further twisted into rebellion against him. The root of her *antinomianism* (opposition to and breach of the law) was actually the *legalism* that was darkening her understanding, dulling her senses, and destroying her affection for her heavenly Father. Now, like a pouting child of the most generous father, she acted as though she wanted to say to God, "You never give me anything. You insist on me earning everything I am ever going to have."

This may not look like the legalism with which we are familiar. But it lies at its root. For what the Serpent accomplished in Eve's mind, affections, and will was a divorce between God's revealed will and his gracious, generous character. Trust in him was transformed into suspicion of him by looking at "naked law" rather than hearing "law from the gracious lips of the heavenly Father." God thus became to her "He-whose-favor-has-to-be-earned."

It is this—a failure to see the generosity of God and his wise

[11] Significantly the tree is described in similar terms to all the other trees in the garden. Cf. Gen. 2:9 with 3:6.

and loving plans for our lives—that lies at the root of legalism and drives it.

It bears repeating: *in Eve's case antinomianism (her opposition to and rejection of God's law) was itself an expression of her legalism!*

When this distortion of God's character is complete, we inevitably mistrust him; we lose sight of his love and grace; we see him essentially as a forbidding God. Geerhardus Vos well expresses this in another context:

> Legalism is a peculiar kind of submission to God's law, *something that no longer feels the personal divine touch in the rule it submits to.*[12]

Legalism is simply separating the law of God from the person of God. Eve sees God's law, but she has lost sight of the true God *himself*. Thus, abstracting his law from his loving and generous person, she was deceived into "hearing" law only as negative deprivation and not as the wisdom of a heavenly Father.

This is the distortion, the "lie about God," that has entered the bloodstream of the human race. It is the poison that mutates into antinomianism both in the form of rebellion against God and as a false antidote to itself. Scratch anyone who is not a Christian, and this (whatever they may *say*) is their heart disposition. Any profession to the contrary is itself a further form of self-deception.

Thus the essence of legalism is rooted not merely in our view of law as such but in a distorted view of God as the giver of his law. In the human psyche (not only in the intellect, which is never an isolated part of our being), truth has been exchanged for the lie. God becomes a magnified policeman who gives his law only because he wants to deprive us and in particular to destroy our

[12] Geerhardus Vos, *The Self Disclosure of Jesus*, ed. and rev. J. G. Vos (1926; repr. Nutley, NJ: Presbyterian & Reformed, 1953), 17; emphasis added. See also Geerhardus Vos, *The Kingdom and the Church* (Philipsburg NJ: Presbyterian & Reformed, 1972), 60–61.

joy. The "lie" that we now believe is that "to glorify God" is not, indeed cannot be, "to enjoy him for ever," but to lose all joy. When the tragic exchange took place Adam and Eve, and with them their entire progeny, with one exception, lost the instinct to say, believe, and taste faith's vision of "God my exceeding joy"[13] and to make the simple confession of faith:

> You make known to me the path of life;
>   in your presence there is fullness of joy;
>   at your right hand are pleasures forevermore.[14]

What God united (and which no man, or woman, should have put asunder), namely, his glory and our joy, have been divorced. Thus, except through the gospel, it is no longer possible for a man or woman to know their "chief end."

These considerations give us some clues as to why legalism and antinomianism are, in fact, nonidentical twins that emerge from the same womb. Eve's rejection of God's law (antinomianism) was in fact the fruit of her distorted view of God (legalism).

Legalism can, therefore, be banished only when we see that the real "truth about God" is that when we glorify him we also come to "enjoy him forever," and with him enjoy everything he has given us.[15] To the unbeliever this is incomprehensible. But it is the happy first principle of the believer's life.[16]

Once the "lie about God"[17] was injected into the human genome, so to speak, it took up permanent lodging deep in the human psyche. It is the default heart condition of the natural man. The theological and pastoral ramifications of this are substantial. For what we often think of as "legalism," either in the non-Christian or in the Christian, is in fact a symptom of an issue much bigger, more

[13] Ps. 43:4.
[14] Ps. 16:11.
[15] 1 Tim. 6:17.
[16] The allusion here is of course to the Westminster Assembly's Shorter Catechism, question and answer 1.
[17] Rom. 1:25.

fundamental, more radical, and further reaching than the question of the role of the law. At that level, legalism and antinomianism seem to be simple opposites—all that is needed, it seems, is right doctrine. But the more basic issue is: How do I think about God, and what instincts and dispositions and affections toward him does this evoke in me? At that level legalism and antinomianism share a common root that has invaded not only mind but heart, affections, and will—how we feel toward God as well as the doctrine of God we profess.

Legalism is, therefore, not merely a matter of the intellect. Clearly it is that, for how we *think* determines how we live. But we are not abstract intellects. And legalism is also related to the heart and the affections—how we *feel* about God. We do not relate to God in an affection- and emotion-free context, creaturely cerebellum to Creator cerebellum as it were, but as whole persons—mind, will, dispositions, motivations, and affections in varying degrees of integrity or disintegration.

Within this matrix legalism at root is the manifestation of a restricted heart disposition toward God, viewing him through a lens of negative law that obscures the broader context of the Father's character of holy love. This is a fatal sickness.

Paradoxically, it is this same view of God, and the separation of his person from his law, that also lies at the root of antinomianism. The bottom line in both of these *-isms* is identical. That is why the gospel remedy for them is one and the same. Boston has a perceptive note in this context:

> The Antinomian principle, That it is needless for a man, perfectly justified by faith, to endeavour to keep the law and do good works, is a glaring evidence that legality is so engrained in man's corrupt nature, that until a man truly come to Christ, by faith, the legal disposition will still be reigning in him; let him turn himself into what shape, or be of what principles he will in religion; though he run into Antinomianism, he will carry

> along with him his legal spirit, which will always be a slavish and unholy spirit.[18]

Legalism is embedded in the human heart virtually from the very day of man's creation[19] and resides in us from conception.

It is, however, all the more complex an issue among God's people if their pastors themselves have the same legal streak that flows from distorted instincts toward the Lord but confuse those instincts with a gospel truth. For then not only is the truth exchanged for the lie, but the lie is treated as though it were the truth. It is failure here that leads to the mistake of prescribing a dose of antinomianism to heal legalism, and vice versa, rather than the gospel antidote of our grace-union with Christ.

The issues raised by the Marrow Controversy therefore sink into the deep foundations of ministry. If we have legalistic spirits, their breath is felt in everything we do, including the counsel we give to others. This is a matter of the heart, as Boston had learned from his own encounter with the *Marrow*.

It cannot be too strongly emphasized, therefore, that everyone is a legalist at heart. Indeed, if anything, that is the more evident in antinomians.

The Nature of Legalism

Dictionaries tend to define *legalism* in terms of its externals. Thus, for example, the *Concise Oxford Dictionary:*

> legalism: n. (Theol.) preference of the Law to the Gospel, doctrine of justification by works; exaltation of law or formula, red tape.[20]

Life is rarely as straightforward as dictionary definitions. That is certainly true here. There is more to legalism than merely a *doctrine*

[18] In Edward Fisher, *The Marrow of Modern Divinity* (Ross-shire, UK: Christian Focus, 2009), 207.
[19] The author of the *Marrow* held that the fall took place on the same day as creation. Boston shared that view, along with other theologians whom he cites. Ibid., 67.
[20] *Concise Oxford Dictionary of Current English*, 5th ed., ed. H. W. and F. G. Fowler, rev. E. McIntosh and G. W. S. Friedrichson (Oxford, UK: Oxford University Press, 1964), s.v. "legalism."

of justification by works rather than by grace. Otherwise legalism would be cured relatively easily. Boston's comments to John Drummond at the 1717 General Assembly could have been limited to: "I found chapters XI and XIX of the Confession of Faith enormously helpful" (the chapters "Of Justification" and "Of the Law of God"). "You should study them!"

But legalism does not easily yield its ground to a five-minute appointment with one's pastoral physician:

> Dr. Pastor: How can I help you today? You have a problem?
>
> Fred Legality: Yes! I seem to have a problem with legalism. I was wondering if you could advise me and perhaps write a prescription for me.
>
> Dr. Pastor: Certainly, Mr. Legality. This is a common problem. You are mistakenly thinking that you can be justified by works. Thankfully there is an immediate cure. Let me first explain my diagnosis, and then I will prescribe the remedy. Because we are sinners, we cannot justify ourselves. But here is the remedy. It is wonderfully powerful. I am glad I can give you the good news: Christ died for your sins. If you trust in what Christ has done, you are then justified by grace, not by works. So you must stop trusting in your own efforts. You understand?
>
> Fred Legality: Well, yes.
>
> Dr. Pastor: Good! Then the prognosis is excellent. I am glad to tell you that you are no longer a legalist! You are cured! But—in case you have a relapse, you understand—remember what I said.
>
> Fred Legality: Well . . .
>
> Dr. Pastor (in response to Fred Legality's weak smile): I am glad I have been able to help. Have a good day now. Would you mind

asking my next patient to come in, please? I think her name is Janis Antinomian. Didn't you used to date her? But try not to engage her in conversation; she has become one of my most difficult patients!

Granted that is a caricature.[21] In the course of pastoral ministry we discover that legalism is not such a straightforward sickness. It is more like the many-headed Hydra of Lerma, which Heracles slew in the second of his twelve labors.[22] It is multidimensional and multilayered. It takes many forms and has many faces. Its presenting symptoms can be hard to diagnose, analyze, and treat. It can prove to be almost intractable. That will be especially true if we have become immune to gospel medicine as a result of unwise self-medication prescribed in one of the latest popular books on getting the best out of your Christian life.

But the essence of legalism, as we have seen, is a heart distortion of the graciousness of God and of the God of grace. For that reason, as now becomes clear, legalism is, necessarily, not only a distortion of the gospel, but *in its fundamental character it is also a distortion of the law*.

This is why when Paul deals with legalism, he does not do so at the expense of the law. Rather he explains its proper role within the context of the gospel: "Do we then overthrow the law by this faith?" He replies vigorously, "By no means! On the contrary, we uphold the law."[23]

The gospel never overthrows God's law for the simple reason that both the law and the gospel are expressions of God's grace. Therefore the reverse is true: grace confirms the law and its true character.

The legalism that distorts *grace* is also the legalism that distorts *law* from its God-given character and function and beneath that has

[21] With apologies to Edward Fisher, author of the *Marrow*, for plagiarizing his dialogical style.
[22] "Hercules" to the Romans.
[23] Rom. 3:31.

distorted the character of the God who gave it.[24] This issue lay at the heart of the opposition of the Pharisees to Jesus.

Would a New Perspective Help?

Take, for example, the Pharisees. Traditionally they have often been portrayed as dictionary-definition legalists whose creed was a straightforward form of works righteousness. But particularly since the late 1970s,[25] much scholarly energy has been expended by contemporary scholarship to correct this impression. Judaism (and therefore Pharisaism), it is contended, was a religion of grace. Some have therefore argued that the "conversion" of Saul of Tarsus was not so much a conversion as a "call." And if it was a conversion, it was certainly not from "works" to "grace" since by definition Judaism, the religion of the Old Testament, was a religion of grace from beginning to end. This is "the New Perspective on Paul," although it extends beyond Paul to a new perspective on Judaism (at least for non-Jews). It has played a sufficiently major role in recent scholarship to have merited its own abbreviation (NPP).

It would be inappropriate here to discuss this in any detail.[26] Suffice it to say that the New Perspective is surely right to hold that the religion taught in the Old Testament was a religion of grace. Reformed theology has consistently held this view from Calvin onward. In various places the Confession of Faith articulates the unity of the two Testaments of Scripture, of God's covenant dealings with

---

[24] By the same token, to preempt our later discussion, antinomianism also distorts both the grace and the law of God.

[25] By general consensus E. P. Sanders, *Paul and Palestinian Judaism* (London: SCM, 1977), serves as the catalyst for the modern discussion, although the contemporary debate has forerunners in earlier work.

[26] The most convenient comprehensive study is the two-volume set *Justification and Variegated Nomism*, ed. D. A. Carson, P. T. O'Brien, and M. A. Seifrid (Grand Rapids, MI: Baker Academic, 2001–2004); vol. 1, *The Complexities of Second Temple Judaism* (2001); vol. 2, *The Paradoxes of Paul* (2004). The references and bibliographical materials in these volumes indicate the extent to which the New Perspective has become something of a minor industry. As medieval theologians proved their mettle by writing commentaries on Peter Lombard's *Four Books of Sentences*, so contemporary New Testament scholars have almost by necessity had to express their "view" of the New Perspective on Paul.

his people, and of the way of salvation in Christ.[27] The Bible is an extended narrative of God's grace from start to finish.

But what is true *at the level of God's revelation* is not necessarily true *at the level of religious practice*. In both Old and New Testament periods the "religion of grace" was all too frequently turned into externalism, a legalistic spirit, and a presumption that God would be gracious because of who his people were and what they had done. Had grace "reigned" throughout the Old Testament epoch, there would have been less need for prophets and less excoriation of the people for the way they dis-graced their God of grace.

Furthermore, when we turn to the Gospels it is clear that even if appeal was made to the language of "grace," the actual religion of many of the Pharisees and those they influenced was dominated by a legalistic spirit. Hence Jesus told one of his most powerful parables "to some who trusted in themselves that they were righteous."[28] And it was surely not merely our Lord's fertile imagination that led him to depict one of his characters saying to his master: "I was afraid of you, because you are a severe man. You take what you did not deposit, and reap what you did not sow."[29] That was a transcript of the heart language his sensitive ears had heard even when the words were never used. It is the legalism of serpentine theology. It blatantly exchanges the truth of God for the lie.[30] The Savior would hardly have described those living in the grace of God with such devastating words as he once did when he exposed the Pharisees as either "whitewashed tombs" or as a "brood of vipers."[31]

Paul gives us his "old perspective on Saul" in these terms: "I myself have reason for confidence in the flesh . . . as to righteous-

---

[27] Confession of Faith, 7.5.6; 8.6; 19.6.3, 7.
[28] Luke 18:9.
[29] Luke 19:21.
[30] This is brought out in the parable of the Pharisee and the tax collector with great subtlety and skill. The Pharisee is portrayed as giving thanks to God (a recognition of his grace!) for what he himself has accomplished that enables him to see himself as superior to the tax collector. No "miserable sinner" confession here, nor any consciousness that he is "the least of all Pharisees, the greatest of sinners." For all the language of "grace" ("I thank you that . . ."), the Pharisee is a legalist at heart.
[31] Matt. 23:27, 33.

ness under the law [or, in the law], blameless." But now he rejoices in "not having a righteousness of my own that comes from the law, but that which comes through faith in Christ, the righteousness from God that depends on faith."[32]

Some exponents of the New Perspective on Paul have complained that the apostle has been read through Reformation-tinted spectacle lenses, as if the issue between the Reformers and the Roman Catholic Church were identical to that between Jesus and the Pharisees or Paul and the Judaizers—a conflict between grace and works, one side holding to "salvation by grace" and the other side to "salvation by works."

But this is scholarship detached from both historical and pastoral reality and misses the real parallel. For the situation on the ground was and is more complex and more subtle than this.

The Reformers were conceived in the womb of the theology of the medieval church. It was obsessed with the notion of grace. No period in church history has given more attention to the question, How do we receive grace? But what the Reformers grasped was that where the language of grace abounds, it is possible for the reality of legalism to abound all the more. The problem was that when "grace" was spelled out in existential terms, it turned out not to be grace at all. It had become a sacramental phenomenon. As the individual cooperated with infused grace, it was hoped

[32]Phil. 3:4, 6, 9. What happened to him can be pieced together from the clues that lie scattered throughout his letters and Luke's record of his life in the Acts of the Apostles (which, since Luke was not with him in his earlier life, is presumably informed by Paul's own perspective). Paul tells the Galatians that he had been "advancing in Judaism beyond many of my own age among my people, so extremely zealous was I for the traditions of my fathers" (Gal. 1:14). This is tantamount to saying that he was quietly confident that he had advanced beyond *all* of his peer group. But then—significantly in the synagogue frequented by his fellow countrymen from Cilicia (and therefore presumably also by himself)—he encountered Stephen but could not "withstand the wisdom and the Spirit with which he was speaking" (Acts 6:9–10). At last a superior is encountered! But this means also a rival. Was it this that first brought to the surface the deep internal exposure of the tenth commandment (Rom. 7:7–8)? One who has advanced beyond others has little reason to covet what anyone else possesses. But Stephen had something he, Saul, clearly lacked; Saul knew Stephen was his superior. Now jealousy, coveting what another possessed, albeit a person he hated, came to life. Faced with two possible responses (to join Stephen in his faith in Christ or to get rid of him), Saul chose the latter and in doing so he discovered that he was spiritually dead—as he indicates in Rom. 7:7–12. There is more conviction of sin in the story of Saul of Tarsus than much New Perspective theology allows.

that one day his or her faith would be suffused by perfect love.[33] At that point grace would have made the person righteously justifiable.[34]

But grace is not an infused substance. And, in the New Testament, justification is not the hoped-for end-product of the subjective working of grace with which the believer cooperates. It is the declaration of God that takes place at the very beginning of the Christian life. The medieval view led to the virtual impossibility of assurance; the biblical view led to the Reformation explosion of it.

Profession without Possession?

By its very nature God's grace finds the *only* reason for its exercise in God himself, *never* in us. God did not choose his people because of what they were.[35] But their sense of his gracious choice of them very subtly slid into an entitlement mentality that eventually dis-graced grace. That was true among the old-covenant people, among the Pharisees, in the pre-Reformation church, and also, alas, in the post-Reformation church in Scotland, not to mention elsewhere.[36]

The Church's Confession of Faith remained unaltered. But it would be naïve scholarship that extrapolated from what was *professed* to what was *preached* and indeed from what was preached to what was *possessed*. Every pastor should know this and therefore should never assume that everyone listening to him has been gripped by the wonder of God's grace—even if they have confessed the church's creed. As gospel ministers from Paul to the present day have acknowledged, few pastoral problems are as carefully disguised as the subtle mingling of a profession of grace with a legalistic heart. "Grace" is not denied; it is diluted, or distorted, and

[33] *Fides formata caritate.*

[34] It was against this background that Rome accused the Reformers of teaching justification as a "legal fiction."

[35] Deut. 7:7.

[36] For this story in the Church of England, see C. FitzSimons Allison, *The Rise of Moralism: The Proclamation of the Gospel from Hooker to Baxter* (New York: Seabury Press, 1966).

disarmed of its power. *The Marrow of Modern Divinity* acted as a kind of litmus test of precisely this spiritual reality.

John Colquhoun of Leith, a "Marrow Man" born out of due season, shrewdly comments:

> A man is to be counted a legalist or self-righteous if, while he does not pretend that his obedience is perfect, he yet relies on it for a title to life. Self-righteous men have, in all ages, set aside as impossible to be fulfilled by them that condition of the covenant of works which God had imposed on Adam, and have framed for themselves various models of that covenant which, though they are far from being institutions of God, and stand upon terms lower than perfect obedience, yet are of the nature of the covenant of works. The unbelieving Jews who sought righteousness by the works of the law were not so very ignorant or presumptuous as to pretend to perfect obedience. Neither did those professed Christians in Galatia who desired to be under the law, and be justified by the law, of whom the apostle therefore testified that they had "fallen from grace" (Galatians 5:4), presume to plead that they could yield perfect obedience.
>
> On the contrary, their public profession of Christianity showed that they had some sense of their need of Christ's righteousness. But their great error was that they did not believe that the righteousness of Jesus Christ alone was sufficient to entitle them to the justification of life; and therefore they depended for justification partly on their own obedience to the moral and the ceremonial law. It was this, and not their pretensions to perfect obedience, that the apostle had in view when he blamed them for cleaving to the law of works, and for expecting justification by the works of the law.
>
> By relying for justification partly on their own works of obedience to the moral and ceremonial laws, they, as the apostle informed them, were fallen from grace; Christ had become of no effect to them. And they were "debtors to the whole law" (Galatians 5:3–4).

Here, Colquhoun is showing that Paul pushes the Galatians to the logical conclusion of their position, which they failed to see in their joining of works and grace. He continues:

> By depending for justification partly by their obedience to the law, they framed the law into a covenant of works, and such a covenant of works, as would allow for imperfect instead of perfect works; and by relying partly on the righteousness of Christ, they mingled the law with the gospel and works with faith in the affair of justification. Thus they perverted both the law and the gospel, and formed for themselves a motley covenant of works.[37]

This same distortion appears when the gospel is preached to the natural man. Boston was all too familiar with the instinct of the awakened individual to say, "I will now try much harder, and I will do better." It seems logical: I realize I have failed. I must reverse this failure by doing better. But it is serpentine logic, for it simply compounds the old legal spirit. It is the natural instinct of the once-antinomian prodigal who, when awakened, thinks in terms of working his way back into the favor of his father.[38]

The proclamation of the gospel is a repudiation of doctrinal legalism. But *what the heart hears* ("I have failed somehow, and I know I must try harder") often draws forth a response of experimental legalism. This goes very deep. It is commonplace to say that one can have a legalistic head and a legalistic heart. But it is also all too possible to have an *evangelical head* and a *legalistic heart.* It was this that the Marrow Men found themselves confronting, several of them first in themselves, for one of the diseases the *Mar-*

---

[37] John Colquhoun, *A Treatise on the Law and Gospel*, ed. D. Kistler (1859; repr., Morgan, PA: Soli Deo Gloria, 1999), 18–19. Colquhoun (1748–1827) has been little noticed outside of his native Scotland (and even there scant attention has been paid to him) and rarely appears in dictionaries of church history and biography. But he was in his day a leading (perhaps the leading) evangelical minister in the Church of Scotland. He is now remembered only for his shrewd comment to students who requested book recommendations from him: "Noo, I daurna [dare not] advise ye to read *The Marrow o' Modern Deeveenity*, for ye ken [know] the Assembly condemned it. But they didna [didn't] condemn Tammas Bowston's notes on *The Marrow*"!

[38] "Treat me as one of your hired servants" (Luke 15:19).

row exposed was the subtle thought that my growth in holiness strengthens my justification. Confirm it? Yes. But strengthen it? Never! Does this sound slightly antinomian? Of course—*but only if one is listening with legalistic ears.*

The situation was further complicated by the fact that their opponents professed a comprehensive orthodoxy in the Reformed tradition of the Confession of Faith. But it took an angular statement like the Auchterarder Creed and an edgy book like the *Marrow* to light a taper that smoked out legalist hearts. It sometimes does. Together the creed and the *Marrow*, like litmus paper—of marginal significance in and of itself—revealed at a touch the presence of acid or alkaline, legalism or grace, in the heart and mind. In truth the Marrow Brethren were not antinomians, but the moment their teaching entered the conversation it exposed the legal "temper" of Christians and non-Christians alike in its true colors.

Legalism, then, is almost as old as Eden itself. In essence it is any teaching that diminishes or distorts the generous love of God and the full freeness of his grace. It then distorts God's graciousness revealed in his law and fails to see law set within its proper context in redemptive history as an expression of a gracious Father. This is the nature of legalism. Indeed we might say these are the *natures* of legalism.

5

THE ORDER OF GRACE

The reason the Auchterarder Creed caused such a violent reaction was that it struck an exposed spiritual nerve in affirming that repentance is not a qualification for coming to Christ. The *Marrow* then further exposed a nerve by stressing that sanctification makes no contribution whatsoever to justification. This was surely an inducement to antinomianism and a life of indifference to the law of God?

The "Backstory"

The full significance of the Marrow Controversy becomes even clearer when we set it within the further dimensions of its wider theological context.

Thomas Boston was particularly burdened by the way in which repentance was being given not only a logical but a chronological priority over faith in the *ordo salutis* (the ordering of the various aspects of the application of redemption).

Over the years in the Reformed tradition in Scotland and elsewhere, a subtle change had taken place in relation to the Reformed *ordo salutis*. Into this context the Auchterarder Creed had injected the view that in the gospel offer of Christ crucified and risen, no prior conditions were attached. There is no intermediate step to be taken that lies between the sinner and receiving the Savior. Repentance does not precede faith in an individual's coming to Christ.

The *Ordo Salutis*[1]

The concept of *ordo salutis* has long been associated with Reformed theology, although its earliest post-Reformation occurrence seems to have been in a Lutheran context. But the expression itself is of much earlier provenance, occurring at least as early as the tenth century in the poetic writings of Odo, Abbott of Cluny.[2] In post-Reformation theology it was increasingly used within the context of the application of the work of Christ to the individual. In its best formulations its intention was to lay bare the internal logic and interrelations of the various aspects of this application, not to delineate a temporal process in which the individual passed from one stage to another.

We have seen that William Perkins employed the metaphor of a "chain" to describe how election, regeneration, faith, justification, mortification and vivification, and repentance and new obedience are related to each other within the context of the individual's relationship to Christ.[3] The metaphor gained such traction in evangelical theology, especially in relation to Romans 8:29–30, that its heuristic and metaphorical nature has often been forgotten. One repercussion of this has been the way in which the various aspects of redemption, viewed as individual links in the chain, follow one another, and each in turn precedes the next. This then had a ten-

[1] For the concept of *ordo salutis* in a systematic context, see the discussion in Sinclair B. Ferguson, *The Holy Spirit*, Contours of Christian Theology (Downers Grove, IL: IVP Academic, 1996), 94–113.

[2] Odo (879–942) employed it in the context of the accomplishment of redemption.

[3] Perkins here was influenced by the work of Theodore Beza (1519–1605). Calvin's colleague and successor in Geneva, Beza had published his *Tabula Praedestionis* (Geneva, 1555) in order to counter the views of Jerome Bolsec, who had opposed Calvin's teaching. The "table" appeared in England first in 1575 in a translation by William Whittingham, onetime colleague of John Knox.

dency to shift the perspective from the logical to the chronological and especially to transfer focus from Christ to the specific benefits of the gospel.[4]

It was within this context that questions about the relationship between faith and repentance surfaced and in their wake the issue of whether repentance preceded or followed faith, and if so in what sense.

Penance or Repentance?

Behind the Reformation conflict lay late medieval discussions on how we receive grace. Imprisoned as it was within the Latin Bible of Jerome (the Vulgate),[5] the church had read Jesus's exhortation "repent" as *paenitentiam agite*,[6] and interpreted it as "do penance." The biblical idea of repentance therefore became associated with, if not limited to, specific concrete acts that a priest could prescribe for sin as part of the sacramental system. For sinners this became the prerequisite for the reception of further grace as, slowly (but rarely rather than surely), the first infusion of grace at baptism was worked out through the sacramental system to its consummation in full justification.[7] With the cooperation of the recipient, if faith were ever fully suffused with perfect love for God (*fides formata caritate*) the individual could finally be justified—indeed *righteously*

---

[4] There may be a metaphorical or symbolic "chain" in Rev. 20:2, but despite the history of the metaphor, one is not even implied in Rom. 8:29–30, and it is important not to confuse the metaphor with what Paul actually says.

[5] Completed in AD 404, the *Vulgate* was confirmed by the counter-Reformation Council of Trent "to be regarded as authentic (*pro authentica*) in public readings, disputations, sermons, and expositions, and let no one dare or presume to reject it on any grounds." Council of Trent, Session 4, April 8, 1546, "Decree on the Vulgate Edition of the Bible and on the Manner of Interpreting Sacred Scripture," in Heinrich Denzinger, *Compendium of Creeds, Definitions, and Declarations on Matters of Faith and Morals*, rev. and ed. P. Hünermann, 43rd ed. (San Francisco: Ignatius Press, 2012), 369.

[6] Matt. 4:17.

[7] In this *ordo salutis*, penance was and is described as "the second plank": "Christ instituted the sacrament of Penance for all sinful members of his Church: above all for those who, since Baptism, have fallen into grave sin, and have thus lost their baptismal grace and wounded ecclesial communion. It is to them that the sacrament of Penance offers a new possibility to convert and to recover the grace of justification. The Fathers of the Church present this sacrament as 'the second plank [of salvation] after the shipwreck which is the loss of grace.'" J. Ratzinger and Christoph Schönborn, *Introduction to the Catechism of the Catholic Church* (San Francisco: Ignatius Press, 1994), 363.

so since "grace" had produced internally a righteousness that could ground justification.

God thus justified those whom grace had *already made righteous*. In this sense justification was "by grace." But it was not *sola gratia*. It took place at the end of an extended and cooperative internal process. Yet it was insisted that it is grace that produces righteousness and does so in such a way that the righteousness of God is revealed in what we might call "the justification of those made righteous by grace."

The young men who were on the cutting edge of the newly birthed Reformation movement realized, as they read Erasmus's edition of the Greek New Testament, that Jesus's message was not *paenitentiam agite* ("do penance"), but *metanoeite* ("repent").[8] Repentance is not a discrete external act; it is the turning round of the whole life in faith in Christ.

Luther quite literally "nailed" this difference when he posted his Ninety-Five Theses in Wittenberg. His first thesis read: "When our Lord Jesus Christ said 'repent' he meant that the whole of the Christian life should be repentance." Repentance then is not the punctiliar decision of a moment but a radical heart transformation that reverses the whole direction of life. In the context of faith the repentant sinner is immediately, fully, and finally justified—at the very beginning of the Christian life. No wonder joy was released and assurance flowed!

Faith First?

But the question still remained: How is evangelical repentance related to faith?

Against this background in medieval theology, Calvin had insisted on giving the priority to faith. Only within the context of faith taking hold of Christ in whom we find the grace of God to us

[8] Matt. 4:17.

can repentance be evangelical. It cannot, therefore, take precedence over faith either logically or chronologically, since then it would be a work prior to and apart from faith. Calvin naturally always had repentance as penance in his sights when he wrote.[9]

A century later the Westminster Divines were at pains to emphasize the grace context for "repentance unto life":

> Repentance unto life is an evangelical grace. . . . By it a sinner, out of the sight and sense of the odiousness of sin, not only of its danger, but also of the filthiness and odiousness of his sins, as contrary to the holy nature and righteous law of God, *and upon the apprehension of his mercy in Christ to such as are penitent*, so grieves for and hates his sins as to turn from them all unto God, purposing and endeavoring to walk with him in all the ways of his commandments.[10]

Thus, within the confessional tradition to which Boston belonged, repentance takes place within the context of faith's grasp of God's grace in Christ. The latter motivates the former, not vice versa.

Boston was emphatic on this point. While we cannot divide faith and repentance, we do distinguish them carefully:

> In a word, gospel repentance doth not go before, but comes after remission of sin, in the order of nature.[11]

The implications of this for preaching the gospel had liberated Boston: Christ should be presented in all the fullness of his person and work; faith then directly grasps the mercy of God in him, and as it does so the life of repentance is inaugurated as its fruit.[12]

[9] John Calvin, *Institutes of the Christian Religion*, trans. F. L. Battles, ed. J. T. McNeill (Philadelphia: Westminster Press, 1960), 3.3.1–2.
[10] Westminster Confession of Faith, 15.1–2; emphasis added.
[11] Thomas Boston, *The Whole Works of the Late Reverend Thomas Boston*, ed. S. M'Millan, 12 vols. (Edinburgh, 1848–1852), 6:109; cf. 6:77–78.
[12] Ibid., 6:78.

The *Marrow* had already put its finger on this point in a conversation between Nomista the legalist and Evangelista the minister:

> Nomista: But yet, sir, you see that Christ requires a thirsting,[13] before a man come unto him, but which, I conceive, cannot be without true repentance.
>
> Evangelista: In the last chapter of the Revelations, verse 17, Christ makes the same general proclamation, saying, "Let him that is athirst come;" and as if the Holy Ghost had so long since answered the same objection that yours is, it follows in the next words, "And whosoever will, let him take of the water of life freely," even without thirsting, if he will for "him that cometh unto me, I will in nowise cast out," John vi.37. But because it seems you conceive he ought to repent before he believe, I pray tell me what you do conceive repentance to be, or wherein does it consist?
>
> Nomista: Why, I conceive that repentance consists in a man's humbling himself before God, and sorrowing and grieving for offending him by his sins, and in turning from them all to the Lord.
>
> Evangelista: And would you have a man to do all this truly before he come to Christ by believing?
>
> Nomista: Yea, indeed, I think it is very meet he should.
>
> Evangelista: Why, then, I tell you truly, you would have him do that which is impossible. For, first of all, godly humiliation, in true penitents, proceeds from the love of God their good Father, and so from the hatred of that sin which has displeased him; and this cannot be without faith.

[13] The reference is to Isa. 55:1.

> *2dly*, Sorrow and grief for displeasing God by sin, necessarily argue the love of God; and it is impossible we should ever love God, till by faith we know ourselves loved of God.
>
> *3dly,* No man can turn to God, except he be first turned of God; and after he is turned, he repents; so Ephraim says, "After I was converted I repented," Jer. xxxi.19. The truth is, a repentant sinner first believes that God will do that which he promiseth, namely, pardon his sin, and take away his iniquity; then he rests in the hope of it; and from that, and for it, he leaves sin, and will forsake his old course, because it is displeasing to God; and will do that which is pleasing and acceptable to him. So that first of all, God's favor is apprehended, and remission of sins believed; then upon that cometh alteration of life and conversation.[14]

Boston set his seal to these words and indicated in lengthy notes that this was his own understanding of the way of salvation.[15] Repentance is suffused with faith; otherwise it is legal. But then without repentance, faith would be no more than imagination.

For all that the Marrow Brethren were suspected of encouraging antinomianism, no member of Boston's congregation in Ettrick would ever have imagined him to be anything but wholly innocent of the charge. Indeed the very year the Auchterarder Creed was being scrutinized and condemned at the General Assembly, Boston preached extensively on the theme he had taken up as his "ordinary":

[14] Edward Fisher, *The Marrow of Modern Divinity* (Ross-shire, UK: Christian Focus, 2009), 162. Nomista responds by saying that Christ taught that repentance precedes faith, to which Evangelista gives an extended response. Ibid., 162–64.

[15] One potential confusion in the minds of those who, while themselves evangelical, opposed the *Marrow* as antinomian, may have been under the mistaken assumption that the only alternative to "forsaking sin in order to come to Christ" was to say that one may come to Christ and continue in sin—the very point Paul repudiates in Rom. 6:1ff. But Boston realized that this binary logic was an illustration of the fallacy *tertium non datur*—in ordinary parlance, "it must be one or the other." In fact there is a third way, namely, that forsaking sin is an indispensable accompaniment of coming to Christ but not a precedent to faith in him. How so? In Paul's categories in Romans 6, the person who by faith is united to Christ in his death and resurrection for justification in that same union has died to the reign and dominion of sin. It would therefore be a contradiction of who he or she is in Christ to go on sinning. Union with Christ is again a structural foundation; omit it and the building collapses. For a succinct treatment of Boston on union with Christ, see Philip G. Ryken, *Thomas Boston as Preacher of the Fourfold State*, Rutherford Studies in Historical Theology (Carlisle, UK: Paternoster, 1999), 184–220.

the absolute necessity of repentance, the danger of delaying it, and for good measure an additional, powerful message, "The extraordinary case of the thief on the cross no argument for delaying repentance."[16]

In all this Boston and the Marrow Brethren seem to be one with Calvin.

At the end of the day we cannot divide faith and repentance chronologically. The true Christian believes penitently, and he repents believingly. For this reason, in the New Testament either term may be used when both dimensions are implied; and the order in which they are used may vary. But *in the order of nature*, in terms of the inner logic of the gospel and the way its "grammar" functions, repentance can never be said to *precede* faith. It cannot take place outside of the context of faith.[17]

Calvin does indeed have in mind the pre-Reformation notion that the gospel command to repent means to do penance. But his thinking extends beyond that:

> Both repentance and forgiveness of sins—that is, newness of life and free reconciliation—are conferred on us by Christ, and both are attained by us through faith. . . .
>
> Now it ought to be a fact beyond controversy that repentance not only constantly follows faith, but is also born of

[16] Boston, *Works*, 6:468. Boston also addressed the question of the necessity of repentance as a "case of conscience" in *Works* 6:76–99. For the series of sermons on repentance, see *Works*, 6:377–481. The two sermons on the thief on the cross were preached in June 1717 and were clearly immediately preceded by the others. This means that at the time Boston had gone to the General Assembly in Edinburgh and heard the Auchterarder Creed condemned ("I believe that it is not sound and orthodox to teach that we forsake sin in order to our coming to Christ, and instating us in covenant with God"), he was in fact preaching a series of powerful sermons on the absolute necessity of repentance and the folly of imagining that one could delay in doing so.

[17] Sometimes the summons accompanying the preaching of the gospel is: (1) Repent! Matt. 3:2: Jesus preached the kingdom of God and called men to repent; Acts 2:38: in response to Peter's sermon, men are to repent and be baptized in the name of Jesus Christ; Acts 17:30: God now commands men everywhere to repent. (2) Sometimes, however, the summons is specifically to believe: John 3:16; cf. Acts 16:30: What must I do to be saved? Believe in the Lord Jesus Christ. It is noteworthy that in Acts 17:34 where the response of *repentance* was required (cf. 17:30 above), the response of the few converts is described as *believing*. (3) On other occasions the summons is given to repent and believe: Mark 1:15, in response to the proclamation of the kingdom good news. It seems clear from this that while denoting different elements in conversion to Christ, both faith and repentance are so essential to such conversion that the one cannot exist apart from the other, and, as a consequence, the one may be used where both are intended, as though either faith or repentance can function as a synecdoche for conversion (faith and repentance). Faith will always be penitent; repentance will always be believing if genuine.

> faith. For since pardon and forgiveness are offered through the preaching of the gospel in order that the sinner, freed from the tyranny of Satan, the yoke of sin, and the miserable bondage of vices, may cross over into the Kingdom of God, surely no one can embrace the grace of the gospel without betaking himself from the errors of his past life into the right way, and applying his whole effort to the practice of repentance. There are some, however, who suppose that repentance precedes faith, rather than flows from it, or is produced by it as fruit from a tree. Such persons have never known the power of repentance, and are moved to feel this way by an unduly slight argument.
>
> . . . Yet, when we refer the origin of repentance to faith we do not imagine some space of time during which it brings it to the birth; but we mean to show that a man cannot apply himself seriously to repentance without knowing himself to belong to God. But no one is truly persuaded that he belongs to God unless he has first recognized God's grace.[18]

Returning, Running, Refusing

The power of this perspective is, of course, already present in our Lord's parable of the prodigal son. Even if the parable is read as having only one main point in view, that burden is expressed in several dimensions. In terms of our discussion we might call it, from one point of view, "The parable of the Free Grace Savior"; from another, "The parable of the En-Graced Antinomian"; and from yet another (and in context perhaps the most pointed), "The parable of the Dis-Graced Legalist."

The prodigal contemplates returning home because he knows his needs can be supplied in his father's home:

[18] Calvin, *Institutes*, 3.3.1–2. Further, for Calvin repentance is the reality of regeneration, which for him is the conversion of the whole of life in mortification and vivification. Hence his (otherwise startling) chapter title in *Institutes* 3.3: "Our Regeneration by Faith: Repentance." (Lest the point be missed, in the later Reformed theological categorization these words, "regeneration by faith," would have sounded distinctly Arminian, giving faith precedence over regeneration!).

> But when he came to himself, he said, "How many of my father's hired servants have more than enough bread, but I perish here with hunger!"

But while there is the supply of his needs in the home of his father, he is—very naturally—still wrestling with the remnant of the Edenic poison, the God as He-whose-favor-is-to-be-earned lie. What else could the father be to such a sinful son?

> I will arise and go to my father, and I will say to him, "Father, I have sinned against heaven and before you. I am no longer worthy to be called your son. *Treat me as one of your hired servants.*"

As he approaches home his once-despised father breaks all social convention (the boy should have been received with a shaming ceremony). Instead he runs to greet him. The prodigal now stammers out his rehearsed words through the hugs and kisses of his father:

> Father, I have sinned against heaven and before you. I am no longer worthy to be called your son.

But the final rehearsed words, "Treat me as one of your hired servants" are smothered by his father's embrace! He will not have his son home only on condition that he "does penance" in order to work his way back into his father's grace. He does not need to "repent enough" to be accepted.

Poignantly there is in the heart of the same father a deep burden for his elder son. He again leaves the house to find him. Luke's introduction to Jesus's narrative makes clear that it is this brother, not the prodigal, who forms the climax to the story: "The Pharisees and the scribes grumbled, saying, 'This man [Jesus] receives sinners and eats with them.'" That grumbling is echoed in the complaint of the elder son: "He was angry."

The tenor of the elder brother's response is well captured in the New International Version:

> Look! All these years I've been slaving for you and never disobeyed your orders. Yet you never gave me even a young goat so I could celebrate with my friends.

To which the father responds in love:

> Son, . . . all that is mine is yours.[19]

What Jesus unmasks here is a legalistic heart, one that has imbibed the poison of Eden.[20] Such a heart sees the Lord as a slave master and not a gracious Father, as restrictive rather than generous. Everything the Father has is available to him. But the elder son's heart is closed, and as far as he is concerned nothing is his. He was at home, but he was in a more distant place than his younger brother. He thought he had to earn by right what he could only enjoy by grace.

What is particularly illuminating is that we are given the impression that only in the context of a lavish display of grace did the hidden poison of the elder brother's legalistic disposition fully manifest itself. Perhaps the same was true of the Pharisees? And was it, correspondingly, the lavishness of grace in the Marrow teaching that also caused so much heart irritation?

This is thought to be Jesus's best-loved parable, usually because our eyes are on the prodigal and his father. But as with jokes, so with parables: there is a principle in both of "end stress." The "punch line" comes at the end. That being the case the alarming message here is that the spirit of the elder brother, the legalist, is more likely to be found near the father's house than in the pig farm—or in concrete terms, in the congregation and among the

[19] Luke 15:1–2, 11–32. The father had "divided his property between them," (v. 12). Note also how the elder brother refers to the prodigal as "this son of yours," not as "this brother of mine."

[20] Notice the echoes of Gen. 3:1 and Gen. 1:26–30 in the narrative.

faithful. And sometimes (only sometimes?), it appears in the pulpit and in the heart of the pastor.

Then it becomes dangerously infectious.

But what causes it?

Reflection on the Marrow Controversy and the literature it spawned suggests that a legalistic spirit can usually be traced back to the same basic principles, no matter what mask it might wear.

Justification by Grace Alone—Got It?

The idea that justification by faith is the standing or falling article of the church is typically associated with Martin Luther. It is also, surely, the standing or falling article of the individual Christian. The strength or weakness of our grasp of justification by faith is integrally related to our freedom and joy in Christ.[21]

Free justification by grace alone through faith alone in Christ alone lies at the heart of the application of redemption. The faith that unites us to Christ also sucks in every spiritual blessing in him: peace with God, exultation in the hope of the glory of God, in tribulations, and even in God himself. There is no condemnation for the believer, no prison-cell existence. For what the law could not do in that it was weak through our flesh, God has done. He sent his Son in the likeness of the flesh of sin and for sin to condemn sin in the flesh so that the righteous requirements of the law might be fulfilled in them. The spirit of bondage is gone.[22]

Earlier in his argument in Romans, Paul had employed an intriguing piece of gospel logic:[23]

---

[21] My concern here is not to comment on the long-standing discussion of whether justification or union with Christ is the architectonic principle in the application of redemption. They are in the New Testament inseparable, since faith, grace, and justification are each, in different respects, "in Christ." Justification and union, imputation and impartation, are not alternatives. Neither exists apart from the other. They should *never* be set over against each other.

[22] Rom. 5:1, 3, 11; 8:1–4, 15.

[23] Rom. 3:27.

> Question: If justification is by grace alone, by faith alone, in Christ alone—what becomes of our boasting?[24]
>
> Answer: Boasting is excluded.
>
> Question: On what principle? On the principle of works?

We should pause before reading further in Paul's dialogue.

The answer here is, surely, yes. For Paul has been insisting that boasting *is* excluded because we have all sinned and fallen short of the glory of God. We cannot justify ourselves by our works. We have broken God's law, whether the law embedded in God's image at creation or the law revealed at Sinai.

So it is true that boasting is excluded by the principle of works; we have no works that are able to ground our boasting.

But, in the event, this is *not* the answer Paul gives, because it is not the logic he uses *in this context*:

> Question: On what principle (is boasting excluded)? On the principle of works?
>
> Answer: No, not on the principle of works.
>
> Question: On what principle then?
>
> Answer: On the principle of grace.

Paul's reasoning is both unexpected and profound. It is true that our lack of works makes boasting impossible. But the principle, or law, of works as such does not a priori exclude boasting. Were we able to adhere to it, we could say, "I did it my way." Potentially we would have something in which to boast.

So the principle or law of works excludes boasting de facto. It is excluded a posteriori but not a priori.

But the principle or law of grace rules out all possibility of boast-

[24] Whether he speaks here and later in his own voice or in the voice of an interlocutor is not essential to determine for our purposes.

ing a priori! It takes all contribution to justification out of our hands and leaves it entirely in God's hands. Grace rules out all qualifications by definition. Grace therefore eliminates boasting; it suffocates boasting; it silences any and all negotiations about our contribution before they can even begin. By definition we cannot "qualify" for grace in any way, by any means, or through any action.

Thus it is understanding God's grace—that is to say, *understanding God himself*[25]—that demolishes legalism. Grace highlights legalism's bankruptcy and shows that it is not only useless; it is pointless; its life breath is smothered out of it.

Sometimes Christians are eager to go on to the "deeper truths" of the Christian life. There is, of course, a genuine progress in understanding that marks maturity.[26] But in reality what we need is to dig down deeper into the first principles of the gospel.

And yet the legal spirit so easily creeps into our thinking. It does so particularly in two areas.

1) Our Thinking about the Gospel Offer

In his *Christ Dying and Drawing Sinners to Himself*, Samuel Rutherford (than whom there have been few higher Calvinists) makes what may seem to be a startling and, perhaps to some, an alarming statement:

> Reprobates have as fair a warrant to believe in Christ as the elect have.[27]

But deny Rutherford's words and we confuse the objective and subjective works of God and make his offer of Christ to us dependent on something within us.

James Durham, a younger contemporary of Rutherford, provides us with an illustration of how this was expressed in the preaching of

---

[25] It can never be repeated too often or too loudly that in Scripture "grace" is not a *res* ("a thing"). It is neither substance nor commodity outside of the person of God himself.
[26] Cf. the lament of the author in Heb. 5:11–14.
[27] Samuel Rutherford, *Christ Dying and Drawing Sinners to Himselfe* (London, 1647), 442.

the gospel. In a communion sermon "Gospel Preparations Are the Strongest Invitations," on the text Matthew 22:4 ("Everything is ready. Come to the wedding feast"), he addresses the issue of "those to whom the offer is made":

> It is not one or two, or some few that are called, not the great only, nor the small only, not the holy only, nor the profane only, but ye are all bidden; the call comes to all and every one of you in particular, poor and rich, high and low, holy and profane.

Then Durham continues:

> We make this offer to all of you, to you who are *Atheists*, to you that are *Graceless*, to you that are *Ignorant,* to you that are *Hypocrites,* to you that are *Lazy* and *Lukewarm*, to the civil and to the profane, we pray, we beseech, we obtest you all to come to the wedding; Call (saith the Lord) *the blind, the maimed, the halt*, &c and bid them all come, yea, *compel them to come in*. Grace can do more and greater wonders than to call such; it can not only make the offer of marriage to them, but it can make up the match effectually betwixt Christ and them.
>
> We will not, we dare not say, that all of you will get Christ for a Husband; but we do most really offer him to you all, and it shall be your own fault if ye want him and go without him. And therefore, before we proceed any further, we do solemnly protest, and before God and his Son Jesus Christ, take instruments this day, that this offer is made to you and that it is told to you in his name, that the Lord Jesus is willing to match with you, even the profanest and most graceless of you, if ye be willing to match with him, and he earnestly invites you to come to the wedding.[28]

[28] James Durham, *The Unsearchable Riches of Christ, and of Grace and Glory in and through Him* (Glasgow: Alexander Weir, 1764), 58–59. This passionate illustration of the free offer of the gospel is set within a reference to Boston's favorite words in Isa. 55:1. Philip G. Ryken has listed Boston's library and reading. While there is no evidence that Boston himself had access to this particular work, he was familiar with several of Durham's other works. Ryken, *Thomas Boston as Preacher of the*

Those words provide a good test of whether we have fully grasped the implications of the gospel of Christ, because they underline the principle that the warrant to believe in Christ does not lie in us but in Christ.

Later in the seventeenth century, Robert Traill took up the same point:

> Is it desired, that we should forbear to make a free offer of God's grace in Christ to the worst of sinners? This cannot be granted by us: for this is the gospel faithful saying and worthy of all acceptation (and therefore worthy of all our preaching of it), that Jesus Christ came into the world to save sinners, and the chief of them, I Tim. i.15. This was the apostolic practice. . . . They began at Jerusalem, where the Lord of life was wickedly slain by them; and yet life in and through his blood was offered to, and accepted and obtained by many of them. . . .
>
> Shall we tell men, that unless they be holy, they must not believe on Jesus Christ? that they must not venture on Christ for salvation, till they be qualified and fit to be received and welcomed by him? This were to forbear preaching the gospel at

Fourfold State, 312–20. For Durham as for Boston, there are no conditions or qualifications required in us that ground the warrant for the gospel offer. The terminology of "conditions" has become so badly muddied as to be unhelpful, and in this context it might be wiser to avoid it altogether in speaking of faith's role. If it is used, it needs to be made clear that the "condition" is instrumental and receptive rather than contributory. In the context of introducing his critique of antinomianism John Flavel defends the use of "condition" in *Planēlogia, A Succinct and Seasonable Discourse of the Occasions, Causes, Nature, Rise, Growth, and Remedies of Mental Errors*, in *The Works of John Flavel* (1691; repr. Banner of Truth, 1968), 3, 420–21. Interestingly his nineteenth-century editor enters a rare footnote in disagreement. Many of the earlier Reformed writers could have more clearly expressed the idea that God's covenants are not "conditional" in the sense that they require our response in order to be *established* but that their established promises of blessing and cursing are effected in terms of faith and obedience or unbelief and disobedience. They are monopleuric in foundation and dipleuric in outworking. What the citation above from Durham underlines is that Boston stood in the best Scottish tradition of free and full-hearted gospel preaching. Durham's sermon "Gospel Preparations" continues beyond the above appeal for another fifteen pages in which he dismantles objections to and rejections of Christ before his final appeal: "And now to conclude, Is there not need, great need to come? And have ye not good warrant to come? [i.e. to the wedding]. . . . And if ye have no garments, rings, or jewels (to speak so) to adorn you, he will give these to you. Come forward then, come, come O come, and let it be a day of covenanting with him. And in sign and token thereof, give up your names to him; and for confirmation take the seal of his covenant, the sacrament with your hand, and bless him with your heart, that so heartily welcomes you. And the blessing of God shall come upon you that come on these terms." *Unsearchable Riches*, 73–74. Who would not have wished to be present to respond to such words and to sit at the Lord's Table?

all, or to forbid all men to believe on Christ. For never was any sinner qualified for Christ. He is well qualified for us, I Cor. i: 30; but a sinner out of Christ hath no qualification for Christ but sin and misery. Whence should we have any better, but in and from Christ? Nay, suppose an impossibility that a man were qualified for Christ; I boldly assert, that such a man would not, nor could ever believe on Christ. For faith is a lost, helpless condemned sinner's casting himself on Christ for salvation; and the qualified man is no such person.

Shall we warn people, that they should not believe on Christ too soon? It is impossible that they should do it too soon. Can a man obey the great gospel command too soon, 1 John iii.23? or do the great *work of God* too soon, John vi.28, 29?[29]

Legalism also creeps into

2) Our Thinking about the Relationship between Sanctification and Justification

An element of this threatened the young Galatian church. Having begun with Christ through the Spirit fulfilling in them the things that the law required, now they were ending with the flesh by adding to Christ. The old seduction of qualifications, additions, and personal contributions had bewitched them.[30]

The Colossian church was also threatened by gospel-diluting teaching. Having received Christ and having come to fullness of life in him, they were being offered a new blessing, a fullness not hitherto known by justifying faith. But there were conditions that

[29] Robert Traill, *A Vindication of the Protestant Doctrine concerning Justification*, in *The Works of the Late Reverend Robert Traill*, 2 vols. (1810 original, 4 vols.) (Edinburgh: Banner of Truth, 1975), 1:263. Traill (1642–1716) was a deeply committed "Covenanter," who, as a late teenager, had stood on the scaffold as a companion with James Guthrie at his execution in 1661. He later joined his father in Holland before returning to minister in London. He was captured and temporarily imprisoned on the Bass Rock in 1677 during a visit to Scotland. He continued to serve as a Presbyterian minister in London until his death.

[30] Gal. 3:1–6.

lay between them and this fullness: things not to handle, or to eat; ascetic practices that would lead them to the fullness.[31]

This was higher-life sanctification by lower-life qualification. But what does it accomplish? Says Paul,

> In demanding that you qualify for fullness, this teaching is evacuating you of the power of justification and sanctification, which are yours in Christ, in whom you have died, been buried, and raised, and whose ascension has brought you into life in the heavenly realms. By contrast, since you are in Christ, all of whose benefits are now yours, of course you must put off everything that is inconsistent with being in him and grow in those graces that express a life like his.[32]

The "plus" on offer is actually a conditionalism that will bankrupt. Hence Paul's call to walk in Christ just as we first received him—by grace through faith, apart from works, yet working by love.[33]

Covenant of Works or Rule of Life?

To speak of the law as a "covenant of works" or as a "rule of life" is, recognizably, the theological language of the seventeenth and eighteenth centuries, not of the present one. It is the language of the *Marrow*, of the Marrow Men, and of the tradition of the Confession of Faith. It may sound alien, employing unfamiliar categories. But whatever one's personal theological tradition, this shorthand expresses a significant truth. The ongoing function of God's law is not to serve as a standard to be met for justification but as a guide for Christian living. Thus, according to the Confession of Faith:

---

[31] Col. 2:6–23.
[32] See Col. 3:1–17.
[33] Col. 2:6–7; Gal. 5:6.

> True believers be not under the law as a covenant of works to be thereby justified or condemned yet it is of great use to them as well as to others as a rule of life.[34]

Whether we employ this time-honored language of "the covenant of works" or not,[35] the point being made is important. For legalism arises not only out of a distortion of the grace of God but also from a warped view of the law of God. We could put it this way: legalism begins to manifest itself when we view God's law as a contract with conditions to be fulfilled and not as the implications of a covenant graciously given to us.

God's *covenant* is his sovereign, freely bestowed, unconditional promise: "I will be your God," which carries with it a multidimensional implication: *therefore* "you will be my people."[36]

By contrast, a *contract* would be in the form: "I will be your God *if* you will live as becomes my people."

It is the difference between "therefore" and "if." The former introduces the *implications* of a relationship that has been established; the latter introduces the *conditions* under which a relationship will be established.

In the history of theology, the definition of doctrine, and the exposition of Scripture, it has often been unhelpfully stated up front that "a covenant is a contract." In the better writers who speak thus, these words are quickly qualified to distinguish divine covenants from commercial contracts.[37] But a clear distinction should be made between the two concepts. "Contract" does not by necessity imply either a sovereign action or a gracious disposition on the part of the contractor. It lacks the unconditional self-giving element present in a covenant ("I will be . . ."). Conditions are written into a contract following negotiations; a covenant is made uncondition-

34 Westminster Confession of Faith, 19.6.

35 The issue of the nomenclature is by no means the point at issue, or under discussion, here. The answer to Shorter Catechism question 12 refers to it as the "covenant of life."

36 Cf. Ex. 6:7; Deut. 7:6; 14:2; Ruth 2:16.

37 Regularly, for example, in Puritan literature and thereafter.

ally. God's covenants carry implications, but none of them is the result of divine-human negotiations. This principle is expressed in two features found in Scripture:

> 1) The New Testament writers had more than one Greek word at their disposal to translate the Hebrew word *berith* ("covenant"): *sunthēkē* and *diathēkē*. They chose *diathēkē*. The presence of the prefix *sun-* ("with," "along with") in *sunthēkē* hints at the probable reason. It was more likely to be interpreted in contractual terms—an agreement two individuals make with (*sun-*) one another, rather than a unilateral disposition one person makes to the other. There is no suggestion that God's covenant was an agreement reached by negotiations and mutually agreed conditions between two parties. No, God's covenant is a gift.
>
> 2) The biblical metaphor that comes chiefly to mind when we think about God's covenant is that of marriage. There is no conditional ("if") clause in a marriage covenant. On the contrary the couple commit themselves to each other unconditionally—"for better or for worse, for richer or for poorer, in sickness and in health, till death do us part." It is out of this unconditional self-giving of one partner that the implications of the covenant are so massive for the other partner. Thus the covenant that carries no conditions (there is no "I will *if* you will"), involves massive implications ("She has . . . *therefore* I must . . .").

Similarly when God made his covenant with his people, the connective between his actions and theirs was not "if" but "therefore." In contemporary terms God stated the *indicative*—his commitment to his people; this in turn gave rise to the *imperative*—the implications for the lifestyle of his people. The implications are the outworking of his declarations.

The nature of the Mosaic covenant was much discussed during the era in which the *Marrow* was written.[38] By no means all theologians and pastors held the same view. But the Confession of Faith adopted the consensus view, seeing the Sinaitic covenant as a further expression of the Abrahamic covenant of grace. It did so because of the background against which the Ten Commandments were originally given, in which (1) God was remembering his covenant with Abraham, Isaac, and Jacob,[39] and (2) God's law itself was prefaced by a statement of its context in his redemption acts in the exodus event. Thus the indicatives of his grace grounded the imperatives of his law:

> *Indicative*: "I am the LORD your God, who brought you out of the land of Egypt, out of the house of slavery."
>
> *Imperative implications*: "You shall have no other gods before me."[40]

Boston's Exception

It is worth noting that at this point Boston expressed one of his (several) differences with *The Marrow of Modern Divinity*, if for no other reason than to illustrate the principle that within generic Reformed theology there has always been a diversity of viewpoint on various issues. Being aware of this saves us from naïvely (but dogmatically!) saying, "The Reformed view is . . . ," when all we are entitled to say is, "The view held by a number of Reformed writers with whom I agree is . . ."![41]

The *Marrow* held that the law given at Sinai was a republica-

[38] Discussed in greater detail in Sinclair B. Ferguson, *John Owen on the Christian Life* (Edinburgh: Banner of Truth, 1987), 20–32.
[39] Ex. 3:6, 16; 4:4–5; 6:1–8.
[40] Ex. 20:2–3.
[41] This is far from being a recipe for a theological free-for-all. The Reformed confessions of faith were consensus documents containing statements agreed to by a majority vote rather than by unanimity. We know, for example, that at the Westminster Assembly the desire was expressed for wording that would enable commissioners to agree to generic Reformed theology without an unnecessary hair-splitting that would disrupt unity in fellowship. It would be a misstep to assume simply because one particular expression of covenant theology became enshrined in the Confession of Faith that all orthodox seventeenth-century Divines shared precisely that view. Some awareness of this is essential for the community life of the church.

tion of the covenant of works. Evangelista expresses the position as follows:

> It was added by way of subserviency and attendance, the better to advance and make effectual the covenant of grace, so that although the same covenant that was made with Adam was renewed on Mount Sinai, yet I say still, it was not for the same purpose.[42]

Thus,

> The ten commandments were the matter of both covenants, only they differed in form.[43]

Boston held that the natural man is "under" the covenant of works; that is, he remains obligated to it and responsible for its breach. But this is because of Eden, not because of Sinai. He is not "in Moses," but he is "in Adam." Nevertheless, under the weight particularly of Galatians 4:24 (Sinai bears children for slavery), Boston held that the Sinai covenant is the covenant of grace, but in it the substance of the covenant of works was repeated for particular subservient ends:

> There is no confounding of the two covenants of grace and works; but the latter was added to the former as subservient unto it, to turn their eyes towards the promise, or covenant of grace.[44]

So in the Mosaic covenant grace was the principle part, even if the content of the covenant of works (i.e., law) seems more conspicuous! This should not drive us to the mistaken conclusion that the covenants were one and the same.

Thus the basic structure at Sinai echoed the structure of life in Eden: God is gracious; he acts sovereignly and gives graciously to

---

[42] Fisher, *Marrow*, 84.
[43] Ibid., 96.
[44] Ibid., 77.

his people.[45] In response to his grace his people desire to please him, obey him, and never grieve him. The law, therefore, and obedience to it must never be abstracted from the character of the Person who gave it. What was true in the old covenant of Sinai is just as true in the new covenant in Christ. For at Calvary God's covenant commitment and its implications are spelled out in large letters: "I have loved you like this; trust and love me in return, for this is my *commandment*, that you love one another as I have loved you."[46] Thus love for the brethren in the New Testament, while motivated by the love of Christ for us, remains simultaneously obedience to the commandment. For love does not ignore the law; rather, it fulfills it.[47]

While then we find our sin exposed by the law, we must not reduce the Decalogue to being merely a rod intended exclusively to beat the backs of sinners. Yes, it may be true that "if it had not been for the law, I would not have known sin."[48] But see it only in that light (as Luther once did, and others since), and we will soon find ourselves succumbing to the poison of Eden all over again.

If we come to think of God as one whose total focus is on exposing our sin, we will become too shortsighted to see his grace. We will be plagued by a spirit of doubting and mistrusting the Father of lights, who gives his good gifts to us.[49] We will find that we have become incapable of responding to him (and his law) within the father-child bond of love. Therefore Boston is emphatic that the way the law exposes sin serves a larger purpose, namely, bringing

[45] In keeping with a number of earlier Reformed theologians (among others, Paul Baynes, Samuel Rutherford, Stephen Charnock, Anthony Burgess, Thomas Watson, and John Owen), Boston speaks about the original divine-human relationship as a gracious one: "And does it seem a small thing unto you, that earth was thus confederate with heaven? This could have been done to none but him whom the King of Heaven delighted to honour. It was an act of grace, worthy of the gracious God whose favourite he was; for there was grace and free favour in the first covenant, though the exceeding riches of his grace, as the apostle calls it (Eph. 2.7), were reserved for the second." *Human Nature in Its Fourfold State* (London: Banner of Truth, 1964), 48 [*Works,* 8:18]. For him there is grace in creation, albeit this should not be confused with *saving* grace.

[46] See John 15:12. See also 2 John 4–6.

[47] Rom. 13:10. In the same way, obedience to the Sinaitic law in the old covenant was motivated by love for the Lord. Indeed that was the greatest commandment (Deut. 6:4–6).

[48] Rom. 7:7.

[49] James 1:17.

us to see our need of, and then to discover the joy in, fatherly grace and forgiveness. Such a balance is crucial to a right view of God, of grace, *and* of the law.

This is the point of the distinction the Confession of Faith makes between the law as a covenant of works and as a rule for life. Of course, before we are in Christ, all we will see in the law is our condemnation. But, as Paul is at pains to stress, the law is good, and just, and holy.[50] And we need to understand, sense, feel, and then delight in the *grace of law*.[51] For unless we are persuaded that God has shown his grace in his law as well as in his Son, all we will hear and see at Sinai is thunder and lightning.

Here, again, is John Colquhoun:

> The distinction of the divine law, especially into the law as a covenant of works and as a rule of life, is a very important distinction. It is . . . a scriptural distinction; and it is necessary in the hand of the Spirit to qualify believers for understanding clearly the grace and glory of the gospel, as well as the acceptable manner of performing every duty required in the law. To distinguish truly and clearly between the law as a covenant and the law as a rule is, as Luther expressed it, "the key which opens the hidden treasure of the gospel." No sooner had the Spirit of truth given Luther a glimpse of that distinction than he declared that he seemed to be admitted into Paradise, and that the whole face of the Scripture was changed for him. Indeed, without a spiritual and true knowledge of that distinction, a man can neither discern, nor love, nor obey acceptably the truth as it is in Jesus.[52]

True, the law is not the means of justification, except in the sense that Christ has kept it for us. But its substance is the moral shape

---

[50] Rom. 7:12.

[51] Ernest Kevan's study of this title retains its value as an informative and comprehensive summary of Reformed teaching in the period of the Confession of Faith: E. F. Kevan, *The Grace of Law: A Study in Puritan Theology* (London: Kingsgate, 1964).

[52] John Colquhoun, *A Treatise on the Law and Gospel*, ed. D. Kistler (1859; repr. Morgan, PA: Soli Deo Gloria, 1999), 40.

that salvation takes. It is, after all, through the gospel-gift of the Spirit that "the law" is written in the heart—not as a "covenant of works," but as a "rule of life." Even if we are unfamiliar with this terminology, we need to become familiar with the biblical truth it seeks to express.

Diagnosis and Remedy

In Romans 7:14 the apostle Paul gives expression to a profound cry of grief and, perhaps, frustration: "We know that the law is spiritual, but I am of the flesh, sold under sin."

How did this teaching factor into the perspective of Boston and his friends?

Believers are free now from the law "as a covenant of works." Christ has both kept God's commandments for us and paid the penalty of their breach in our place. We are free from the condemnation and the reign of sin. Paul has already made this clear in Romans 3:21–6:23.

But we are not yet free from the presence of sin, and until that day dawns we may still be haunted by the specter of the law seen (as we once saw it exclusively) as a condemning power. True, we who were once sold under sin, upon whom sin had closed the mortgage (as A. T. Robertson puts it), have now been purchased by the precious blood of Jesus Christ. We are no longer under law but under grace. Yet so long as the law uncovers sin in our lives,[53] we are liable to fall back into the old legal view of ourselves.

This is why the psychology of the old life can take much longer to shift than its theology. We understand the gospel, yet there is a continuity in the person who lived under the law's condemnation and knew nothing of God's grace in Christ. We have moved into a new house fully paid for. But it may be a long time before it loses all the vestiges of its former owner. So with us: there remains

[53] Which, it should be noted, Paul virtually personifies in Romans 7, just as he had personified sin in Rom. 5:12–7:24.

in us much that can easily stimulate the legalistic instincts of our past. Thus many Christians find that the sunshine of God's grace in Christ is obscured, and they walk uncertainly in the dark, instead of in the light. They need to learn that Jesus is "more full of grace than I of sin."[54] John Bunyan's Pilgrim was not the first nor the last to wander out of the way toward the house of "Mr. Legality."[55]

This was evidently a major concern to Thomas Boston. Christians are indeed "dead to the law," and yet, he notes with John Owen–like penetration:

> In the best of the children of God here, there are such remains of the legal disposition and inclination of heart to the way of the covenant of works, that as they are never quite free of it in their best duties, so at sometimes their services smell so rank of it, as if they were alive to the law, and still dead to Christ. And sometimes the Lord for their correction, trial, and exercise of faith, suffers the ghost of the dead husband, the law, as a covenant of works, to come in upon their souls and make demands on them, command, threaten, and affright [frighten] them, as if they were alive to it, and it to them. And it is one of the hardest pieces of practical religion, to be dead to the law in such cases.[56]

In terms of the marriage metaphor Paul uses in Romans 7:1–6, the old marriage to the law is finished. Yet many in the second marriage (to Christ) may still be haunted by the memory of the former husband. There is only one remedy: to live in the awareness that the new husband abounds in more grace than the abusive husband did in condemnation. It is this that will produce what Thomas Chalmers famously described as "the expulsive power of a new affection." This is gospel christology, gospel theology, and gospel psychology too.

---

[54] From John Wesley's hymn "O Jesus Full of Truth and Grace," v. 1.
[55] John Bunyan, *The Pilgrim's Progress* (1678), ed. Roger Sharrock (Harmondsworth, UK: Penguin, 1965), 50–55.
[56] Fisher, *Marrow*, 176.

6

SUSPICIOUS SYMPTOMS

The danger of legalism is that it builds up again what Christ has torn down.[1] It distorts and may actually destroy the gospel. It is inimical to the grace of God in Christ. It lies at the heart of many pastoral problems and is one of the most common spiritual sicknesses. Unfortunately it is an infectious disease, especially if a pastor or preacher has contracted it. So it is important to be able to recognize some of its common symptoms.

A (Self) Righteous "Temper"

Legalism produces what our forefathers called a self-righteous "temper." Of course it can do that in the limited modern sense of the word *temper*—"anger" or "rage." But in the older sense the word is closer to our word *temperament*—a person's basic disposition. *Temper* can be controlled, at least to an extent; *temperament*, however, cannot be hidden. It is like the breath of a smoker or the scent of a pleasing perfume. It discloses itself in a variety of ways, some more subtle than others.

[1] Gal. 2:18.

Think of the Pharisee in Jesus's parable of the Pharisee and the tax collector.[2]

Pharisees lived "according to the strictest party of . . . religion."[3] The name itself is probably derived from the root "to separate." Pharisaism was essentially a conservative "holiness movement." So the Pharisee was a man deeply exercised about personal and religious holiness in the details of life. Indeed the Pharisee Jesus pictures praying in the temple went beyond the specific requirements of the law. Listen to his prayer. He thinks of himself as:

- Not like other men. (By definition—he is, after all, a Pharisee.[4])
- A Ten Commandments man. (He alludes to at least three of them.)
- Able to compare himself favorably with others. (He does so specifically with a tax collector who entered the temple simultaneously.)
- A man punctilious in his disciplines. (He fasts twice a week. The law included more feasts than fasts and *required* fasting only once a year on the Day of Atonement[5]).
- A self-sacrificing man. (He tithed *everything*. The law required tithing of only crops, fruit, and animals.[6] Apparently the Pharisee's tithing extended beyond income to his possessions.)

Who is this man?

Luke tells us that Jesus told the parable "to some who trusted in themselves that they were righteous, and treated others with contempt."[7] But *Jesus himself did not tell his original hearers this*. Indeed we are given the impression that his hearers were probably led along by the Pharisee's hint that he was "not like . . . this tax collector." Surely the Pharisee was God's man, the righteous one

[2] Luke 18:9–14.
[3] Acts 26:5.
[4] The probable derivation is "a separated one."
[5] Lev. 16:29, 31. Other fasts were introduced but the text that notes them (Zech. 8:19) stresses that they are to be turned into feasts!
[6] Lev. 27:30–32.
[7] Luke 18:9.

who could leave the temple assured he was justified before God. It could not be the miserable tax collector, could it? For, apart from being a tax collector and therefore by definition associated with "sinners," he:

- Could not even lift his eyes to heaven—which was expected in prayer etiquette.[8]
- Beat his breast in the light of his obvious sinfulness.
- Cried out to God to be "merciful" (literally, "propitiated") to him—since no sacrifice was prescribed for his high-handed transgressions.
- Acknowledged he was "a sinner."

There was, surely, only one answer to Jesus's implied question: "So which of these two men went home from temple worship that day justified, righteous in the sight of the Holy God of heaven?"

We are over-familiar with this parable.

We know "the right answer."

We have been immunized against the unexpected, indeed stunning truth.

It was the tax collector.

How can contemporary Christians recapture the sense of shock at hearing Jesus's conclusion?

In one sense the answer is simple. It should shock us because evangelical Christians may existentially have more in common with the Pharisee than with the tax collector. Those into whose temperaments justification by grace has fully permeated:

- Do not look down on another person—including another Christian. The instinct to do so is one of the most obvious telltale signs of a heart from which legalism has not yet been fully or finally banished; for it implies that we have merited grace more than another.

---

[8] See John 17:1.

- Do not assume that there is anything in our devotion to the Lord that is the reason for God's acceptance of us rather than of somebody else who lacks it.

- Do not assume that it is on the grounds of a decision we made, or for that matter our years of commitment to Christ, that we are accepted before God.

- Do not despise ("treat with contempt," in Luke's expression) an embarrassing breach of etiquette, or outward show of sorrow, in another person.

So, when did you last beat your breast and say, "God, be merciful to me, a sinner"?

The Grace Exposé

In several of his parables Jesus seems to expose the legalistic spirit by describing massive outpourings of God's grace in deeply countercultural ways. In his teaching, grace is unexpected, and so its appearance takes us by surprise and evokes very basic reactions, exposing our hearts.

Thus the welcome of grace the father gives to his prodigal son brings to the surface the elder brother's legalistic temperament.

In a similar way it is the tax collector and not the Pharisee who is justified.

Bare law cannot accomplish this. It is the gospel's emphasis that we are justified apart from the law, period—no qualifications, no "ifs" and "buts"—that exposes the sickness.

Similar symptoms appear in the parable of the laborers in the vineyard.[9] The laborers were hired at different times during the day: at the third, sixth, ninth, or eleventh hour. They are paid in reverse order. Those who have worked longest are paid last. They are thus able to calculate the hourly rate at which the master pays

---

[9] Matt. 20:1–16.

the latecomers. They receive the amount that was promised to the earliest workers! So naturally the latter anticipate a wage hike for themselves; already they are calculating their bonuses:

> Now when those hired first came, they thought they would receive more, but each of them also received a denarius [as had those who began work at the last hour!]. And on receiving it they grumbled at the master of the house.[10]

In context the parable is making a larger point about the flow of redemptive history, and perhaps about the ingathering of the Gentiles. But within that context it is fascinating to see Jesus unpick the human heart. Had the all-day laborers not seen the latecomers receive their wages, they would presumably have accepted their payment without comment. It is the Master's exhibition of grace that evokes their "righteous" indignation. Now we hear their murmuring spirit as they calculate what they have really deserved because of their works, in the light of what others have received in grace.

This is the grace exposé. Without the demonstration of grace, the true nature of their hearts would not have been revealed.

Of course we may assume that later on they told each other that their murmuring was an aberration. They were not usually "like that." But the truth is their reaction was a revelation. It had never appeared before simply because they had never encountered such grace before.

This "legal temper" has many faces.

Sometimes it manifests itself in our service of God. Others (with lesser gifts, shorter experience, poorer preparation) are given positions in the church, and we are passed over. We are irked, not legalistic! But, to the contrary, what is irking us is the grace of God, which irritates us because deep down we still think that grace should always operate on the principle of merit, as a reward for,

[10] vv. 10–11.

or at least a recognition of, our prior faithful service. After all, shouldn't the one who is faithful in little be given much?

Every form of jealousy, all coveting for oneself of what God has given to others, all seeing God's distribution of gifts as related to performance rather than his fatherly pleasure and enjoyment, is infected with this. At the end of the day, it means my sense of personal identity and worth has become entwined with performance and its recognition rather than being rooted and grounded in Christ and his de-merited grace. This too is a subtle form of legalism. It emerges from my soul as though God's grace to others drew it out of me like a powerful magnet. Grace lances the boil of merit.

At other times it is exposed in the motivations that lie behind our obedience. Here is John Colquhoun once more:

> When a man is driven to acts of obedience by the dread of God's wrath revealed in the law, and not drawn to them, by the belief in His love revealed in the gospel; when he fears God because of His power and justice, and not because of His goodness; when he regards God more as an avenging Judge, than as a compassionate Friend and Father; and when he contemplates God rather as terrible in majesty than as infinite in grace and mercy, he shows that he is under the dominion, or at least under the prevalence of a legal spirit. . . . He shows that he is under the influence of this hateful temper . . . when his hope of divine mercy is raised by the liveliness of his frame in duties, and not by discoveries of the freeness and riches of redeeming grace, offered to him in the gospel; or when he expects eternal life not as the gift of God through Jesus Christ, but as a recompense from God for his own obedience and suffering, he plainly shows, that he is under the power of a legal spirit.[11]

So legalism has these and many other faces. What the author of the *Marrow*, and those who appreciated his book, realized was

[11] John Colquhoun, *Treatise on the Law and Gospel*, ed. D. Kistler (1859; repr. Morgan, PA: Soli Deo Gloria, 1999), 143–44.

that at times only *shock therapy* recalibrates the mind, will, and affections rooted in a legal frame. Indeed they assumed that the fact that Paul was accused of antinomianism was an indication that they themselves were on the right track.[12]

A Spirit of Bondage

Legalism also creates its own bondage in the soul. John Bunyan knew much of this through personal experience and long observation of those who came to him for gospel medicine. In *Pilgrim's Progress* he describes the struggles of Christian's friend Faithful.

Faithful encounters "a very aged man . . . Adam the First," who invites him to stay with him in the town of Deceit. He offers him all manner of pleasures (including marriage to his three daughters!). When Christian later asks Faithful what his response was, he says with stark honesty:

> Why, at first I found myself somewhat inclinable to go with the Man, for I thought he spake very fair; but looking in his forehead as I talked with him, I saw there written, Put off the old Man with his deeds.

As Faithful made his escape,

> I felt him take hold of my flesh, and give me such a deadly twitch back, that I thought he had pulled part of me after himself: This made me cry, "O *wretched Man!*" So I went on my way up the hill.

But then as he was about halfway up the hill, another dramatic encounter took place:

[12] Cf. the vigorous comments of D. M. Lloyd-Jones, which are of interest here, although they are by no means unique or even original: "This free grace of God in salvation is always exposed to that charge of antinomianism. . . . If you do not make people say things like that sometimes, if you are not misunderstood and slanderously reported from the standpoint of antinomianism, it is because you do not believe the gospel truly and you do not preach it truly." D. Martyn Lloyd-Jones, *Romans 2:1–3:20: The Righteous Judgment of God* (Edinburgh: Banner of Truth, 1989), 187. Cf. also his comments in D. Martyn Lloyd-Jones, *Romans 6: The New Man* (Edinburgh: Banner of Truth, 1972), 9–10.

> I looked behind me, and saw one coming after me, swift as the wind; so he overtook me. . . .
>
> So soon as the Man overtook me, he was but a word and a blow: for down he knocked me and laid me for dead. But when I was a little come to myself again, I asked him wherefore he served me so? He said, "Because of my secret inclining to Adam the First"; and with that he struck me another deadly blow on the breast, and beat me down backward; so I lay at his foot as dead as before. So when I came to myself again, I cried to him for mercy; but he said, "I know not how to show mercy," and with that knocked me down again. He had doubtless made an end of me, but that one came by, and bid him forbear.

Christian then asks: "Who was that, that bid him forbear?" Faithful responds:

> I did not know him at first, but as he went by, I perceived the holes in his hands, and his side; then I concluded that he was our Lord. So I went up the Hill.

Then Christian explains it all:

> That man that overtook you, was Moses, he spareth none, neither knoweth he how to show mercy to those that transgress his Law.

And Faithful comments:

> I know it very well, it was not the first time that he has met with me.[13]

What Bunyan here calls Faithful's "secret inclining to Adam the First" is related to Paul's metaphor of our marriage to our first husband. The memory of him, which returns like a ghost to a haunted house—the out-of-the-blue sense that we have been permanently

[13] John Bunyan, *The Pilgrim's Progress* (1678), ed. Roger Sharrock (Harmondsworth, UK: Penguin, 1965), 104–6; emphasis original.

marred by that first marriage, the despondency that we can never be attractive to our new husband Jesus Christ, our sliding back into nightmares about our previous "abusive relationship"—conspires to bring a sense of condemnation. That in turn becomes a creeping paralysis in our relationship to the Lord and brings with it a loss of our sense of pardon. We are guilty, failures, ashamed. We must do better to get back into his graces. But we keep failing. We cry to the law to show some mercy; but bare law contains no mercy. It is powerless to pardon. Moses, in this sense, can only beat us into a bondage frame of spirit.

Then our only hope is to have, with Faithful, a clear sight of the nail scars in the hands of Jesus Christ our second husband. For the gospel tells us that it was while we were still weak, still sinners—while we were enemies—Christ died for us.[14] It is only through the free, patient, loving grace of our second husband, the second man, the last Adam, Jesus Christ, that we can be delivered from a bondage frame of spirit. This the law cannot do. The personal, spiritual, mental, emotional, temperamental release comes only when we grasp the fact that what the law could not do, because of our weak flesh, God has done for us in Christ. The abused bride must drink in her new husband's love and fix her eyes on him.

This concern with legalism is in fact the ultimate "backstory" of *The Marrow of Modern Divinity*. Its author ("E. F.") gives this personal testimony:

> Let me confess ingenuously. I was a professor of religion at least a dozen years before I knew any other way to eternal life, than to be sorry for my sins, and ask forgiveness, and strive and endeavour to fulfil the law, and keep the commandments, according as Mr. Dod[15] and other godly men had expounded them;

---

[14] Rom. 5:6–10.

[15] John Dod (1549–1645), because of both his longevity and his spiritual gifts, was already "a legend in his lifetime" and widely esteemed by seventeenth-century Puritans. He was variously nicknamed "Faith and repentance Dod" and "Decalogue Dod" (after his best-selling *A Plaine and Familiar*

> and truly, I remember I was in hope I should at last attain to the perfect fulfilling of them; and in the mean time, I conceived that God would accept the will for the deed; or what I could not do, Christ had done for me.
>
> And though at last, by means of conferring with Mr. Thomas Hooker[16] in private, the Lord was pleased to convince me that I was yet but a proud Pharisee, and to show me the way of faith and salvation by Christ alone, and to give me (I hope) a heart in some measure to embrace it; yet, alas! through the weakness of my faith, I have been, and am still apt to turn aside to the covenant of works; and therefore have not attained to that joy and peace in believing, nor that measure of love to Christ, and man for Christ's sake, as I am confident many of God's saints do attain unto in the time of this life. The Lord be merciful unto me, and increase my faith![17]

Bunyan may have been right to say that it was Moses who beat Faithful for his secret inclining to Adam the First. But ultimately this is the work of Satan, for Paul's words in Romans 7:11—"Sin, seizing an opportunity through the commandment, deceived me and through it killed me"—need to be read against the background of Genesis 3. There is a malevolent personal presence behind "sin" in Paul's words. The Serpent did precisely what Paul describes: he used the commandment to deceive Eve about the nature of the commandment giver. This in turn produced in her a legal and bondage spirit that led to death. She saw only one law—the negative

---

Exposition of the Tenne Commandements [London, 1604], written with his neighboring minister Robert Cleaver).

16 Thomas Hooker (1586–1647) was a fellow of Emmanuel College, Cambridge, the so-called hotbed of Puritanism. It was founded in 1584 by Elizabeth I's servant Sir Walter Mildmay. Granting it a charter, Elizabeth commented, "I hear, Sir Walter, that you have been erecting a Puritan foundation," to which Mildmay replied that he had planted an acorn "which, when it become an oak, God alone knows what will be the fruit thereof." Within twenty years, to be an "Emmanuel man" was to be suspected of Puritan leanings. Hooker served as a lecturer (i.e., Bible expositor) at Chelmsford Cathedral. Suppressed under Archbishop William Laud in 1629 he eventually made his way via Rotterdam to the Massachusetts Bay Colony. There he became the pastor of the First Church in Newton (Cambridge), where he exercised a powerful and wide-ranging ministry. It was said of him that "he was a person who, while doing his Master's work, would put a king in his pocket." Cotton Mather, *Magnalia Christi Americana*, 2 vols. (1852; repr. Edinburgh: Banner of Truth, 1979), 1:53.

17 Edward Fisher, *The Marrow of Modern Divinity* (Ross-shire, UK: Christian Focus, 2009), 41.

one—not the many blessings of God's commands.[18] She saw only prohibition—not the person, full of wisdom and love, as the heavenly Father he is. Having found a landing place here in the case of Eve, Satan continues to land in the same territory in our lives too. But now he has grown from a serpent into a dragon exercising his malicious deceptive ministry.[19]

Ever since, Satan has been driving people to the law as a contract, pressing down on our failure to keep its terms, confirming our worst fears about our relationship to God, and blackmailing us into further bondage in our legalism. Again, Boston comments—notice the final phrase:

> While the law retains its power over a man, death has its sting, and sin its strength against him; but if once he is dead to the law, wholly and altogether set free from it, as it is the covenant of works; then sin hath lost its strength, death its sting, *and Satan his plea against him.*[20]

The children of God hear the whispers of the Evil One: "Look, you have sinned. You have broken God's law. You are under condemnation. You are not qualified to be a believer." Nor, surely, is there a gospel minister to whom he has not added the words, ". . . far less fit to be a pastor." He knows he cannot destroy the salvation of God's people; but he is bent, indeed hell-bent—as he was in Eden—on destroying our peace, liberty, and joy in God.

Where can we find refuge? The master spiritual counselor John Newton provides the answer:

> Bowed down beneath a load of sin,
> By Satan sorely pressed,
> By war without, and fears within,
> I come to thee for rest.

---

[18] Gen. 1:28–31; 2:16.
[19] Rev. 12:9. As Serpent he deceived the woman; now grown to become "a great red dragon" he deceives "the whole world" (Rev. 12:3, 9).
[20] Fisher, *Marrow*, 178; emphasis added.

> Be thou my shield and hiding-place,
> That, sheltered by thy side,
> I may my fierce accuser face,
> And tell him Thou hast died.[21]

There and there alone is liberty from bondage.

A Cure?

What, then, is the remedy for legalism?

At the stage we have reached in reflecting on the *Marrow*, it scarcely needs to be said.

It is grace. But it is not "grace" as commodity, grace as substance. It is grace in Christ. For God's grace to us *is* Christ.

Yes, it is the atonement; but not atonement as theory, or as an abstract reality, something that has an identity of its own outside of and apart from the Lord Jesus. For Christ himself, clothed as he is in his gospel work, *is* the atonement—"He is the propitiation for our sins."[22]

The remedy therefore is the one that healed Paul of the deep disease of legalism. It is not difficult to imagine that he too knew what it was to be beaten by Moses. He was after all "the chief of sinners."[23] But here is what he discovered:

> Whatever gain I had, I counted as loss for the sake of Christ. Indeed, I count everything as loss because of[24] the surpassing worth of knowing Christ Jesus my Lord. For his sake I have suffered the loss of all things and count them as rubbish, in order that I may gain Christ *and be found in him, not having a righteousness of my own that comes from the law, but that which comes though faith in Christ, the righteousness from God that depends on faith*.[25]

---

[21] From John Newton's hymn "Approach My Soul the Mercy Seat."
[22] 1 John 2:2.
[23] See 1 Tim. 1:15.
[24] Note that Paul does *not* write "*in exchange for* the surpassing worth."
[25] Phil. 3:7–9.

The remedy is that prescribed by Charles Wesley, discovering that these words are true:

> O Jesus, full of truth and grace,—
> *More full of grace than I of sin . . .*[26]

Where sin abounds, where the law condemns, there grace abounds all the more *even* to the chief of sinners. Indeed *especially* to the chief of them, for the more sin there has been, the more God's grace has abounded. This is the flood tide that drowns legalism in its tracks.

If it is said that such free grace will lead people to conclude, "Let us go on sinning that grace may abound"; we are on safe ground. For that was the conclusion some people drew from what Paul called "my gospel." But antinomianism can never be its fruit, as he demonstrated[27] and as we shall see in the next chapter.

---

[26] Emphasis added. One potential "Reformed" objection to citing Wesley's words in this connection might arise from those who share the generic Reformed distinctive that Christ died to save only the elect, but hold that he did so by paying the exact total penalty due for each of and all the sins of the elect—no less, but also no more (rather than the view that what Christ accomplished in itself on the cross qualifies him to save any and all whom the Lord elects and calls). This suggests that even within the Reformed view of particular redemption ("limited atonement") there are different approaches to how the atonement functions. To consider this issue would require essay-length discussion, but in these pages the undergirding view is that Christ's sufferings would not have been decreased or increased depending on the exact number of the elect. In relation to Wesley's words, "grace" is not to be thought of as a commodity that can increase or decrease in amount according to the equation governing the sufferings of Christ. In short, the "more grace in Christ" than "sin in me" principle is established by the fact that in Christ we are not only pardoned (and thus brought back to Edenic innocence) but also "counted righteous" with the final and indissoluble righteousness of Christ. God's grace in Christ not only takes us back to creation Eden; it secures us for the glorified Eden. Those who are justified in Christ are as righteous in the sight of God, and as permanently so, as is Christ himself. For the only righteousness by which we are righteous *is* Christ's righteousness.

[27] Rom. 6:1ff.

7

FACES OF ANTINOMIANISM

The controversy aroused by *The Marrow of Modern Divinity* was about more than a book. Along with the Auchterarder Creed, the *Marrow* proved to be a litmus test—particularly of ministers and their ministry—often revealing hearts and minds as alkaline or acidic, grace filled or legalism tending.

The issues involved, as we have also seen, related both to the exposition of the Scriptures and the exegesis of the human heart.

Accused

The Marrow Men were accused of holding and encouraging a number of views that were contrary to Reformed orthodoxy. *Antinomianism* featured at the top of the list.

As a matter of historical record the Marrow Brethren held tenaciously to the teaching of the Confession of Faith. They believed that God's law remains as a rule of life for the Christian believer. In fact part 2 of the *Marrow* is an exposition of the Ten Commandments.

Yet the accusation was not altogether surprising. The message of part 1 of the *Marrow* sought to echo Paul's emphasis that where sin abounds, grace super-abounds, and that there are no qualifications for coming to Christ.

But more than that, Marrow theology insisted that levels of sanctification can neither increase nor diminish our justification. To the legalist the gospel of the Marrow Brethren sounded suspiciously like antinomianism.

The issue was not a new one in the seventeenth and eighteenth centuries.

Jesus was never accused in his lifetime of being a legalist. But the issue of antinomianism did arise. John the Baptist lived an abstemious life and baptized penitents. Jesus by contrast made relatively few positive references to the law, ignored scribal shibboleths, on occasion spoke in almost violent language to the Pharisees, went to dinner parties with sinners—and did not baptize anyone. As his opponents gathered their dossier against him, they were getting ready to charge him as being "antinomianism incarnate." After all, did he not encourage indifference to the law of Moses?[1] Their carping criticism against him was that he sat loose to the demands of the law, sailed close to the anti-Sabbatarian wind, and did not keep his disciples in good discipline.

So we are confronted here with an old problem. Does the gospel dismantle the law? It was a consolation to the Marrow Brethren that the preaching and teaching of both Jesus and Paul aroused the same questions and criticism.[2]

But antinomianism, like legalism, has many faces.

Strands in the Thread

The term *antinomian* has its roots in the Lutheran Reformation. Luther's early theology and writing in some senses simply tracked his own spiritual experience. On occasion he seems to have reached his views in the process of writing about them. In particular the deep sense of bondage he had known, followed by his overwhelm-

[1] Mark 2:1–3:6 records a series of such incidents, including a pursuit of Jesus and his disciples through the grain fields one Sabbath afternoon. We are left wondering why such scrupulous Pharisees were not at home studying Torah! See Mark 2:23–24.

[2] Rom. 3:31. The accusation that he dismantled the divine law was a critical factor in the condemnation of Paul, and one that pursued him all the way from Asia to Jerusalem. See Acts 21:27–28. Jesus's response is found at length in Matt. 5:17–48.

ing sense of deliverance, left its mark on the vigor of his speech about the condemning law of God. His basic hermeneutic for understanding the Bible was to ask the question of every passage: Is this law, or is this gospel? That principle had its value, but it could easily produce a distortion so that at times Luther seemed to portray the law exclusively as an enemy.

It was in this context that his friend Johannes Agricola (1492–1566) drew what he thought were the logical conclusions of this radical contrast between law and gospel—the abolition of any role for the law in the Christian life. He expounded this "antinomianism" first in debate with Philip Melanchthon[3] and then later with Luther himself. In the 1530s Melanchthon had begun to employ the notion of the so-called *tertius usus legis*, that the law was a guide for the Christian life. In reaction Agricola basically rejected any role for the law. He had become *antinomian* (*anti* = against; *nomos* = law), although he later withdrew from his earlier views.

While the debate with Agricola was essentially intramural, many on the radical edges of the Anabaptist movement went to extremes that threatened the stability and reputation of the Reformation. This injected into the bloodstream of the Reformed churches a deep sensitivity to, and fear of, antinomianism. Any theology that saw the law in poor light was seen as the first domino in a series to fall, leading to a total collapse.

Waves of antinomianism followed, of different kinds and degrees, and continued to beat on the shores of international Reformed theology well into the seventeenth century and beyond.[4]

[3] Philip Melanchthon (1497–1560) became professor of Greek at the University of Wittenberg in 1518 and a close colleague and confidant of Luther. The first edition (1521) of his *Loci Communes*, which grew out of his exposition of Romans, already treated the issues of law and gospel.

[4] Earlier studies took note of antinomianism in the Puritan era. See chap. 2 of Gertrude Huehns, *Antinomianism in English History: With Special Reference to the Period 1640–1660* (London: Cresset Press, 1959), 25–42. The fresh wave of interest in the early modern period of British history and the seventeenth century in particular has brought a number of recent studies with a specific focus on antinomianism—inevitably with varying theological presuppositions, including Tim Cooper, *Fear and Polemic in Seventeenth-Century England: Richard Baxter and Antinomianism* (Farnham, UK: Ashgate, 2001); David R. Como, *Blown by the Spirit: Puritanism and the Emergence of an Antinomian Underground in Pre–Civil-War England* (Stanford, CA: Stanford University Press, 2004). For the narrative in New England, see, inter alia, David D. Hall, *The Antinomian Controversy, 1636–1638: A Documentary*

For our purposes the simplest way to think of antinomianism is that it denies the role of the law in the Christian life. Its big text (somewhat paradoxically[5]) is Romans 6:14: "You are not under law but under grace."

In contrast, the Confession of Faith taught that while the law is not a covenant of works for the believer, it nevertheless functions as a rule of life.

We saw earlier how careful we need to be with our use of category terms. Not all "antinomians" are either identical or equal. Some who propositionally have held the antinomian view have nevertheless had reputations for godly living. We need to remember the apostolic injunction that the Lord's servant must not be quarrelsome. He must not dispute merely about words. He must remember that he is to act and speak with gentleness to those who hold opposing views.[6]

Robert Traill is once again a wise guide for us:

> Let us not receive reports suddenly of one another. In times of contention, many false reports are raised, and rashly believed. This is both the fruit and the fuel of contention. For all the noise of Antinomianism, I must declare, that I do not know (and I have both opportunity and inclination to inquire) any one Antinomian minister or Christian in London, who is really such as their reproachers paint them out, or such as Luther and Calvin really wrote against.[7]

Antinomianism manifests itself in different forms.

History (Middletown, CT: Wesleyan University Press, 1968); William K. B. Stoever, *A Faire and Easie Way to Heaven: Covenant Theology and Antinomianism in Early Massachusetts* (Middletown, CT: Wesleyan University Press, 1978); Theodore D. Bozeman, *The Precisionist Strain: Disciplinary Religion and Antinomian Backlash in Puritanism to 1638* (Chapel Hill, NC: University of North Carolina Press, 2004). For the later development of antinomianism in England, see Peter Toon, *The Emergence of Hyper-Calvinism in English Nonconformity, 1689–1765* (London: Olive Tree, 1967). A recent discussion drawing on seventeenth-century writers in both historical and contemporary discussion is Mark Jones, *Antinomianism: Reformed Theology's Unwelcome Guest* (Phillipsburg, NJ: P&R, 2013).

[5] "Paradoxically," since Rom. 6:1–23 is Paul's *locus classicus* exposition to counter antinomianism.

[6] 2 Tim. 2:22–26.

[7] Robert Traill, *A Vindication of the Protestant Doctrine Concerning Justification*, in *The Works on the Late Reverend Robert Traill*, 2 vols. (1810 original, 4 vols.) (Edinburgh: Banner of Truth, 1975), 1:281.

Dogmatic Strand

In view here are theologians who hold that the law of God is abrogated in its entirety for a believer.

This was the position of the English Antinomians like John Saltmarsh, John Eaton, and Tobias Crisp.[8] It was a view that tended to be associated with hyper-Calvinism. Here divine indicatives so overwhelmed divine imperatives that biblical balance was lost. Great emphasis was placed on the fact that believers walk in the Spirit, who now dwells in them—and his indwelling, not the written law, rules and guides the Christian's life. But this gave a less than satisfactory explanation of why it is that the Spirit is said to write *the law* on our hearts and minds in regeneration. It is difficult to see how, in the context of Jeremiah, this excludes the Decalogue.[9]

Although in one sense antinomianism is the "opposite" error from legalism, in another sense it is the "equal" error, for it similarly abstracts God's law from God's person and character (which undergoes no change from old to new covenant). It fails to appreciate that the law that condemns us for our sins was given to teach us how not to sin.

Moreover, it would hardly do to say that the law is irrelevant because believers are now indwelt by the Spirit. The commandments remain "holy and righteous and good."[10] Furthermore the specific exhortations of the new covenant lead to the fulfilling of

[8] Of interest here is that John Flavel's analysis and critique of antinomianism had an introductory address to readers signed by a number of Divines, including John Howe, Nathaniel Mather, and Increase Mather. These Divines had been signatories to a testimony that the works published as those of Tobias Crisp had indeed been transcribed by his son. Contrary to their expectation, this was published with Crisp's sermons, which contained sentiments that were widely regarded as antinomian (including by Flavel). This address is of interest because it illustrates the desire of these men to avoid extremes of condemnation. Indeed while recognizing that some of Crisp's statements have antinomian tendencies, they noted that other strands in the material stressed the inseparability of justification and sanctification, and that evidences of grace do serve to reassure an individual that the faith by which he experiences assurance is in fact genuine. See *The Works of John Flavel*, 6 vols. (1820; repr. London: Banner of Truth, 1968), 3:413–18. The authors comment on such issues: "If every passage that falls from us be stretched and tortured with the utmost severity, we shall find little to do besides accusing others, and defending ourselves, as long as we live. A spirit of meekness and love will do more to our common peace, than all the disputation in the world," 3:413. In whatever manner we interpret this self-defense, the words are themselves worth weighing.

[9] Heb. 8:10; 10:15, citing Jer. 31:33.

[10] Rom. 7:12.

the old-covenant law.[11] Hyper-Calvinistic antinomianism placed such an emphasis on the prevenient, eternal, electing, distinguishing grace of God that any emphasis on the place of the law seemed prejudicial to it. Linked with this was a doctrine of justification from eternity and an emphasis on the immediacy of the witness of the Holy Spirit apart from the evidences of a holy life. In an attempt to rid themselves of the resmuggling of good works into the foundation of justification, the hyper-Calvinists confused foundation and superstructure, ground and evidence.

The logical development of this was to view the law as inimical to the preaching of grace. Antinomianism therefore had no relevant place in the Christian life for the practical syllogism (that a Spirit-transformed life lived in conformity to God's law is evidence of God's saving grace). Those who, having been justified in eternity, experienced the Spirit bearing witness with their spirits that they are the children of God needed no such objective rule. In one sense they were operating with an over-realized personal eschatology, as though the strong and subtle influence of sin had been destroyed.

But such doctrinal antinomianism was far from the spirit of a Thomas Boston or any of his colleagues.[12]

Exegetical Strand

In addition to its dogmatic form (but closely related to it) antinomianism in the strict sense is defended by specific exegetical considerations,[13] arguing that any view, such as that of the Westminster Divines—that there is a threefold division in the law and that one of these divisions (the moral law) continues to function—is an imposition on the biblical text.

The taxonomy of the law, that sees it in terms of a "threefold

[11] Eph. 6:1–3 is perhaps the most obvious illustration of this.

[12] Boston, it will be remembered, did not even read to the end of John Saltmarsh's book before returning it to its owner. In sharp contrast, he *bought* his parishioner's copy of the *Marrow*!

[13] In these various categorizations the term *antinomian* is used without the vituperative freight that it frequently carries in polemical literature. We might well wish for a different shorthand terminology, but as Calvin realized with the expression "free will"—it is what it is!

division,"[14] goes back beyond the Reformation at least as far as Thomas Aquinas.[15] Probably a majority of contemporary biblical scholars (including evangelicals) reject this as a theological grid overlaid on the biblical data, an *epexegetical imposition* rather than an *exegetical conclusion*. In this view the Mosaic law was simply that: one law code.

The notion that there was distinct ceremonial law that has now been fulfilled and abrogated, civil law that governed the people as a nation that has now ceased to function since God's people are an international community, and moral law (the Ten Commandments) is thus viewed as alien to the Scriptures. The beauty of the traditional threefold division lies only in the eye of the beholder, not in the biblical text. The law of Moses, in its entirety, has ceased to have a binding role in the new covenant. It has, as the law of Moses, simply been brought to an end. It has no binding authority in the life of the believer. The law of Moses governed its own epoch; it does not govern the new epoch inaugurated by Christ. We are "not under law but under grace,"[16] and live in the Spirit.

The issues involved in this debate are too wide-ranging and far-reaching to be given satisfactory resolution here. But it is important *from the point of view of the Marrow Brethren* to explain their view of the law. For, paradoxically, today they would more likely be accused of legalism than of antinomianism![17] Several general observations will help us to follow their thinking:

[14] In my own view it would be more felicitous to speak of the "threefold *dimensions*" of the law rather than to use the term *divisions*, since as the Confession of Faith notes, "Beside this law, commonly called moral, God was pleased to give to the people of Israel as a church under age, ceremonial laws, containing several typical ordinances, partly of worship, prefiguring Christ, his graces, actions, sufferings and benefits; and partly, holding forth divers instructions of moral duties. All which ceremonial laws are now abrogated, under the New Testament" (19.3). Here the ceremonial and the moral are not divisions between laws but dimensions of laws. The Confession itself did not use the language of "divisions."

[15] See Thomas Aquinas, *Summa Theologica*, 1a IIae QQ 99–108, trans. Fathers of the English Dominican Province (New York: Benziger, 1948), 2:1,031–119.

[16] Rom. 6:14.

[17] Virtually all evangelical scholars who espouse exegetical antinomianism nevertheless de facto uphold the substance of the Ten Commandments as expressive of a gospel-centered lifestyle, because of the way in which they form the substance of New Testament exhortations. The dominant exception is the fourth (Sabbath) commandment. In some senses this highlights the extent to which the Sabbath command serves as something of a theological litmus test. It is evident that both the *Marrow* and the

> It should be a working principle of our interpretation of Scripture that it does not set law and grace over against each other in absolute terms.
>
> When John says that "the law was given through Moses; grace and truth came through Jesus Christ," the relationship he sees between grace and law is not antithetical but complementary. Christ's ministry (grace and truth/reality) fulfills Moses's ministry (law/shadow/type). This is further elaborated by the verbs John employs: law was *given*, but Christ *came.*[18]
>
> When (in Romans 6:14) Paul affirms that we are not "under law," he is not denying that the law continues to be relevant. He had been accused of precisely this.[19] But already (in Romans 3:31) he had stressed that rather than "overthrow" the law, the gospel functions to "uphold" it. After all, "we know that the law is good, if one uses it lawfully,"[20] since it is "holy and righteous and good," and "spiritual."[21]
>
> The new covenant in Christ establishes the law not only externally, but also internally. Christ died "in order that the righteous requirement of the law might be fulfilled in us, who walk not according to the flesh but according to the Spirit."[22]

Thus what the author of Hebrews calls the "becoming obsolete" of the old covenant[23] is held hand in glove with his affirmation of Jeremiah's vision of the new covenant:

Marrow Brethren subscribed to the view that, like the other commands in the Decalogue, the Sabbath command should be viewed as pre-Sinaitic and therefore not abolished with the end of the Mosaic administration. Specifically this command illustrates the multidimensionalism view of the Mosaic law, since there were in the Sabbath commandment under Moses both moral and ceremonial dimensions. The perspective of at least one strand in Puritan thought was that, as coming from the hand of Moses, the believer has nothing to do with the law; but as coming from the hand of Christ in the beginning of the new creation, the believer is, through marriage to Christ, an in-law to the Decalogue.

[18] John 1:17. The movement here may be compared to that in Heb. 1:1–2, from fragmentary, varied, and episodic to fulfillment and finality in Christ.

[19] Acts 21:28.

[20] 1 Tim. 1:8.

[21] Rom. 7:12, 14.

[22] Rom. 8:4. Here too there is an echo of Jer. 31:33 and especially Ezek. 36:25–27.

[23] Heb. 8:13.

For this is the covenant that I will make with the house
of Israel
after those days, declares the Lord:
I will put my laws into their minds,
and write them on their hearts,
and I will be their God,
and they shall be my people.[24]

The citation is repeated.[25] Given the emphasis the author of Hebrews places on these words, we are surely bound to ask: *Which laws* are written into our minds and on our hearts? The most obvious answer is: What other law would the first readers understand but the Decalogue? Since the author of Hebrews teaches that the ceremonial patterns of the old covenant have been fulfilled in Christ, he could not have meant them. And since Hebrews was written to those who now have "no lasting city" and therefore no longer see themselves as citizens of a state with its capital in Jerusalem,[26] they are no longer a people governed by the civil regulations intended for life in the land.

Too Easily Dismissed?

The seventeenth-century Reformed writers who upheld the continuing obligation of the Decalogue are often dismissed as inflexible in their thinking. But an often overlooked (if known at all) indication of their *flexibility* is found in their discussions of whether the Christian receives the Decalogue from the hands of Moses or from the hands of Christ. As the *Marrow* noted, the Christian is, according to Paul, "not . . . outside the law of God but under the law of Christ."[27]

---

[24] Heb. 8:10.

[25] In Heb. 10:16.

[26] Heb. 13:14.

[27] 1 Cor. 9:21. Edward Fisher, *The Marrow of Modern Divinity* (Ross-shire, UK: Christian Focus, 2009), 188. A measure of restoration to Eden takes place in regeneration, since "man at first stood *in* law, rather than *under* law—being formed to the spontaneous exercise of that pure and holy love, which is the expression of the Divine image, and hence also to the doing of what the law requires." Patrick Fairbairn, *The Revelation of Law in Scripture* (Edinburgh: T & T Clark, 1868), 45; emphasis original.

Behind this lies a sophisticated biblical theology.

Depending on the "tradition" of theological education in which we have been reared, we tend to be introduced to "biblical theology" from different sources. Indeed the phrase itself means different things to different people. The majority of theological teachers and students did not suck in biblical theology with their mother's milk (to rework some words of Calvin), and have accessed it through relatively recent literature; in addition they are often little versed in the theological literature of the sixteenth and seventeenth centuries. It is easy therefore to fall into the error of assuming that biblical theological, redemptive historical, and exegetical perspectives have been known and employed only relatively recently. We therefore need to be on our guard against the overworked canard that the authors of the Confession of Faith used a "proof text" method in doing their theology.

This is an example of "the heresy of modernity" in at least two ways. First, the Westminster Divines were deeply opposed to producing a confession with proof texts and did so only under duress at the command of the English Parliament. But, in addition, biblical theology itself is much older than its history as an academic discipline. As C. S. Lewis well notes, we moderns can all too easily be like people entering a conversation at eleven o'clock not realizing that it began at eight o'clock.

The truth is that there is an intricate weaving of exegesis and biblical and redemptive historical theology behind the wording of the Confession, and this is nowhere more certain than in its treatment of the law of God.[28]

[28] That the best of the seventeenth-century authors did not see themselves as "proof-texters" is particularly well (and in this context relevantly) illustrated in the contemporaneous work of Anthony Burgess, *Vindiciae Legis*. Burgess was a member of the Third Committee of the Assembly charged with framing the original wording for the chapter "Of the Law of God," which was remitted for study on November 18, 1645, and finally voted on in the Assembly on September 25, 1646. In the interim Burgess was invited by the ministers of London to deliver a series of lectures on the theme. It is these thirty lectures that, by a request of the ministers dated June 11, 1646, were published as *Vindiciae Legis*. A reading of them suggests the close agreement between the Confession of Faith and Burgess in both the doctrinal statements and the biblical exegesis that lay behind them. The lectures were delivered within a scholastic framework; that is to say, they are composed of responses

Epochal Theology

The classical view of Reformed orthodoxy viewed the law of God in terms of three epochs.

1) Creation

At his creation God's image, male and female, reflected his character. Obedience to God in terms of a holy (devoted to God) lifestyle was intuitive and "natural." The man and the woman were created as the image of God, the macrocosmic Lord, and were called to imitate him by exercising microcosmic lordship.[29] The pattern of the Lord of the macrocosm was therefore embedded into the life rhythm of the lords of the microcosm. Thus God's seventh-day rest was the paradigm for theirs.[30] Many but not all Puritans took Paul's comment on Gentiles' being "a law to themselves. . . . They show that the work of the law is written on their hearts"[31] to be a reference to the vestiges of this basic element in the human constitution as divine image. In this sense, as John Owen wrote, the law was "connatural" to man, and his "domestic, his old acquaintance . . . his familiar, his friend."[32]

2) Moses

Paul writes that "the law came in . . ."[33] The reference is (a) to the Mosaic administration and (b) to the Decalogue in particular, as

---

to sixty-two questions. But their substance (in distinction from their format) reveals a deep sense of biblical-theological thinking and a sensitivity to the flow of redemptive history from Genesis to Revelation. This is not to claim that contemporary biblical theologians would necessarily agree with Burgess. But the fact of the matter is that it is difficult to find two works of contemporary biblical theology that entirely agree with each other! My point here is exclusively to underline that to dismiss Burgess and his contemporaries on the grounds that they were "proof texting" rather than engaging in serious biblical theology is simply to display a lack of familiarity with the basic source materials.

[29] This is the thrust of Gen. 1:26–28. The *imago dei* (v. 26) is not defined as dominion (v. 28). But *dominion* is an expression of divine image bearing.

[30] Gen. 2:1–3. Implied here is that the statement "God blessed the seventh day and made it holy" (v. 3) must apply to God's intention for men and women, not to his blessing the day for himself (he had no need to either bless or sanctify a day for himself).

[31] Rom. 2:14–15.

[32] John Owen, *An Exposition upon Psalm* CXXX (London, 1668), in *The Works of John Owen*, 24 vols., ed. W. H. Goold (Edinburgh: Johnstone & Hunter, 1850–1855), 6:389.

[33] Rom. 5:20.

his later discussion in Romans 7:1–24 makes clear. This for Paul is the law "written . . . on tablets of stone . . . carved in letters on stone."[34] So the giving of the law through Moses has some important characteristics.

First, the law is now given in an objective written form, and its inscription is external to man, not only internal as it was in Eden.

Second, there is a "glory" related to the law, albeit—when placed beside the glory of new covenant ministry of the Spirit—*comparatively speaking* it has no glory at all.[35]

This *comparative* way of highlighting the epochal development that is marked by Pentecost is characteristic of Paul and important to notice. He employs it already in Galatians. Believers have, in redemptive historical terms, transitioned from an era of being heirs but slaves, to a new epoch of being mature sons who enjoy the presence of the Spirit of adoption and use Jesus's mode of address to God as they cry, "Abba! Father!" (*No Old Testament believer ever cries, "Abba! Father!"*). Of the Old Testament believer Paul writes, "The heir, as long as he is a child, is no different from a slave, though he is the owner of everything, but he is under guardians and managers until the date set by his father."[36]

A radical antithesis is suggested: once slave, now son.

Yet this is a comparative antithesis, not an absolute one. If one may venture an illustration from personal experience: when I was in elementary school, those were the happiest days of my life *until* I progressed to high school. Those days really were the happiest days of my life *until* I went to university. Now we are really talking about the happiest days of my life—*until* graduation. Then, free from classwork, exams, professors—this is freedom at last! Thus, *from the perspective of the age of fulfillment*, elementary school, high school, yes, even university, all seem like imprisonment with

[34] 2 Cor. 3:3, 7.
[35] 2 Cor. 3:7–11.
[36] Gal. 4:1–7.

teachers as the jailers. *But at the time, it was possible to find joy and pleasure in each epoch.*

Here, then, a fuller understanding of a prior epoch is possible only from within a later epoch. In the same way, the Old Testament believer tasted rich blessings within the context of the Mosaic administration. But *by comparison* with the fullness of grace in Christ, they pale into insignificance.[37] Grasp this, and we come to see that Paul does not deny that there is divine glory in the law. His language is not pejorative but comparative.

Third, the Decalogue's commands are cast in a largely negative form (eight of them are negations; only two are positive exhortations).

Negation is, in fact, the simplest form of command. (This is illustrated by the fact that the two positive commands open out into a thousand questions about how to fulfill them: How do we keep the Sabbath? How do we honor parents when we have married, are rearing children of our own, and belong to a new family unit? By comparison the application of the negatively framed commands is more straightforward and discussable only at the margins).

We understand this if we are parents. We do not first try to explain to infants how electricity works and then tell them not to stick a screwdriver into the electric socket. We first do only the latter, warning them that it may do them harm and cause them pain. Perhaps several years will elapse before we provide them with a positive explanation of how electricity works. The negative command is more straightforward, simpler, and requires less explanation.

Fourth, the commandments are set within a specific historical-sociological context in which people make idols and bow down to them, servants are owned not merely employed, families extend beyond the nuclear unit to households, and people live in an agrarian economy owning oxen and donkeys.

[37] Cf. John Calvin, *Institutes of the Christian Religion*, trans. F. L. Battles, ed. J. T. McNeill (Philadelphia: Westminster Press, 1960), 2.9.1.

Fifth, the commandments have extended codicils attached to them because they are to be applied:

i) to a specific people group—God's uniquely called-out-and-called-together ones who are to form the womb within which the messianic promises would be preserved.

ii) within a specific time frame—until Messiah comes.

iii) with provisions in the application of these ten laws to the whole of society to govern them as a specific state in one particular land to keep them "holy," distinct from other nations, all with a view to Messiah coming.

iv) with provisions made for ceremonial regulations and actions that would provide preliminary pictures, constantly repeated, of how pardon for sinners, and reconciliation with and access to God, would ultimately be provided by God himself.

Sixth, these ten commandments were to be regarded as belonging to a distinct category within the law as a whole. They were clearly related to, yet distinct from, the application of them to civil life and worship. This was so fundamental to understanding the dynamic of God's law that it was expressed physically in three ways, often overlooked:

> i) Only the Decalogue element in the legal code was written by God.[38]
>
> ii) Only the Decalogue was specifically inscribed in stone.
>
> iii) Only the Decalogue was deposited in the ark of the covenant.[39] Its location, in the ark and under the mercy seat or covering, is surely expressive of the way in which the blood sprinkled on the mercy seat symbolically atones for the breach of the commandments underneath it. This, as Boston notes, is vivid symbolism in which "justice satisfied, and judgment fully executed" are represented.[40]

---

[38] Ex. 24:12.

[39] Ex. 25:16.

[40] Fisher, *Marrow*, 102.

It was also made explicit that the applications of the law were given for the people "to observe in the land that you are crossing the Jordan to possess."[41] This explains the focus of these laws on a national homeland. Thus God taught in emblematic form that the Decalogue was foundational, its applications secondary, contextualized, and temporary. This was further emphasized in the recognition that the sacrificial system was pictorial and sacramental and pointed to a future sacrifice that would be fully efficacious to deal with sin.[42]

3) Christ

The law of God, thus written on tablets of stone and sealed within the ark of the covenant, is now rewritten by the Spirit and sealed in the hearts of believers. External regulation once again becomes inner disposition, albeit within the context of sanctification having begun but glorification not yet being consummated. It is apparent that neither the civil nor the ceremonial dimensions of the law are included in this "writing."

Like Old Testament *prophecy* then, so with Old Testament *law*, *it is in the light of its fulfillment that the real structures that were always present in God's ancient word are fully revealed.*

Thus, for the Marrow Brethren and their precursors, a careful observation of the context in which the law of God was given, a tracing of its story throughout the whole Bible—in a word, a biblical theological, Christocentric approach to the law—underscored that like all Gaul, God's law is "divided into three parts"—unified indeed because divinely given, and yet multidimensional in character, function, and historical reach. The fact that the unified law "breaks down" into its constituent dimensions in Christ is an indication that those dimensions were native to the law itself.

Thus only in Christ do the law's aspects and divisions—"dim-

---

[41] Deut. 6:1 NIV.

[42] The logic of Heb. 7:23–25; 10:1–4, while embedded in a book of the new covenant, expresses an understanding that was possible in the Mosaic epoch, since its logic is not dependent on the incarnation of Christ but on the repetition of the sacrifices.

ensions"—become clear. But what is *brought to light* by his coming is not *created* by his coming. Rather, Christ's coming makes clear what was always there.[43]

B. B. Warfield's comment on the relationship between the Old and the New Testament revelation is apropos here:

> The Old Testament may be likened to a chamber richly furnished but dimly lighted; the introduction of light brings into it nothing which was not in it before; but it brings out into clearer view much of what is in it but was only dimly or even not at all perceived before. . . . Thus the Old Testament revelation of God is not corrected by the fuller revelation which follows it, but is only perfected, extended and enlarged.[44]

It is within this perspective that the Marrow Brethren believed that the three-dimensional character and the ongoing significance of the Decalogue were mandated not by "traditionalism," or by "proof texting," but by a careful biblical-theological handling of the text of the whole of Scripture.

But there are also experimental expressions of antinomianism.

Experimental Strand

The extent of fear of and concern about antinomianism in the seventeenth and eighteenth centuries can be measured by a comment

[43] Lest the "scholarship" of the Westminster Divines be regarded as hopelessly outmoded and premodern, and predetermined by a nonbiblical-theological a priori grid, it is salutary to note Bruce K. Waltke independently validating their biblical theology view by adopting similar exegetical arguments to those of the Divines. Bruce K. Waltke, in *Theonomy: A Reformed Critique*, ed. William S. Barker and W. Robert Godfrey (Grand Rapids, MI: Zondervan, 1991), 70–72. As Professor Waltke indicates, a clear distinction was made not only between the Decalogue and its ancillary applications but also between ceremonial and civil laws. The former are given in Exodus 25–40 and in Leviticus, not in Deuteronomy. In this sense, while there is a divine unity in the law, it is like the unity of a beam of light that when passing through a prism reveals the constituent colors that have not been seen by the naked eye. In the case of the law of God, as with the prophecies of the coming of the Messiah, it becomes clear only in Christ that there is in the law a permanent foundation (Decalogue) and a temporary ceremonial as well as a local and interim civil application. The former remains; the latter are abrogated in different ways. The ceremonies come to an end. While the civil laws give us hints about righteous government, they no longer constitute the law code Christians should seek to have established in the various nations to which they belong. We may draw appropriate analogies to our own contexts from the concreteness of application of the Decalogue to a particular people in a particular temporal, geographical, and religio-social context in the past. This fulfillment-clarifying principle is seen in relation to Christ when it becomes clear that the prophesied coming of Christ has first- and second-coming dimensions.

[44] B. B. Warfield, *Biblical Doctrines* (New York: Oxford University Press, 1929), 141–42.

by the New England minister Thomas Shepard: "Those who deny the use of the law to any that are in Christ become patrons of free vice under the mask of free grace."[45] Antinomianism of that order had manifested itself on the margins of nonconformity. But clearly the concern was that in any aberration from orthodoxy there is an inbuilt "domino effect"—so that doctrinal and exegetical antinomianism would eventually lead to a full-fledged rejection of biblical imperatives altogether and would turn the grace of God into lasciviousness[46] in a manner reminiscent of the doggerel

> Free from the law, O blessed condition,
> I can sin as I please and still have remission.

Antinomianism has an everyday and mundane form, for example, in the professing Christian who responds to his passenger's anxious glance at his speedometer with a "We're not under law; we're under grace."

At one level it would be appropriate to say: "Actually you are under the law—Indiana Law, or Pennsylvania Law, or Scots Law—and there is a flashing light behind you to prove it!"

But in terms of our theology of the Christian life, responding "But you *are* under the law" would in any case not really deal with the problem. It would miss its real heart. For the deepest response to antinomianism is not "You are under the law" but rather

> You are despising the gospel and failing to understand how the grace of God in the gospel works! There is no condemnation for you under the law because of your faith-union with Christ.

---

[45] Thomas Shepard (1605–1649) was fifteen when he entered Emmanuel College, Cambridge. Ordained in the Church of England, he was barred from preaching under Archbishop Laud. He sailed to Massachusetts and became minister of the First Church of Cambridge. A vigorous opponent of antinomianism, he was involved in the trial of Anne Hutchinson at the height of the New England antinomian controversy. His exposition of the parable of the ten virgins is marked by such rigor that John ("Rabbi") Duncan, nineteenth-century professor of Hebrew at New College, Edinburgh, once famously remarked that "Shepard is fine, but I wish I were as good as one of his hypocrites!" John M. Brentnall, ed., *"Just a Talker": Sayings of John ("Rabbi") Duncan* (Edinburgh: Banner of Truth, 1997), 183.

[46] Jude 4 (KJV).

> But that same faith-union leads to the requirements of the law being fulfilled in you through the Spirit. Your real problem is not that you do not understand the law. It is that you do not understand the gospel. For Paul says that we are "in-lawed to Christ."[47] Our relationship to the law is not a bare legal one, coldly impersonal. No, our conformity to it is the fruit of our marriage to our new husband Jesus Christ.

Practical antinomianism has many forms today. One of them is the secular gospel of self-acceptance masquerading as Christianity. "Since God accepts me the way I am, I ought not to get straitjacketed by the law of God—what God wants is that I be myself." This has very concrete expressions in what are euphemistically described as "lifestyle choices": "This is how I am, God is gracious, and [implied: unlike you, if you disagree with me] he accepts me as I am, and therefore I will remain as I am."

At one level the problem is indeed rejection of God's law. But underneath lies a failure to understand grace and ultimately to understand God. True, his love for me is not based on my qualification or my preparation. But it is misleading to say that God accepts us the way we are. Rather he accepts us *despite the way we are. He receives us only in Christ and for Christ's sake.* Nor does he mean to leave us the way he found us, but to transform us into the likeness of his Son.[48] Without that transformation and new conformity of life we do not have any evidence that we were ever his in the first place.

At root then antinomianism separates God's law from God's person, and grace from the union with Christ in which the law is written in the heart. In doing so it jeopardizes not simply the Decalogue; it dismantles the truth of the gospel.

---

[47] 1 Cor. 9:20–21.

[48] Rom. 8:29.

8

CAUSES AND CURES

Antinomianism takes various forms. People do not always fit neatly into our categorizations, nor do they necessarily hold all the logical implications of their presuppositions.[1] Here we are using "antinomianism" in the theological sense: rejecting the *obligatory* ("binding on the conscience") nature of the Decalogue for those who are in Christ.

Antinomianism, it was widely assumed in the eighteenth century, is essentially a failure to understand and appreciate the place of the law of God in the Christian life. But just as there is more to legalism than first meets the eye, the same is true of antinomianism.

Opposites Attract?

Perhaps the greatest misstep in thinking about antinomianism is to think of it *simpliciter* as the opposite of legalism.

It would be an interesting experiment for a budding doctoral student in psychology to create a word-association test for Christians. It might include:

[1] While it is important and legitimate to lay bare theological presuppositions, it is not always the case that individuals are comprehensive and consistent in following through their implications, and it is important not to impute a belief in those implications where they are in fact denied by an individual. This is an overstep common in polemical writing. It remains proper, however, to point out the logical implications of presuppositions.

Old Testament	Anticipated answer → New Testament
Sin	Anticipated answer → Grace
David	Anticipated answer → Goliath
Jerusalem	Anticipated answer → Babylon
Antinomianism	Anticipated answer → ?

Would it be fair to assume that the instinctive response there at the end would be "Legalism"?

Is the "correct answer" really "Legalism"? It might be the right answer at the level of common usage, but it would be unsatisfactory from the standpoint of theology, for antinomianism and legalism are not so much antithetical to each other as they are both antithetical to grace. This is why Scripture never prescribes one as the antidote for the other. Rather grace, God's grace in Christ in our union with Christ, is the antidote to both.

This is an observation of major significance, for some of the most influential antinomians in church history acknowledged they were on a flight from the discovery of their own legalism.

According to John Gill, the first biographer of Tobias Crisp, one of the father figures of English antinomianism:[2] "He set out first in the legal way of preaching in which he was exceeding jealous."[3]

Benjamin Brook sets this in a larger context:

> Persons who have embraced sentiments which afterwards appear to them erroneous, often think they can never remove too far from them; and the more remote they go from their former opinions the nearer they come to the truth. This was unhappily

[2]Tobias Crisp (1600–1643) was educated at Eton and Christ's College, Cambridge, and became a fellow of Balliol College, Oxford. He was appointed rector of Newington, Surrey, and later of Brinkworth, Wiltshire, where he seems to have been a devoted pastor to his congregations. He died of smallpox in 1643, probably contracted as he diligently visited the sick. Three volumes of his sermons were soon published under the title *Christ Alone Exalted.* As a result of the sermons his name became associated with John Saltmarsh and others. His editor, Robert Lancaster, denied that Crisp was guilty of antinomianism, but he was viewed with suspicion by the Westminster Divines. John Gill, a predecessor of C. H. Spurgeon, was Crisp's first biographer.

[3]John Gill, "Memoirs of the Life of Tobias Crisp, D. D.," in Tobias Crisp, *Christ Alone Exalted*, 3 vols. (London: John Bennett, 1832), 1:*vi*.

> the case with Dr. Crisp. His ideas of the grace of Christ had been exceedingly low, and he had imbibed sentiments which produced in him a legal and self-righteous spirit. Shocked at the recollection of his former views and conduct, he seems to have imagined that he could never go far enough from them.[4]

But Crisp, in keeping with others, took the wrong medicine.

The antinomian is by nature a person with a legalistic heart. He or she becomes an antinomian in reaction. But this implies only a different view of law, not a more biblical one.

Richard Baxter's comments are therefore insightful:

> Antinomianism rose among us from an obscure Preaching of *Evangelical Grace*, and insisting too much on tears and terrors.[5]

The wholescale removal of the law seems to provide a refuge. But the problem is not with the law, but with the heart—and this remains unchanged. Thinking that his perspective is now the antithesis of legalism, the antinomian has written an inappropriate spiritual prescription. His sickness is not fully cured. Indeed the root cause of his disease has been masked rather than exposed and cured.

There is only one genuine cure for legalism. It is the same medicine the gospel prescribes for antinomianism: understanding and tasting union with Jesus Christ himself. This leads to a new love for and obedience to the law of God, which he now mediates to us in the gospel. This alone breaks the bonds of both legalism (the law is no longer divorced from the person of Christ) and antinomianism (we are not divorced from the law, which now comes to us from the hand of Christ and in the empowerment of the Spirit, who writes it in our hearts).

Without this both legalist and antinomian remain wrongly related to God's law and inadequately related to God's grace. The marriage of duty with delight in Christ is not yet rightly celebrated.

---

[4] Benjamin Brook, *Lives of the Puritans*, 3 vols. (London, 1813), 2:473.
[5] Richard Baxter, *Apology for A Nonconformist Ministry* (London, 1681), 226; emphasis added.

Ralph Erskine,[6] one of the leading Marrow Brethren, once said that the greatest antinomian was actually the legalist. His claim may also be true the other way around: the greatest legalist is the antinomian.

But turning from legalism to antinomianism is never the way to escape the husband whom we first married. For we are not divorced from the law by believing that the commandments do not have binding force, but only by being married to Jesus Christ in union with whom it is our pleasure to fulfill them. Boston himself is in agreement with this general analysis:

> This Antinomian principle, that it is needless for a man, perfectly justified by faith, to endeavour to keep the law, and do good works, is a glaring evidence that legality is so engrained in man's corrupt nature, that until a man truly come to Christ, by faith, the legal disposition will still be reigning in him; let him turn himself into what shape, or be of what principles he will in religion; though he run into Antinomianism he will carry along with him his legal spirit, which will always be a slavish and unholy spirit.[7]

A century later, the Southern Presbyterian pastor and theologian James Henley Thornwell (1812–1862) noted the same principle:

> Whatever form, however, Antinomianism may assume, it springs from legalism. None rush into the one extreme but those who have been in the other.[8]

---

[6] Ralph Erskine (1685–1782) was the younger brother of Ebenezer Erskine (1680–1754) under whose father's ministry Thomas Boston had been brought to Christ. In 1737 he followed his brother into the "Associate Presbytery," which Ebenezer and others formed in 1733 (although Ebenezer was not formally deposed from the Church of Scotland until 1740). Both brothers were among the "Representers" or Marrow Brethren. Their new denomination divided over the Burgess Oath in 1747, after which numbers of members left for the New World and became one half of the root of the Associate Reformed Presbyterian Church (the other half being the Reformed Presbyterians, or Covenanters, who had similarly emigrated). Ralph is best known today for his *Gospel Sonnets*. These reflect his habit of "winding down" from his pulpit exertions at the end of the Lord's Day by turning the themes of his preaching into verse.

[7] Edward Fisher, *The Marrow of Modern Divinity* (Ross-shire, UK: Christian Focus, 2009), 221.

[8] J. H. Thornwell, *The Collected Writings of James Henley Thornwell*, 4 vols. (1871–1873; repr. Edinburgh: Banner of Truth, 1974), 2:386.

Here, again, is John Colquhoun, speaking of the manifestation of this in the life of the true believer:

> Some degree of a legal spirit or of an inclination of heart to the way of the covenant of works still remains in believers and often prevails against them. They sometimes find it exceedingly difficult for them to resist that inclination, to rely on their own attainments and performances, for some part of their title to the favor and enjoyment of God.[9]

If antinomianism appears to us to be a way of deliverance from our natural legalistic spirit, we need to refresh our understanding of Romans 7. In contrast to Paul, both legalists and antinomians see *the law* as the problem. But Paul is at pains to point out that *sin, not the law* is the root issue. On the contrary, the law is "good" and "righteous" and "spiritual" and "holy."[10] The real enemy is indwelling sin. And the remedy for sin is neither the law nor its overthrow. It is grace, as Paul had so wonderfully exhibited in Romans 5:12–21, and that grace set in the context of his exposition of union with Christ in Romans 6:1–14. To abolish the law, then, would be to execute the innocent.

For this reason it is important to notice the dynamic of Paul's argument in Romans 7:1–6. We have been married to the law. A woman is free to marry again when her husband dies. But Paul is careful to say *not* that the law has died so that we can marry Christ. Rather, it is the believer who was married to the law who has died in Christ. But being raised with Christ, she is now (legally!) free to marry Christ as the husband with whom fruit for God will be brought to the birth. The entail of this second marriage is, in Paul's language, that "the righteous requirement of the law might be fulfilled in us, who walk not according to the flesh but according to the Spirit."[11]

---

[9] John Colquhoun, *A Treatise on the Law and Gospel*, ed. D. Kistler (1859; repr. Morgan, PA: Soli Deo Gloria, 1999), 223.
[10] Rom. 7:12, 14.
[11] Rom. 8:4.

This is the sense in which the Christian's relationship to the law is that of being an "in-law"![12] We are not related to the law directly as it were, or the law in isolation as bare commandments. The relationship is dependent on and the new fruit of our prior relationship to Christ. In simple terms, just as Adam received the law from the Father, from whose hand it should never have been abstracted (as it was by the Serpent and then by Eve), so the new-covenant believer never looks at the law without understanding that his relationship to it is the fruit of his union with Christ.

Bunyan saw the meaning of Romans 7.[13] An "inclination to Adam the First" remains in all of us. The believer has died to the law, but the law does not die. The law still exists to the believer. But united to Christ the believer is now able to fulfill the law of marriage and bear fruit!

Thus grace, not law, produces what the law requires; yet at the same time it is what the law requires that grace produces. Ralph Erskine sought to put this in verse form:

> Thus gospel-grace and law-commands
> Both bind and loose each other's hands;
> They can't agree on any terms,
> Yet hug each other in their arms.
>
> Those that divide them cannot be
> The friends of truth and verity;
> Yet those that dare confound the two
> Destroy them both, and gender woe.
>
> This paradox none can decipher,
> That plow not with the gospel heifer.[14]

So, he adds,

---

[12] 1 Cor. 9:21 (*ennomos Christou*).

[13] See above, pp. 125–28.

[14] Ralph Erskine, *Gospel Sonnets or Spiritual Songs* (Edinburgh: John Pryde, 1870), 288–89.

To run, to work, the law commands,
The gospel gives me feet and hands.
The one requires that I obey,
The other does the power convey.[15]

Head and Heart

This is a fundamental pastoral lesson. It is not merely a matter of the head. It is a matter of the heart. Antinomianism may be couched in doctrinal and theological terms, but it both betrays and masks the heart's distaste for absolute divine obligation, or duty. That is why the doctrinal explanation is only part of the battle. We are grappling with something much more elusive, the spirit of an individual, an instinct, a sinful temperamental bent, a subtle divorce of duty and delight. This requires diligent and loving pastoral care and especially faithful, union-with-Christ, full unfolding of the Word of God so that the gospel dissolves the stubborn legality in our spirits.

Olney Hymns, the hymnbook composed by John Newton and William Cowper, contains the latter's hymn "Love Constraining to Obedience," which states the situation well:

No strength of nature can suffice
To serve [the] LORD aright;
And what she has, she misapplies,
For want of clearer light.

How long beneath the law I lay
In bondage and distress!
I toil'd the precept to obey,
But toil'd without success.

Then to abstain from outward sin
Was more than I could do;

[15] Ibid., 296.

Now, if I feel its pow'r within,
I feel I hate it too.

Then all my servile works were done
A righteousness to raise;
Now, freely chosen in the Son,
I freely choose his ways.

What shall I do was then the word,
That I may worthier grow?
What shall I render to the LORD?
Is my enquiry now.

To see the Law by Christ fulfill'd,
And hear his pard'ning voice;
Changes a slave into a child,[16]
And duty into choice.

We are dealing here with a disposition whose roots go right down into the soil of the garden of Eden. Antinomianism then, like legalism, is not only a matter of having a wrong view of the law. It is a matter, ultimately, of a wrong view of grace, revealed in both law and gospel—and behind that, a wrong view of God himself.

But what doctrinal issues are at stake in antinomianism?

Why Then the Law?

The issue of the role of the law of God in the new covenant is a question as old as the Sermon on the Mount, as ancient as the Pastoral Epistles, and as fundamental as Paul's question: "Why then the law?"[17]

This was true at the time of the Reformation and during the "Second Reformation" that extended into the Puritan era. The rediscovery of covenant theology led to discussions on the nature and

[16] Newton and Cowper include a footnote reference to Rom. 3:31 at this point.
[17] Matt. 5:17–48; Gal. 3:19; 1 Tim. 1:8.

role of the law. It should therefore not come as a surprise that in the biblical scholarship of the past seventy years, the rediscovery of the significance of covenant thought, both in the ancient Near East in general and in the Old Testament in particular, has been followed by a cottage industry of books and articles on the position of the law.

There are statements in the New Testament that describe the law of God with a certain harshness. Paul can speak about its role in the "ministry of death" and of the "ministry of condemnation" that was associated with it.[18] Furthermore, other statements might seem to suggest that the believer is free from the law.[19] This surely gives antinomianism sufficient grounds for its theological position?

There are, however, a number of important counter-considerations.

Limited Vocabulary?

In an important article written in 1964, prior to the publication of his major commentary on Romans, C. E. B. Cranfield sought to illumine the discussion of Paul's view of the law by pointing out the obvious: Paul employed no working vocabulary for *legalism*, *legalist*, or *legalistic*. He never used such terms. Nor did his vocabulary stretch to the term *antinomian*. He therefore expounded the role of, and misunderstandings of, the law without this verbal and categorical equipment.

This statement of the obvious is not, however, quite so obvious to many readers of the New Testament. There is an inbuilt tendency to assume that if a concept is present in our minds as we read Scripture, it must also have been present in the biblical author's mind. And indeed if we hold a high view of the Scriptures it may be hard for us to accept that some of our conceptual terms were simply not part of the apostolic equipment.

In this context the upshot of Paul's restricted vocabulary is that he did not employ our ready-made theological terms to express the

[18] 2 Cor. 3:7, 9.
[19] Rom. 6:14; 7:4.

key ideas that were later involved in the Marrow Controversy. In his own context he works within the "limitations" of the vocabulary he employs.[20] Thus, writes Cranfield, Paul writes under

> a very considerable disadvantage compared with the modern theologian when he is to attempt to clarify the Christian position with regard to the law.

Cranfield is not saying that Paul did not understand the law the way the church has done. But he is saying that Paul did not use the same linguistic equipment to state his view. He continues:

> In view of this we should I think, be ready to reckon with the possibility that sometimes when he appeared to be disparaging the law, what he really had in mind may not be the law itself, but the misunderstanding and misuse of it for which we have a conventional term, but for which he had none.[21]

While Cranfield may have been right to underscore this lacuna in the commentaries, the theological point itself had been made four hundred years earlier by Calvin:

> To refute their error [i.e., legalism] he [Paul] was sometimes compelled to take the bare law in a narrow sense, even though it was otherwise graced with the covenant of free adoption.[22]

---

[20] This point raises in its wake the large question of the relationship between the biblical text and its vocabulary and the later formulations of our Christian beliefs. It is illustrated by the term *Trinity*. *Trinitas* comes into usage only in the time of Tertullian (160–c. 225). Not only did Paul *not* use the term, but it did not *exist* in his vocabulary. But did he have the concept? If we define the concept by saying, "Trinity means that God is one *ousia* in three *personae*," it seems unlikely that this precise conceptualization was part of Paul's thinking. Does this mean Paul did not believe in the Trinity? The reverse; his letters are shot through with the substance of the later doctrine. A cursory reading of them with an eye to observing how often he coalesces the activity of the persons of the Trinity makes this overwhelmingly clear.

[21] C. E. B. Cranfield, "St. Paul and the Law," *Scottish Journal of Theology* 17 (March 1964): 55. Much of this article is reprinted as part of an appendix ("Essay II") in C. E. B. Cranfield, *A Critical and Exegetical Commentary on The Epistle to the Romans*, 2 vols. (Edinburgh: T & T Clark, 1979), 2:845–62. In his *Commentary*, Cranfield writes that Paul "was surely seriously hampered in the work of clarifying the Christian position with regard to the law" (p. 853). This may not have been the most felicitous way to express the situation, but the central point is nevertheless well taken: Paul had to employ the more general vocabulary at his disposal to denote a precise concept for which he lacked the vocabulary.

[22] John Calvin, *Institutes of the Christian Religion*, trans. F. L. Battles, ed. J. T. McNeill (Philadelphia: Westminster Press, 1960), 2.5.2. Cranfield notes in his commentary that he believed his point had not

Antinomian writers do not normally take cognizance of the exegetical and theological implications of this. But unless we are sensitive to it we will fail to unravel the proper meaning of Paul's attitude to the law.

What we discover in Paul is a simple key to understanding why he can make *both* pejorative and complimentary statements about the law: the ministry that produces death is a ministry of the law that *in itself* is "holy and righteous and good."[23] Its condemning character is not the result of anything inherent in the law, but of the evil that is inherent in us.

Paul vigorously insists on this in Romans 7:7–12; indeed the whole chapter serves to clarify the nature and role of the law. He has come to know sin because of the law. Does this mean that the law itself is somehow sinful?

The passage is bookended by what appears to be an *inclusio*, which stresses the goodness of the law:

> Question: Is the law sin(ful)?
>
> Negatively, in verse 7, he denies that the law is sin.
> Positively, in verse 12, he affirms that the law is holy, righteous, and good.

Within the *inclusio* he makes clear that it is sin, and not the law, that is the culprit:

> Our sin is revealed by the law (v. 7b).
> Our sin is also forbidden by the law (v. 7c).
> Sin is in fact opportunistic with respect to the law (v. 8).
> Sin comes to life in the light of the law (v. 9: like insects when a stone is lifted).
> The law promised life ("Do this and live").

received attention in the literature prior to his 1964 article. Linguistically and exegetically this was probably true. But clearly *theologically* the implications of this had been appreciated by many theologians, as Calvin did in the way he noted the importance of a properly nuanced reading of Scripture.

[23] Rom. 7:12. Note how in this context Paul goes on to explain that we miss the dynamic of the working of the law if we attribute responsibility to it that should be attributed to sin (Rom. 7:13).

Sin turned the law into an instrument of death (v. 10).
Conclusion: It is sin, not the law, that kills us (v. 11)!

Thus it is in the very context in which Paul seems to take such a harsh and negative view of the law—it is the reason for his sin consciousness—that he clarifies its holy nature. It bears the very character of God himself. This is why he—and we—by faith can say, "I delight in the law of God, in my inner being."[24] We must, surely, if it is holy, good, and spiritual.

The antinomian position then, which tends to take negative or pejorative statements about the law in an absolute sense, misses the biblical framework that clarifies the apostolic teaching.

The Grace of God in the Giving of the Law

It is, of course, a hermeneutical mistake so to emphasize the unity of Old and New Testaments and their respective covenants that we fail to recognize their significant diversity.

The epochal difference between the two covenants is such that John can describe it in radical terms when he writes of the Spirit's ministry: "As yet the Spirit *was not* since Jesus was not yet glorified."[25] What is stated here in an *absolute* sense is, however, meant to be understood in a *comparative* sense.

What is true of the Spirit in John's Gospel is, by way of analogy, also true of the law. What is intended to be seen within a comparative context should not be read in absolutist terms. The law came by Moses; grace and truth came through Christ.[26] This contrast is not *absolute*. Apart from other considerations, if it were, Christians would *never* admire the piety of the psalmist in Psalm 1:2 ("His delight is in the law of the Lord") or of Psalm 119:97 ("Oh how I love your law"). But the truth is that Christians instinctively desire

[24] Rom. 7:22.
[25] John 7:39, literal rendering. Clearly John knows of the Spirit's presence and power prior to the death, resurrection, and ascension of Jesus: John 1:32; 3:5–8, 34; 6:63.
[26] John 1:17.

to rise to this,[27] because they recognize—at least at a subliminal level—that the law was the gracious gift of a loving Father, even if, in itself, it does not provide the power to keep it.

If the antinomian responds, "But there is more to Torah-Law than Decalogue," we must insist that while this is true, there is never less. Indeed we are entitled to ask: What is it in Torah that has been written on our minds and in our hearts in the new covenant? Can it be other than the Decalogue we are now empowered to love and keep? It cannot be the ceremonial and civil applications of it. We love the law because it is "spiritual,"[28] that is, it is in harmony with the Spirit. And in the Spirit we delight in the law of God after our "inner being."[29] After all, the Lord Jesus, the man of the Spirit par excellence, loved and fulfilled the law. Nor did he do this as a kenotic, to-be-tolerated-for-the-present means to an end, but because in our humanity he genuinely loved what God's Word told him God himself loved. The writing of the law in our hearts by the Spirit and the indwelling of the law-keeping Lord Jesus in our lives are the explanation of why the same becomes true for us also.

Law in the Context of Redemptive History

It is a basic presupposition in Reformed theology that the glory of God is manifested in redemptive history through the restoration of man as the image of God.[30] God's salvation economy always involves the renewal of what was true of us in creation.

It is true that salvation transcends life at creation in its movement toward glorified reality. But the movement is bi-directional: back to created Eden, forward to re-created and glorified Eden; God's revelation parallels this—it keeps reworking the patterns of earlier revelation and redemption and progresses them.

Nothing is more fundamental to this than the way in which

[27] They do so because Jer. 31:31–33 has come to pass.
[28] Rom. 7:14.
[29] Rom. 7:22.
[30] Rom. 8:29; 2 Cor. 3:18; Eph. 4:22–24; Col. 3:9–10; 1 John 3:2.

divine indicatives give rise to divine imperatives. This is the Bible's underlying grammar. Grace, in this sense, always gives rise to obligation, duty, and law. This is why the Lord Jesus himself was at pains to stress that love for him is expressed by commandment keeping.[31]

It is true that the New Testament teaches us about the law of love. Love is the fulfilling of the law.[32] Indeed, "the whole law is fulfilled in one word: 'You shall love your neighbor as yourself.'"[33] But love is never said to be a replacement for law in Scripture, for several important reasons.

The first is that love is what law commands, and the commands are what love fulfills. The law of love is not a freshly minted, new-covenant idea; it is enshrined at the heart of old-covenant faith and life. It was to be Israel's constant confession: the Lord is one, and he is to be loved in a whole-souled manner.[34]

The second is the often overlooked principle: love requires direction and principles of operation. Love is motivation, but it is not self-interpreting direction.

Paul's exposition of the Christian life in Romans 13:8–10 involves the significant principle that love is the fulfilling of the law. But he spells out for us that the "law" he is talking about in this context is "the commandments"—that is, the Ten Commandments. He cites four of the "neighbor love" commandments (in the order in which they appeared in his Greek Old Testament at Deut. 5:17–21). But he does not isolate these particular commandments (adultery, murder, stealing, coveting); rather he goes on to include "any other commandment."[35]

Commandments are the railroad tracks on which the life empowered by the love of God poured into the heart by the Holy Spirit

[31] John 13:34; 14:23–24; 15:10, 12, 14, 17.
[32] Rom. 13:10.
[33] Gal. 5:14.
[34] Deut. 6:5–6.
[35] Rom. 13:9.

runs. Love empowers the engine; law guides the direction. They are mutually interdependent. The notion that love can operate apart from law is a figment of the imagination. It is not only bad theology; it is poor psychology. It has to borrow from law to give eyes to love.

The Big and the Bigger Picture

We have already considered various aspects of the Bible's big picture. At Sinai God's law was given to govern his people's relationship to him ("religious" or "ceremonial" law) and also their relationship to each other in society ("civil" law). The latter was intended for them as (1) a people redeemed from Egypt, (2) while they lived in the land, (3) with a view to the coming of the Messiah.

But there is a bigger Bible picture, which extends from Sinai both backward and forward.

The exodus was itself a restoration, intended to be seen as a kind of re-creation. The people were placed in a kind of Eden—a land "flowing with milk and honey." There, as in Eden, they were given commands to regulate their lives to the glory of God.[36] Grace and duty, privilege and responsibility, indicative and imperative were the order of the day as they lived before God and with one another.

In addition to or, more accurately, as the foundation of these applications, God gave them the Decalogue. It was simply a transcript in largely negative form, set within a new context in the land, of the principles of life that had constituted Adam's original existence.

Fast-forward to Calvary and the coming of the Spirit. As Moses ascended Mount Sinai and brought down the Law on tablets of stone, now Christ has ascended into the heavenly Mount, but in contrast to Moses, he has sent down the Spirit who rewrites the law not now merely on tablets of stone but in our hearts. There is a recalibration to Eden, albeit in the heart of a person formerly enslaved to sin, bearing its marks, and living in a world still under

[36] The tabernacle and the temple were also reflections of Eden.

the dominion of sin. Now the empowerment is within, through the indwelling of Christ the obedient one, the law keeper, by the Spirit. This is what now provides both motivation and empowerment in the Christian. And this empowerment reduplicates in us what was true for the Lord Jesus—the ability to say, "Oh how I love your law!" Grace and law are perfectly correlated to one another.

Thus, in Christ, what was interim in Old Testament law becomes obsolete. There is an international fulfillment of the Abrahamic promise, given 430 years before Sinai.[37] Now whatever in the Sinaitic covenant was intended (1) to preserve and distinguish the people as a nation in a particular land, and (2) to point them to Christ by means of ceremonies and sacraments, has ceased to be binding on the church.

But by the same token, what was the expression of God's created intention for man remains in place. Restoration to the image of God implies this. And since this is so, the Christian can no more be an antinomian than he can adopt the view that salvation is not the restoration of his life as the image of God.

Thus for the *Marrow* and the Brethren who appreciated it, the law written in the heart was given as part of the grace of creation. As the *Marrow* expressed it:

> Adam heard as much (of the law) in the garden, as Israel did at Sinai; but only in fewer words, and without thunder.[38]

All progressive revelation echoes and advances prior revelation. This broken law was given in a specific interim formulation at Sinai. Now the same law is written in our hearts, the fruit not of creating grace, or of the commands of Sinai, but of the shed blood of Jesus. That shed blood brought Mosaic ceremonies to an end by fulfilling

[37] Gal. 3:17.

[38] Fisher, *Marrow*, 54. Note that there is not *absolute identity* proposed between Sinai and Eden but a real continuity rooted in the notion that the image of God is always called to reflect him; albeit the image is called to do so in differing conditions in whatever one of the "fourfold state" he or she lives: creation, fall, regeneration, or glory.

them; it marked the finale of the civil laws of Israel as God's people now entered a new epoch and became a spiritual nation in all lands, and no longer a socio-political people group preserved in one land.

This, then, seen from various angles, is how mainstream Reformed biblical theology saw the role of the law.

Paradoxically, today it is often statements like those of the Confession of Faith that are accused of a lack of biblical-theological perspective, for failing to understand the place of the law in redemptive history. But to this the Westminster Divines would surely be entitled to respond, "But how can you read the prophets and say they did not understand these distinctions? Were they not the mouthpieces of God, saying: 'It is not sacrifice and burnt offering that come first, but obedience'? Did they not thereby distinguish ceremonial law from moral law?"

Here again we see a parallel between Old Testament prophecy and Old Testament law. The prophets predicted the Christ who would come to save his people. But it was only when those prophecies of his coming passed through the prism of his presence that the whole truth became clear. These "unified" prophecies were in fact always looking forward to a two-stage coming of his kingdom, the first at the incarnation and the second at the consummation. So it is with the law: only in the light of Christ do we clearly see its dimensions.

As the perfect embodiment of the moral law of God, Jesus Christ bids us come to him and find rest (a term loaded with exodus echoes[39]). He also bids us be united to him through faith in the power of the Spirit, so that as he places his yoke (of law) on our shoulders we hear him say, "My yoke is easy and my burden is light."

So we are Ephesians 2:15–16 Christians: the ceremonial law is fulfilled.

We are Colossians 2:14–17 Christians: the civil law distinguishing Jew and Gentile is fulfilled.

[39] See: Ex. 33:14; Deut. 12:9; Josh. 1:13, 15; Isa. 63:4.

And we are Romans 8:3–4 Christians: the moral law has also been fulfilled in Christ. But rather than being abrogated, that fulfillment is now repeated in us as we live in the power of the Spirit.[40]

In Christ then, we truly see the *telos* of the law. And yet as Paul also says, "Do we abrogate the law by teaching faith in Christ? No. We strengthen it. For Christ did not come to abolish it but to fulfill it, so that it might in turn be fulfilled in us." That is why in Romans 13:8–10, Ephesians 6:1, and in other places the apostle takes for granted the abiding relevance of the law of God for the life of the believer.

The Old Testament saint knew that while condemned by the law he had breached, its ceremonial provisions pointed him to the way of forgiveness. He saw Christ as really (if opaquely) in the ceremonies as he did in the prophecies. He also knew as he watched the sacrifices being offered day after day and year after year that this repetition meant these sacrifices could not fully and finally take away sin—otherwise he would not need to return to the temple precincts. He was able to love the law as his rule of life because he knew that God made provision for its breach, pointed to redemption in its ceremonies, and gave him direction through its commandments.

It should not, therefore, surprise us or grieve us to think that the Christian sees Christ in the law. He or she also sees it as a rule of life; indeed, sees with Calvin that Christ is the life of the law because without Christ there is no life in the law.

We appreciate the clarity of the law only when we gaze fully into Christ's face. But when we do gaze there, we see the face of one who said, "Oh how I love your law; it is my meditation all the day"[41]—and we want to be like him.

This is not—as the antinomian feared—bondage. It is freedom. The Christian rejoices therefore in the law's depth. He seeks the

[40] Here it should be noted that the New Testament contrasts the letter with the Spirit but never the substance of the moral law with the Spirit.

[41] Ps. 119:97.

Spirit's guidance for its application, because he can say with Paul that in Christ through the gospel he has become an "in-law."[42]

At the end of the day the antinomian who regards the moral law as no longer binding is forced into an uncomfortable position. He must hold that an Old Testament believer's passionate devotion to the law (of which devotion, curiously, the majority of Christians feel they fall short) was essentially a form of legalism. But it is Jesus himself who shows an even deeper intensity in the law by expounding its deep meaning and penetration into the heart.[43]

Neither the Old Testament believer nor the Savior severed the law of God from his gracious person. It was not legalism for Jesus to do everything his Father commanded him. Nor is it for us.

A Tale of Two Brothers

In some ways the Marrow Controversy resolved itself into a theological version of the parable of the waiting father and his two sons.

The antinomian prodigal when awakened was tempted to legalism: "I will go and be a slave in my father's house and thus perhaps gain grace in his eyes." But he was bathed in his father's grace and set free to live as an obedient son.

---

[42] Again the principle is that he is *ennomos Christou*, "in-law" through his marriage to Christ. One might think here of the way in which, for example, the *Rules of Golf*, authoritatively issued by the United States Golf Association and The Royal and Ancient Golf Club of St. Andrews, are never regarded as "legalistic" by those who play golf. And to be an "antinomian" golfer and ignore the rules leads to disqualification. Fascinatingly, the governing bodies of golf publish a surprisingly large book giving guidance on the details of the application of the rules to every conceivable situation on a golf course—and to some that are virtually inconceivable! The rules, and their detailed application, are intended to enhance the enjoyment of the game. My edition (2010–2011) extends to 578 pages with a further 131 pages of index. The person who loves the game of golf finds great interest and pleasure, even delight, in browsing through these applications of the *Rules of Golf*. It should therefore not greatly stretch the imagination that the Old Testament believer took far greater pleasure at a higher level in meditating on and walking in the ways of God's law. It is passing strange that there should be so often among Christians a sense of heart irritation against the idea that God's law should remain our delight. Our forefathers from Luther onward grasped this principle, and, as a result, through the generations those who made use of the standard catechisms learned how to apply God's Word and law to the daily details of life. It is a mysterious paradox that Christians who are so fascinated by rules and principles that are necessary or required in their professions or avocations respond to God's ten basic principles with a testy spirit. Better, surely, to say, "Oh how I love your law!" It should be no surprise that there appears to be a correlation between the demise of the law of God in evangelicalism and the rise of a plethora of mystical ways of pursuing guidance, detaching the knowledge of God's will from knowledge of and obedience to God's Word.

[43] Matt. 5:17–48.

The legalistic older brother never tasted his father's grace. Because of his legalism he had never been able to enjoy the privileges of the father's house.

Between them stood the father offering free grace to both, without prior qualifications in either. Had the older brother embraced his father, he would have found grace that would make every duty a delight and dissolve the hardness of his servile heart. Had that been the case, his once antinomian brother would surely have felt free to come out to him as his father had done, and say: "Isn't the grace we have been shown and given simply amazing? Let us forevermore live in obedience to every wish of our gracious father!" And arm in arm they could have gone in to dance at the party, sons and brothers together, a glorious testimony to the father's love.

But it was not so.

It is still, alas, not so.

Yet this is still true:

> There is therefore now no condemnation for those who are in Christ Jesus. For the law of the Spirit of life has set you free in Christ Jesus from the law of sin and death. For God has done what the law, weakened by the flesh, could not do. By sending his own Son in the likeness of sinful flesh and for sin, he condemned sin in the flesh, in order that the righteous requirement of the law might be fulfilled in us, who walk not according to the flesh but according to the Spirit.[44]

And the invitation still stands:

> Come, everyone who thirsts,
>   come to the waters;
> and he who has no money,
>   come, buy and eat!
> Come, buy wine and milk

[44] Rom. 8:1–4.

without money and without price.
Why do you spend your money for that which is not bread,
and your labor for that which does not satisfy?
Listen diligently to me, and eat what is good,
and delight yourselves in rich food.[45]

This full and free offer of Christ, this dissolution of the heart bondage that evidences itself in both legalism and antinomianism, this gracious obedience to God to which our union with Christ gives rise as the Spirit writes the law into our hearts—this is still the marrow of modern divinity. Indeed it is the marrow of the gospel for us all. It is so because the gospel is Christ himself, clothed in its garments.

[45] Isa. 55:1–2.

9

THE MARROW OF ASSURANCE

At the General Assembly of the Church of Scotland in 1721 James Hog had brought a representation on behalf of the Marrow Brethren defending *The Marrow of Modern Divinity*. A Commission of the General Assembly had responded with twelve questions to which the Marrow Brethren replied in detail in March 1722.[1]

The eighth query read as follows:

> Is knowledge, belief, and persuasion, that Christ died for me, and that he is mine, and that whatever he did and suffered, he did and suffered for me, the direct act of faith, whereby a sinner is united to Christ, interested in him, instated in God's covenant of grace? Or, is that knowledge a persuasion included in the very essence of that justifying act of faith?

The issues raised here were ones that long preceded the period of the Marrow Controversy. Is assurance possible? How is it to be obtained? And *of what exactly*, are we assured? Since this topic is so germane to our actual enjoyment of salvation, it has often touched raw nerves in the church for more than one reason.

---

[1] The queries, along with the responses, are printed in Edward Fisher, *The Marrow of Modern Divinity* (Ross-shire, UK: Christian Focus, 2009), 345–76.

False Assurance

For one thing, it is possible to have false assurance. After all, the Sermon on the Mount virtually ends with Jesus saying:

> Not everyone who says to me, "Lord, Lord," will enter the kingdom of heaven. . . . On that day many will say to me, "Lord, Lord, did we not . . . cast out demons in your name, and do many mighty works in your name?" And then will I declare to them, "I never knew you; depart from me, you workers of lawlessness."[2]

Later, writing to the multi-gifted Corinthians, Paul would issue a similar warning: someone may be willing to be martyred ("deliver up my body to be burned") yet lack the central evidence of being genuinely a Christian.[3]

It is also possible for a true believer to be harassed with doubts; to be, in words much loved in the days when the *Marrow* was being penned, "A child of light walking in the darkness."[4] The Psalms also bear especially eloquent testimony to this kind of experience: "I had said in my alarm, 'I am cut off from your sight'";[5] "In the day of my trouble I seek the Lord," says Asaph; "in the night my hand is stretched out without wearying; my soul refuses to be comforted."[6]

If that is true, then indeed William Perkins wisely entitled his famous work *A Case of Conscience. The Greatest that Ever Was: How a man may know whether he be the childe of God, or no. Resolved by the Word of God.*[7]

If we are to set these issues in their proper perspective, then we need in fact to begin long before the 1720s and indeed prior to the Reformation.

---

2 Matt. 7:21–23.
3 1 Cor. 13:1–3.
4 See Isa. 50:10.
5 Ps. 31:22.
6 Ps. 77:2.
7 Published in 1592.

From Jerusalem to Rome

The Scriptures underscore the reality of both false assurance and lack of assurance. It is also clear that the New Testament church was baptized into a deep and pervasive sense of assurance. Jesus encourages his disciples by telling them that although they may suffer persecution, they are blessed because their "reward is great in heaven"; Paul is sure that nothing can separate us from the love of God in Christ; Peter reassures us that there is an imperishable inheritance that is guarded in heaven for those whom God is guarding.[8]

The post-apostolic church, less clear as it was on the nature of the gospel, nevertheless seemed to pulsate with the sense that the death and resurrection of Christ brought both forgiveness and also a glorious assurance. But by the dawning of the early Middle Ages and the time of Pope Gregory I ("The Great"),[9] assurance was increasingly regarded as rare, and even, supposing it were possible, undesirable and a potential source of antinomianism.

In fact this reservation is indicative of a lingering concern and problem—the fear that a person who has assurance of salvation may use this as a pretext for living in a self-centered and self-absorbed fashion. A similar, if not identical, objection characteristically arises in relationship to election and predestination and to unconditional grace. While it is surely right to be concerned about any form of moral indifference, the undergirding error here is a failure to understand how the gospel works, and especially the significance and implications of the believer's grace union with Christ.

At the height of the Middle Ages we find Thomas Aquinas[10] taking a more measured approach. Thomas argued that assurance might come by various means, for example by special revelation, or by signs of grace in one's life. But he set the tone for the pre-

[8] Matt. 5:12; Rom. 8:38–39; 1 Pet. 1:4–5.
[9] 540–604.
[10] 1225–1274.

Reformation church in holding that while special revelation was reserved for the few (like Paul), yet the evidences of the marks of grace are always less certain. So assurance was possible. It could be inferred *conjecturaliter* from good works. But since the grace of the righteousness produced in us (on the basis of which we are justified) was always beyond immediate perception, one could have no full certainty of the relationship between this grace and its fruit in one's own life.

With the increasing sacramentalizing and objectifying of grace, therefore, the medieval *ordo salutis* was designed to lead the individual sinner from congruent merit to condign merit in final justification. But how could one know that grace had so worked that the individual whose faith was suffused with love for God (*fides formata caritate*) was now "righteous" and therefore righteously justifiable by God?

This is the point that is reached at the close of the pre-Reformation scholastic period by, for example, Gabriel Biel.[11] No one can *by ordinary means* be sure within the *ordo salutis* that perfect justification has been accomplished through the infusion of grace. While that position did not go unchallenged,[12] either before (for example, by the nominalist John Duns Scotus) or later during the Council of Trent (1545–1563), it was to become classic post-Tridentine doctrine. Thus Trent, without a universal rejection of the possibility of assurance, castigated "the vain confidence of heretics" (aka the Reformers!) and rejected the notion that believers ought by definition to have assurance, and affirmed that

> no pious person ought to doubt of the mercy of God, or the merit of Christ, and of the virtue and efficacy of the sacraments.

[11] C. 1425–1495. The landmark work placing Biel in the story of theology remains Heiko Oberman, *The Harvest of Medieval Theology: Gabriel Biel and Late Medieval Nominalism* (Cambridge, MA: Harvard University Press, 1963).

[12] In the interests of historical integrity it is important to remember that while Roman Catholic theology appears from the outside to be monolithic, it is not so from within. As is well known, even at the Council of Trent (1545–1563) there were arguments in favor of doctrinal views more Lutheran and Reformed than the Tridentine theology ultimately expressed.

But then, having apparently held out hope, Trent continues:

> Even so each one when he regards himself, and his own weakness and indisposition, may have fear and apprehension touching his own grace; *seeing that no one can know with a certainty of faith, which cannot be subject to error, that he has obtained the grace of God.*[13]

In some ways as significant, because so stark, is the manner in which that view, carefully articulated and guarded by Trent, was defended by the vigorous polemics of Cardinal Robert Bellarmine,[14] who went so far as to write:

> The principle heresy of Protestants is, that saints may obtain to a certain assurance of their gracious and pardoned state before God.[15]

While the expressed fear of Rome was that assurance would lead to a libertarian approach both in personal morals and ecclesiastical authority, there was clearly a further and more sinister element. As the Reformation was to demonstrate, if assurance of salvation is a reality, then the necessity of the extended sacramental process leading to final justification becomes null and void. Moreover, if assurance can be enjoyed by all at the beginning of the Christian life rather than—in only a few cases—be realized by the end of the Christian life, the power of the church is immediately reduced. What it cannot give, it cannot take away.

It was this, in part, that made the Reformers teach that Rome

---

[13] Council of Trent, Session 6, On Justification, First Decree, Chapter 9 (January 13, 1547); emphasis added.

[14] Robert Bellarmine (1542–1621) is perhaps best known as the cardinal inquisitor who informed Galileo that he was not permitted to teach Copernican science. He was canonized in 1930 and made a doctor of the church in 1931. Following the Gunpowder Plot in England in 1605 and the proclamation of the Oath of Allegiance to James VI and I the following year (essentially a rejection of papal authority and influence), Bellarmine was drawn into discussions with Roman Catholic priests in England with the twofold result that James wrote a critique of him in 1609, and Bellarmine came to be viewed as the major apologist for Roman Catholicism. For most of the rest of the seventeenth century Bellarmine became a discussion and debating partner in treatises on central gospel doctrines.

[15] *De Justificatione Impii*, 3.2.3, *Disputationes de Controversiis Christianae Fidei adversus huis Temporaris Haereticos*, 4 vols., Cologne, 1619.

had stolen the glorious birthright of Christians out of their own pockets and kept the children of God walking as children of darkness without the light of assurance.

Post Tenebras—Darkness?

From one point of view, therefore, the Reformation was born out of the womb of the rediscovery of *certitude*—spiritual certainty or assurance. In this sense, Luther's spiritual experience, and perhaps also Calvin's, must be understood as a search for a truly evangelical way of assurance of salvation. Certainty was a major issue for the Reformers and their protagonists. How can we be sure of Scripture, of Christ, of grace, of salvation? The Reformation watchwords give reply: Scripture establishes its own authority, salvation is by grace alone, through Christ alone, received in faith alone. Thus Reformed theology at its best and wisest spoke with one voice: it is possible to have assurance of salvation without extraordinary revelation. The first recipients of Scripture had it; saints throughout the ages have had it; we may have it too. The Confession of Faith stated it front and center: believers—

> may in this life be certainly assured that they are in a state of grace, and may rejoice in the hope of the glory of God.[16]

But much hangs on those three letters, "may." Medieval theology did not absolutely deny the possibility of assurance but certainly assumed its rarity among Christians. The Westminster Divines insisted on the possibility of assurance for all believers but did not assert its universality among Christians. At the end of the day then, the question remains: Is this simply a spectrum of less and more? Is assurance normal or abnormal? To put this in its most basic terms, in the post-Reformation church the issue became whether assurance was "of the essence of faith."

[16] Westminster Confession of Faith, 18.1.

The Confession of Faith, having affirmed that all genuine Christians can enjoy assurance, had gone on to say:

> This infallible assurance doth not so belong to the essence of faith, but that a true believer may wait long, and conflict with many difficulties before he be partaker of it.

And then it further balanced these words by affirming that the believer

> may, without extraordinary revelation, in the right use of ordinary means, attain thereunto [i.e., assurance].[17]

In its 1720 "Act concerning a Book, entitled, *The Marrow of Modern Divinity*," the General Assembly of the Church of Scotland had accused the *Marrow* of teaching that assurance is of the essence of faith, and it appealed to both Scripture and the Westminster Divines to vindicate its judgment.[18] The Marrow Brethren, in response, argued that in fact their own view was consistent with the best Reformed Divines and with the Confession and catechisms of the church.[19] With measured indignation they wrote:

> The main of the condemned passages the query refers to . . . being in matter the same with what has commonly been taught in the Protestant churches, and, in words of the renowned Mr. John Rogers of Dedham, (a man so noted for orthodoxy, holiness, and the Lord's countenancing of his ministry, that no sound Protestants in Britain or Ireland, of what denomination soever, would, in the age wherein he lived, have taken upon them to condemn as erroneous) his definition of faith, which we have as follows: "A particular persuasion of my heart that

---

[17] Ibid., 18.3. The wording of the Larger Catechism, question 81, was "Assurance of grace and salvation not being of the essence of faith, true believers may wait long before they obtain it."

[18] The Assembly appealed to Isa. 1:10; Rom. 8:16; and 1 John 5:13; as well as to chapter 17.1 and 17.3–4 of the Confession, and questions 81 and 172 of the Larger Catechism.

[19] Fisher, *Marrow*, 361–70. This section includes a single incandescent sentence of some 650 words of protest to the effect that the Brethren were in harmony with the theological tradition they had been suspected of abandoning! Their opponents, in their view, fail to distinguish the assurance of faith from the assurance of sense. Ibid., 364–65.

> Christ Jesus is mine, and that I shall have life and salvation by his means; that whatsoever Christ did for the redemption of mankind, he did it for me." Where one may see, though the difference in words be almost none at all, *yet it runs rather stronger with him than in the* Marrow.[20]

Surveying the history of Scottish theology it is clear that this question of assurance has been one of its longest-standing concerns. Along with the issue of the extent of the atonement, which had also been front and center in the Marrow Controversy, it would come to prominence again a century later in the trial of John McLeod Campbell, who was deposed from the ministry for holding (1) that Christ atoned for all humanity and (2) that assurance was of the essence of faith. Although McLeod Campbell's views were by no means a reiteration of Boston's and the Marrow Brethren, the controversy surrounding his views underlines the ongoing importance of the theme in pastoral theology and life.[21]

Frequent appeal has been made in connection with assurance to the alleged differences between the early Reformers and the Puritans, and more precisely between Calvin and the Westminster Divines. It is worthwhile spending a little time on this issue since the suggestion is not infrequently made that there is a direct line traceable from Calvin through the *Marrow* and the Brethren to McLeod Campbell, in that all three held the view that assurance is of the essence of faith. Whatever we make of the last mentioned's views, it seems clear that Boston believed that Marrow theology had been misunderstood.

---

[20] Ibid., 362; emphasis added. As a group the Marrow Brethren together were probably far better read in the Reformed tradition of the English-speaking and -writing pastors and theologians than were their critics, and for that reason it is understandable that there is a certain note of "how dare you?" in their appeal to the words of John Rogers. Rogers (c. 1570–1636), a product of Emmanuel College in Cambridge, was the legendary lecturer at Dedham in Essex from 1605–1636. Thomas Hooker described Rogers as "the prince of all the preachers in England" and was keen to be called to Colchester in order to have more opportunity to hear him preach. Cotton Mather, *Magnalia Christi Americana*, 2 vols. (1852; repr. Edinburgh: Banner of Truth, 1979), 1:334.

[21] Interest in and discussion of McLeod Campbell's views underwent something of a revival in the second half of the twentieth century. See the discussion in Sinclair B. Ferguson, "'Blessed Assurance, Jesus Is Mine'?," in *From Heaven He Came and Sought Her: Definite Atonement in Historical, Biblical, Theological, and Pastoral Perspective*, ed. David Gibson and Jonathan Gibson (Wheaton, IL: Crossway, 2013), 607–31.

In fact, contrary to much of the received scholarship, Calvin, the Westminster Divines, and the *Marrow* in fact have much more in common than the notes on which they may differ—and this is something Boston clearly grasped. Although it may seem a parenthesis to our discussion, it is extremely helpful to see the eighteenth-century debate against this larger background.

Which Way to Ettrick?

It has often been argued that Calvin's view of assurance was quite different from that of the Puritans. One passage is thought to be especially germane:

> Now we shall possess a right definition of faith if we call it *a firm and certain knowledge* of God's benevolence toward us, founded upon the truth of the freely given promise in Christ, both revealed to our minds and sealed upon our hearts through the Holy Spirit.[22]

The wording of the Confession of Faith is, as we have seen:

> This infallible assurance doth not so belong to the essence of faith, but that a true believer may wait long, and conflict with many difficulties, before he be partaker of it.[23]

Many Reformed students (including the most orthodox) have regarded Calvin and Westminster to be virtually irreconcilable here. In its more extreme forms it is said both that while Calvin made assurance of the essence of faith, the Westminster Divines denied it, *and* that Calvin's scheme gave no place to the practical syllogism, while the Westminster Divines emphasized it. If a plea of mitigating circumstances is made, it is usually either that Calvin was overreacting against the complete absence of assurance in the Roman system,

[22] John Calvin, *Institutes of the Christian Religion*, trans. F. L. Battles, ed. J. T. McNeill (Philadelphia: Westminster Press, 1960), 3.2.7; emphasis added.
[23] Westminster Confession of Faith, 18.3.

or that seventeenth-century ministers were dealing with a different pastoral situation from Calvin. But neither of these responses is necessary, or adequate.

For one thing, an inappropriate contrast is being drawn here. In the *Institutes* Calvin is *defining faith*; in the Confession of Faith the Westminster Divines are *describing assurance*. Two related but quite different things are being discussed and contrasted as though they were the same.

In fact when the Westminster Divines define the activity of faith, they speak of it as "accepting, receiving and resting on Christ alone for justification, sanctification and eternal life, by virtue of the covenant of grace."[24] This triptych of elements in faith ("accepting, receiving and resting") clearly constitutes a certain assurance of Christ—we do not accept, receive, and rest on someone we believe to be untrustworthy. Patently what the Divines go on to say four chapters later is that such faith does not exist in a vacuum. It is faith in Christ set within the context of the psychology, life situation, personality, complexes, opposition, difficulties, and damage that together constitute the individual's *sitz im Leben*.

To use formal language, in distinction from the "direct act" of faith in Christ, which implies a certain assurance of him ("He is able to save to the uttermost those who draw near to God through him"[25]), assurance of salvation is a "reflex act." It does not have Christ as its direct object but the believer him- or herself. The direct act of faith says, "Christ is able to save," while the reflex act says, "I am someone who has been saved through faith in Christ."

We need look no further than the *Institutes* to discover that Calvin himself well understood this. He is like a high school chemistry teacher who provides his pupils with a definition but tells them that their laboratory experiment may not work out in exactly these

[24] Ibid., 14.2.
[25] Heb. 7:25.

terms because of experimenter error, contamination of materials, or differences in environmental factors.[26]

Thus Calvin, in the same chapter of the *Institutes*, is able to say:

> The knowledge of faith consists in assurance rather than in comprehension. . . . We add the words "sure and firm" in order to express a more solid constancy of persuasion. For, as faith is not content with a doubtful and changeable opinion, so is it not content with an obscure and confused conception, but requires full and fixed certainty, such as men are wont to have from things experienced and proved. . . . He alone is truly a believer who, convinced by a firm conviction that God is a kindly and well-disposed Father toward him, lays hold on an undoubted expectation of salvation. . . . No man is a believer, I say, except him who, leaning upon the assurance of his salvation, confidently triumphs over the devil and death.[27]

And also:

> But someone will say: "Believers experience something far different: In recognizing the grace of God toward themselves they are not only tried by disquiet, which often comes upon them, but they are repeatedly shaken by gravest terrors. For so violent are the temptations that trouble their minds as not to seem quite compatible with that certainty of faith." Accordingly we shall have to solve this difficulty if we wish the above-stated doctrine

[26] One of the most vigorous critics of Calvin here (as also in his doctrine of the Lord's Supper) was the formidable nineteenth-century Scottish theologian William Cunningham: "It is certainly strange, that a man of such wonderful soundness and penetration of judgment as Calvin should have said, as he did say, 'We shall have a complete definition of faith, if we say that it is a steady and certain knowledge of the divine benevolence towards us, which being founded on the truth of the gratuitous promise in Christ, is both revealed to our minds and confirmed to our hearts by the Holy Spirit.' . . . We cannot but look upon this as an illustration of the pernicious influence of men's circumstances upon the formation of their opinions. . . . Calvin never contradicted himself so plainly and palpably as this." Curiously Cunningham goes on to note that the only way Calvin's statement can be reconciled with what follows is if he is giving a definition of faith that describes "what true faith is, or includes, in its most perfect condition and in its highest exercise." But this, it seems, is exactly what Calvin is doing, and so the profound and acute Cunningham could have given Calvin the benefit of the doubt and acknowledged that he was doing precisely the one thing that renders consistent his exposition. See William Cunningham, *The Reformers and the Theology of the Reformation* (1862; repr. London: Banner of Truth, 1967), 119–20.

[27] Calvin, *Institutes*, 3.2.15, 16, 17.

> to stand. Surely, while we teach that faith ought to be certain and assured, we cannot imagine any certainty that is not tinged with doubt, or any assurance that is not assailed by some anxiety. On the other hand, we say that believers are in perpetual conflict with their own unbelief. Far, indeed, are we from putting their consciences in any peaceful repose, undisturbed by any tumult at all.[28]

Further, Calvin writes of the fact that the disciples were true but weak believers before the resurrection:

> We ought not to seek any more intimate proof of this than that unbelief is, in all men [i.e., who are believers] always mixed with faith.[29]

Thus it is

> he who, struggling with his own weakness, presses toward faith in his moments of anxiety, is already in large part victorious.[30]

And again:

> I have not forgotten what I have previously said, the memory of which is repeatedly renewed by experience: faith is tossed about by various doubts, so that the minds of the godly are rarely at peace—at least they do not always enjoy a peaceful state.[31]

Elsewhere Calvin underlines the extent to which Christ has given us the sacraments in order to minister to assurance.[32] This being the case, two conclusions stand out.

The first is that Calvin distinguishes his definition of faith from his description of Christian experience.

The second is that he holds that assurance is of the essence of

[28] Ibid., 3.2.17.
[29] Ibid., 3.2.4.
[30] Ibid., 3.2.17.
[31] Ibid., 3.2.37. Notice his appeal to experience!
[32] Ibid., 4.16.32; 4.17.1–2.

faith in the sense that Christ is its object; whereas when the believer looks at him- or herself set within the prevailing circumstances of life, and particularly in the context of the conflict of the flesh against the Spirit, he or she never experiences faith in terms of its hermetically sealed definition. Calvin recognized that his definition of what faith is should not be isolated from his description of what the believer actually experiences. Indeed, faith cannot be defined in any other way. It cannot be defined in terms of struggles, doubts, fears, and frailties. It must be defined in terms of wholehearted trust in Christ. But significantly just before his definition of faith, Calvin notes:

> Experience obviously teaches that until we put off the flesh, we attain less than we should like.[33]

If we now ask how Calvin harmonizes this, he gives us his answer:

> In order to understand this, it is necessary to return to that division of flesh and spirit which we have mentioned elsewhere.[34]

In Christ we are no longer dominated by the flesh, but by the Spirit; but we are not yet delivered from the flesh. So long as this eschatological tension exists for the believer, so long will there be—in Calvin's view—a gap between the definition of faith and the actual experience of the believer:

> The greatest doubt and trepidation must be mixed up with such wrappings of ignorance, since our heart especially inclines by its own natural instinct toward unbelief. Besides this, there are innumerable and varied temptations that constantly assail us with great violence. But it is especially our conscience itself that, weighed down by a mass of sins, now complains and groans, now accuses itself, now murmurs secretly, now breaks out in open tumult. And so, whether adversities reveal God's wrath,

[33] Ibid., 3.2.4.
[34] Ibid., 3.2.18.

> or the conscience finds in itself the proof and ground thereof, thence unbelief obtains weapons and devices to overthrow faith.[35]

> The root of faith can never be torn apart from the godly breast, but clings so fast to the inmost parts that, however faith seems to be shaken or to bend this way or that, its light is never so extinguished or snuffed out that it does not at least lurk as it were beneath the ashes . . . but that, though it be assailed a thousand times, it will prevail over the entire world.[36]

That is not really so different from the way in which the Confession of Faith describes the life of the faith that accepts, rests on, and receives Christ:

> This faith is different in degrees, weak or strong; may be often and many ways assailed and weakened, but gets the victory; growing up in many to the attainment of a full assurance through Christ, who is both the author and finisher of our faith.[37]

Finally, it is in this context that Calvin gives some place to sanctification as a help to assurance. He writes:

> The saints quite often strengthen themselves and are comforted by remembering their own innocence and uprightness, and they do not even refrain at times from proclaiming it. . . . The saints by innocence of conscience strengthen their faith and take from it occasion to exult.

He explains very carefully that this is not a denial of salvation by grace:

> [A conscience that is erected on grace] is established also in the consideration of works, so far, that is, as these are testimonies

[35] Ibid., 3.2.20.
[36] Ibid., 3.2.21.
[37] Westminster Confession of Faith, 14.3.

> of God dwelling and ruling in us. . . . Therefore, when we rule out reliance upon works, we mean only this: that the Christian mind may not be turned back to the merit of works as to a help toward salvation but should rely wholly on the free promise of righteousness. But we do not forbid him from undergirding and strengthening this faith by signs of the divine benevolence toward him . . . ; the grace of good works shows that the Spirit of adoption has been given to us.[38]

Calvin did not devote a chapter of his *Institutes* to the theme of assurance. But he had taught, within the context of his exposition of *faith*:

1) There is an assurance in faith, because it accepts and rests on Christ.
2) This assurance of Christ is set within a spectrum as it presses itself into the consciousness of the believer.
3) This distance between the definition and the experience of faith is explained in terms of the conflict between the flesh and the Spirit in which the believer is involved. It is part of the not-yetness of the Christian life.

In contrast with Calvin, the Westminster Divines did devote a separate chapter in their Confession of Faith to the subject of assurance. There they taught that it is possible to have saving faith (which they had already defined as "accepting, receiving, and resting upon Christ alone for justification, sanctification, and eternal life") and yet not enjoy infallible assurance.

Thus Calvin and the Divines focus on two distinct but related loci. They come at the topic of assurance from two different perspectives. But at the end of the day they meet in the middle. Were

[38] Calvin, *Institutes*, 3.14.18. In this context Calvin mentions the same elements to which the Westminster Divines would later refer: faith, evidential works, and the ministry of the Holy Spirit. At this point François Wendel was surely right to say that Calvin's view "contained the germs of later Puritanism." *Calvin: Origins and Developments of His Religious Thought* (New York: Harper & Row, 1963), 276.

it not for the mistaken perspective that has often dogged the way in which Reformed theology has been viewed ("Did they, or did they not, agree with Calvin on this or that point?"), this would have been much clearer. In this instance Calvin's definition of faith was brought so near the eye that the context in which he worked it out was obscured, the different loci which he and the Divines treated ignored, and the way in which their discussions overlap in the middle bypassed.

Confession versus Calvin?

Had these relatively obvious points been recognized, the *Marrow* and its supporters would have been handled with greater circumspection. It seems clear, however, that at this stage the study of Calvin by students of theology had given way to the use of other textbooks that, whatever their merits, lacked the pastoral approach and biblical sensitivity that is a hallmark of the *Institutes*. The both/and approach so characteristic of Calvin thus tended to be dissipated in the either/or treatment of a theological manual.[39]

Boston read the *Marrow* as echoing the entire Reformed theological tradition, and for that reason he found no contradiction

[39] Doubtless this is a topic worthy of broader study. For a survey of theological education in Scotland, see Jack C. Whytock, *An Educated Clergy: Scottish Theological Education and Training in the Kirk and Secession, 1560–1850* (Carlisle, UK: Paternoster, 2007). In the relevant section of this study (pp. 80–143) there is only one reference to the *Institutes*. Boston's theology professor was George Campbell, who, as we have seen, used Leonard van Rijssen's *Compendium Theologiae* and Andrew Essenius's *Compendium Theologiae Dogmaticum*. Boston himself comments on the use of Essenius (*Marrow*, 139) and appeals to the latter as supporting his view and that of the *Marrow*. Three comments are worth making here. The first is to note the extent to which Latin remained the *lingua franca* of education. Since by this time, ability in the use of Latin must have varied considerably, the wisdom of this practice may well be questioned. In the Simson case it proved to be a liability. A professor who gives his lectures in Latin can easily defend himself against accusations of deviant teaching by blaming his students' inability to follow his lectures accurately. Second, even if students struggled with Latin texts, Calvin's *Institutes* had been available in English translation for well over a century and could have been used as a text. If, as seems likely, Calvin was largely neglected in theological education, it was to the detriment of students, for his work shapes thinking specifically for pastoral ministry, biblical exposition, and coherent dogmatic theological thinking. Third, in contrast to this, the textbooks employed seem to have been chosen precisely because they were scholastic in form and style. That might seem understandable in the context of a theological education; but to use scholastic texts exclusively is an unhealthy preparation for ministry in a nonscholastic environment. Intriguingly, given the fact that one would expect a reference to Calvin in any discussion on faith and assurance, it is striking that in Boston's four-thousand-word note on faith, there is no reference to the *Institutes*, although Boston at some point had access to Thomas Norton's translation of the *Institutes*.

between it and the Confession of Faith. He was sufficiently adamant on this point to write his most extensive note in his own edition of the *Marrow* to demonstrate it, arguing in connection with the wording of the Confession of Faith:

> How faith can grow in any to a full assurance, if there be no assurance in the nature of it, I cannot comprehend.[40]

In fact, in the *Marrow* Evangelista had untangled the difference for Neophytus between the direct act of faith in Christ and the reflex development of assurance.[41] If there was a real issue here, it lay not in the doctrine of assurance but in the nature of the gospel offer on which faith laid hold. What the Westminster Divines and Boston following them had recognized was that while it is necessary and proper to define faith, we can never treat it as an abstraction. In the case of weak and doubting persons, our response is not a priori to deny that they have real faith but to seek to discern the seed of faith and nourish it according to the principles of Scripture. In this they simply followed Calvin:

> We cannot imagine any uncertainty that is not tinged with doubt, or any assurance that is not assailed by some anxiety. . . . Believers are in perpetual conflict with their own unbelief. . . . He who, struggling with his own weakness, presses toward faith in his moments of anxiety is already in large part victorious. . . . In order to understand this, it is necessary to return to that division of flesh and spirit which we have mentioned elsewhere. It most clearly reveals itself at this point. Therefore the godly heart feels in itself a division because it is partly imbued with sweetness from its recognition of divine goodness, partly grieves in bitterness from an awareness of its calamity; partly rests upon

[40] Fisher, *Marrow*, 143. The entire note on faith is included as the appendix in this book.

[41] Ibid., 243. In his notes at this point Boston appealed to the authority of Rutherford: "The assurance of Christ's righteousness is a direct act of faith, apprehending imputed righteousness: the evidence of our justification we now speak of, is the reflex light, not by which we are justified, but by which we know that we are justified." Samuel Rutherford, *Christ Dying and Drawing Sinners to Himselfe* (London, 1647), 111.

> the promise of the gospel, partly trembles at the evidence of its own iniquity; partly rejoices at the expectation of life, partly shudders at death. This variation arises from imperfection of faith, since in the course of the present life it never goes so well with us that we are wholly cured of the disease of unbelief and entirely filled and possessed by faith. Hence arise these conflicts; when unbelief, which reposes in the remains of the flesh, rises up to attack the faith that has been inwardly conceived.[42]

In a sense then, like Calvin, Boston well understood that while the theology of faith is simple, the experience of assurance is complex for two reasons. The first is that we are complex, not to say complicated, and assurance impacts on what moderns have tended to call the "self-image," in this instance, "How do I think about myself in relation to God in Christ?" Full assurance is therefore a complex spiritual and psychological process by which confessing, "Christ died for sinners, and I rest on him," becomes, "I am sure that nothing in all creation can separate me from the love of God in Christ Jesus my Lord." In one individual that complexity may be so beautifully simplified that its intricacy goes unnoticed. In others the complexity of their self-consciousness needs to be pastorally untangled before the clear connection between believing in Christ and realizing the implications of that become clear.

To this we will turn in the next chapter of our study.

---

[42] Calvin, *Institutes* 3.2.18.

10

HOW ASSURANCE OF CHRIST BECOMES ASSURANCE OF SALVATION

Assurance is not one-dimensional. That for the Marrow Brethren was the key. Indeed this understanding was already embedded in the *Marrow* itself, in the dialogue between Neophytus and Evangelista that opens an extended discussion of assurance:

> Evangelista: But how do you, neighbor Neophytus; for methinks you look very heavily.
>
> Neophytus: Truly, sir, I was thinking of that place of Scripture, where the apostle exhorts us "to examine ourselves whether we be in the faith or no" (2 Cor. 3:15); whereby it seems to me, that a man may think he is in the faith, when he is not. Therefore, sir, I would gladly hear how I may be sure that I am in the faith.
>
> Evangelista: I would not have you to make any question of it, since you have grounded your faith upon such a firm foundation as will never fail you; or the promise of God in Christ is of a tried truth, and never yet failed any man, nor ever will. Therefore I would have you to close with Christ in the promise, without making any question whether you are in the faith or no;

for there is an assurance which rises from the exercise of faith as a direct act, and that is, when a man, by faith, directly lays hold upon Christ, and concludes assurance from thence.

Neophytus: Sir, I know that the foundation whereon I am to ground my faith remains sure; and I think I have already built thereon; but yet, because I conceive a man may think he has done so when he has not, therefore would I fain know how I may be assured that I have so done?

Evangelista: Well, now I understand you what you mean; it seems you do not want a ground for your believing, but for your believing that you have believed.

Neophytus: Yea, indeed, that is the thing I want.[1]

Here the notion that there is a distinction without separation in our understanding of assurance is brought to the surface—what Reformed theology describes as the direct and the reflex acts of faith. Neophytus has believed (the direct act). What he wants to know is not, "How can I be sure that Christ is able to save me?" but, "How can I be sure that I have believed in the Christ who saves?" It is the difference between confidence in Christ's ability to save and the self-awareness that one has this confidence and is among those whom he saves.

It was precisely in issues like this that Boston and his friends, as working pastors, seemed to find the dialogical form of the *Marrow* so helpful.[2]

For Boston, then, assurance is ours because of a three-dimen-

[1] Edward Fisher, *The Marrow of Modern Divinity* (Ross-shire, UK: Christian Focus, 2009), 243.

[2] Perhaps one might venture the opinion here that this was more effective than the somewhat standardized format of many contemporary books on counseling in which each chapter begins with a variation on: "Sally and John sat opposite me in my office. Their marriage was in ruins" followed by a brief exposition of the resolution and—although, thankfully not always—usually leading to an overly happy-ever-after ending with only a nod to challenges in the future. For what the *Marrow* does is to walk us through the conversation slowly, carefully, point by point. This is much more like real pastoral counseling. Plus it is deeply theological, as all pastoral counseling should be (since at the end of the day our dysfunctions are related to our knowledge of God and our trust in, love for, and obedience to him—or lack of it).

sional ministry of the Spirit: (1) he shines on the Word of God and especially the saving promises of God and gives light in the soul; (2) he shines on his own work in our hearts so that we see the harmony in our lives between justification and sanctification—always in the context of faith; and (3) he acts, from time to time, in such a way that he bears witness with our spirits, and thus to us, that we are God's children.[3]

We can spell out the gospel answer to the question that troubled Neophytus as follows.

Christ and Faith

It bears repeating: assurance of salvation is the fruit of faith in Christ. Christ is able to and does, in fact, save all those who come to him through faith. Since faith is *fiducia*, trust in Christ as the one who is able to save, there is a certain confidence and assurance seminally inherent in faith. The act of faith, therefore, contains within it the seed of assurance. Indeed, faith in its first exercise is an assurance about Christ. This dimension of assurance is therefore implicit in faith. Thus Professor John Murray affirms:

> The germ of assurance is surely implicit in the salvation which the believer comes to possess by faith, it is implicit in the change that has been wrought in his state and condition.

He goes on daringly, but significantly, to add:

> However weak may be the faith of a true believer, however severe may be his temptations, however perturbed his heart may be respecting his own condition, he is never, as regards consciousness, in the condition that preceded the exercise of faith. The consciousness of the believer differs by a whole diameter from that of the unbeliever. At the lowest ebb of faith

[3] Thomas Boston, *The Whole Works of the Late Reverend Thomas Boston*, ed. S. M'Millan, 12 vols. (Edinburgh, 1848–1852), 2:17.

> and hope and love his consciousness never drops to the level of the unbeliever at its highest pitch of confidence and assurance.[4]

One is tempted to ask, Was Professor Murray also among the Marrow Brethren?

But notice: it is in faith and not apart from it that the Christian says, "I take Jesus Christ as my Savior." It is a corollary of this that apart from faith, standing outside of faith, this affirmation cannot be made, and therefore one cannot make the corollary statement, "Jesus is mine." Neither implicit nor explicit assurance exists apart from actual faith.

Why is this so important? It means we cannot have a meaningful pastoral conversation on the following presupposition: "But leaving the reality of my faith aside for the moment, tell me how I can have assurance of salvation."

Both the misunderstanding of, and the wholesale rejection of, the so-called practical syllogism are guilty of a mistaken assumption here. For the practical syllogism does not work without respect to faith. Nor should it be criticized as though it were intended to be an alternative way of experiencing assurance apart from faith.

This is why Evangelista was so concerned to clarify exactly what it was that concerned Neophytus. Since he believes he is a believer, what hinders his enjoyment of assurance is that he has doubts about the genuineness of that faith. He is sure Christ is able to save those who believe; his question is, "How can my faith be confirmed?"

The issue that is being placed under the microscope of pastoral analysis here is then not how we become believers, but how do we know we are believers? This is a matter of self-awareness. It is a reflex act of faith, not its direct act. So any discussion of the topic must take place within the context of faith, never apart from it. There is no alternative route to the assurance of salvation, as if it

[4] John Murray, *Collected Writings of John Murray, vol. 2: Systematic Theology* (Edinburgh: Banner of Truth, 1977), 265.

were legitimate to ask, "Apart from route A (faith), will you take me along route B without faith?"

This proper self-conscious awareness of genuine faith (i.e., that the individual is a true and not a false believer) develops within three dimensions.

Grace and Faith

Faith seeks understanding and is nourished through it. It is possible, of course, to have little knowledge and yet real assurance because faith has nourished itself richly on the knowledge it possesses. Correspondingly, it is possible to have much knowledge and little assurance if an individual responds disproportionately to the knowledge he or she possesses.

In particular, assurance is nourished on a clear understanding of grace and especially of union with Christ and the justification, adoption, and regeneration that are ours freely in him.[5]

The chief enemies of the Christian's assurance at this point are probably three.

The first is our native tendency to drift from the fact that our salvation is all of grace, and even our active participation in its reception is both the fruit of grace and, although active, noncontributory to the salvation itself. It is all too possible to make some progress in growth and sanctification but then ever so subtly slip into thinking that "of course it was appropriate that God was gracious to me—he knew that I would become the growing Christian that I now am."

The second is a phenomenon we have met before in these pages: the difficulty some Christians have in believing that they are freely justified by the Father, who in his love sent his Son for them. They may have been nurtured in a womb of preaching that has portrayed Christ as one who by his sacrifice persuades a wrathful Father to pardon us, in view of what he (Christ) has done. When grace no

[5]Thomas Boston, *Human Nature in Its Fourfold State* (London: Banner of Truth, 1964), 285ff. [*Works*, 8:203ff.].

longer reaches back into the very fountainhead, then deep and suspicious thoughts of God the Father develop, and assurance is not possible. To quote John Owen again:

> Few can carry up their hearts and minds to this height by faith, as to rest their souls in the love of the Father; they live below it, in the troublesome region of hopes and fears, storms and clouds. All here is serene and quiet. But how to attain to this pitch they know not. This is the will of God, that he may always be eyed as benign, kind, tender, loving, and unchangeable therein; and that peculiarly as the Father, as the great fountain and spring of all gracious communications and fruits of love. This is that which Christ came to reveal.[6]

To fail here is, sadly, to lose hold of the harmony of the Trinity and to lose sight of the sheer grace of God in the gospel. God the Father is absolutely, completely, and totally to us what he reveals himself to be to us in Christ.[7] Understand this and sense the light it brings to the mind and affections, and faith strengthens while assurance is nourished.

A third problem here that militates against the enjoyment of assurance is a failure to recognize that justification is *both* final and complete. It is final because it is the eschatological justification of the last day brought forward into the present day. It is complete because in justification we are counted as righteous before the Father as Christ himself, since the only righteousness with which we are righteous is Jesus Christ's righteousness. When faith thus grasps the reality of this inheritance, then Christ himself looms large. This is the key to the enjoyment of assurance precisely because assurance is our assurance that he is a great Savior and that he is ours.

Thus in gospel assurance Christ is central; indeed Christ is everything. Yet contrary to an entire trend in historical theological

---

[6] John Owen, *The Works of John Owen*, 24 vols. ed. W. H. Goold (Edinburgh: Johnstone & Hunter, 1850–1855), 2.23.

[7] See John 14:7, 9b.

scholarship, this does not mean there is no place for the practical syllogism.

Walking in Faith

What, then, is the function of the so-called practical syllogism? In its most basic form it is derived from this simple and all too obvious principle: high degrees of Christian assurance are simply not compatible with low levels of obedience. If Christ is not actually saving us, producing in us the obedience of faith in our struggle against the world, the flesh, and the Devil, then our confidence that he is our Savior is bound to be undermined, imperceptibly at first, but really.

This is why there is a strong link in the New Testament between faithfulness in the Christian walk and the enjoyment of assurance. Obedience strengthens faith and confirms it to us because it is always marked by what Paul calls "the obedience of faith."[8]

This teaching is particularly clear in 1 John. While the Gospel is written with an evangelistic purpose,[9] John's first epistle is written in part to assure believers: "I write these things to you who believe in the name of the Son of God that you may know that you have eternal life."[10] While there is some debate about the exact antecedent of "these things" (does *tauta* refer to the immediately preceding section or to the entire book?), in any event the assurance of his readers is John's burden, and in fact the entire book is an encouragement to assurance.

John picks out four moral characteristics in the life of the believer that encourage assurance.

1) *Obedience to the commands of God.* In various ways he reiterates the teaching of Jesus in the Farewell Discourse in John 14–16: "We know that we have come to know him, if we keep his commandments. Whoever says 'I know him' but does not keep his

[8] Rom. 1:5; 16:26.
[9] John 20:31.
[10] 1 John 5:13.

commandments is a liar, and the truth is not in him."[11] Again the same emphasis reappears later on in the letter:

> Everyone who believes that Jesus is the Christ has been born of God, and everyone who loves the Father loves whoever has been born of him. By this we know that we love the children of God, when we love God and obey his commandments. For this is the love of God, that we keep his commandments.[12]

Despite its claims, therefore, antinomianism ignores the teaching of the apostle of love, who stresses that genuine assurance will go hand in hand with authentic commandment keeping. To him, love and law are not antithetical; they are in-laws. Faith works by love; love expresses itself in obedience. The "obedience of faith" attests the reality of faith.

2) Another way of expressing this is that genuine faith attests itself in *righteous living*. John also teaches us that we are confirmed in the reality of our regeneration by the fruits produced in us by the Spirit, i.e., by a personal character that is consistent with the new family ethos into which we have been born: "If you know that he [i.e., Christ] is righteous, you may be sure that everyone who practices righteousness has been born of him."[13]

3) John also expresses this negatively. Assurance is confirmed by *not sinning*. This is not the context to discuss John's nuance, but we cannot avoid his conclusion that a radical breach with sin is the inevitable concomitant of life in Christ and the evidence that assures us of faith: "We know that everyone who has been born of God does not keep on sinning."[14]

4) Expressed again positively, this means that *walking in love is so much a hallmark of regeneration that it confirms the presence of faith*: "We know that we have passed out of death into life,

[11] 1 John 2:3–4.
[12] 1 John 5:1–3.
[13] 1 John 2:29.
[14] 1 John 5:18. Cf. 1 John 3:6, 9.

because we love the brothers"[15] (i.e., with a love that is not merely in words or in talk but in deed and in truth[16]). Thus "whoever loves [i.e., in the sense previously defined] has been born of God and knows God."[17]

The *Marrow* contains an illuminating dialogue as Evangelista concludes his exposition of the confirmatory effects of faith and responds to a further question prompted by what he has said:

> Neophytus: But, sir, I pray you, let me ask you one question more touching this point; and that is, suppose that hereafter I should see no outward evidences, and question whether I had ever any true outward evidences, and so whether I had ever any true inward evidences, and so whether ever I did truly believe or no, what must I do then?
>
> Evangelista: Indeed it is possible you may come to such a condition; and therefore you do well to provide beforehand for it. Now then, if ever it shall please the Lord to give you over to such a condition, first let me warn you to take heed of forcing and constraining yourself to yield obedience to God's commandments, to the end you may so get an evidence of faith again, or a ground to lay your believing, that you have believed, upon; and so forcibly to hasten your assurance before the time.[18]

In the context of this study, it is appropriate to ask a question here: Would you give this counsel to those struggling with the issue of whether there are real evidences of regeneration and faith in their lives? Is there not something deeply countercultural, even counter-*evangelical* in such counsel? If a friend encouraged you to go to a Christian counselor because you were struggling with such

[15] 1 John 3:14.
[16] 1 John 3:18.
[17] 1 John 4:7; cf. 1 John 4:16.
[18] Fisher, *Marrow*, 247. Boston summarizes this in a note on assurance: "If one examines himself by this infallible rule, he cannot safely take his obedience for a mark or evidence of his being in the state of grace, until he run it up into his faith embracing Christ." Ibid., 197. There is an inbuilt principle of gospel logic at stake here: there is no assurance *of faith* that can be experienced *apart from faith*.

issues, and you received *this* counsel, would you go back for more, or perhaps seek a second opinion? We live in a subculture that has become so used to the "how to," and "you can," and "seven steps" mentality that this counsel seems to cut across our expectations.

Yet Thomas Boston thought it was appropriate (and by no means a counsel to laxness), because it stressed the importance of believing giving rise to obedience, not obedience giving rise to assurance irrespective of believing. Such faith cannot be forced into us by our efforts to be obedient; it arises only from larger and clearer views of Christ. Herein lies the paradox: we want to talk and think about how to get better evidences; Boston is concerned that we get a better grip of Christ. Then the evidences will grow like fruit.

What is in view here is hardly the offer of assurance that is sometimes presented: "Did you believe in Christ? Then it says here in 1 John that you have passed from death to life, so you now have assurance." This is a misstep that inevitably breeds the notion that all Christians *per definitionem* have assurance. On the contrary, what John sets out is assurance that is deeply rooted in the reality of the life of faith. Because it is, it completes the complex of grace that produces in us the evidence of a life that really is being saved.

The reason assurance is the significant issue that William Perkins and others have suggested is that on the one hand it is possible to be a self-deceived hypocrite and on the other hand all too possible to be a genuine Christian who finds it difficult, and is often too hesitant, to draw the glorious conclusion that he is truly the Lord's. It is important therefore to notice that there is a third dimension to coming to a settled assurance of faith in the Savior.

The Spirit and Faith

The direct act of faith is the fruit of the ministry of the Spirit. "No one can say 'Jesus is Lord' except in the Holy Spirit."[19] In a paral-

[19] 1 Cor. 12:3.

lel manner, Paul describes the reflex act of faith as the fruit of the Spirit's ministry in our lives:

> You have received the Spirit of adoption as sons, by whom we cry, "Abba! Father!" The Spirit himself bears witness with our spirit that we are children of God, and if children, then heirs—heirs of God and fellow heirs with Christ.[20]

In an earlier but parallel passage, Paul wrote:

> And because you are sons, God has sent the Spirit of his Son into our hearts, crying, "Abba! Father!"[21]

The similarity in those statements is obvious; the difference is illuminating.

Paul describes assurance in terms that Calvin echoes in his definition of faith—it involves a confidence that God is our Father through Jesus Christ and that we are able to approach him in identical language to that used by the Lord Jesus himself.[22]

In the story of post-Reformation interpretation Romans 8:15–16 has been something of a *crux interpretum*. The Spirit's witness takes place conjointly with our witness that we are God's children and is expressed in the cry, "Abba! Father!" Doubtless in the background here is the Old Testament principle that in a court of law any evidence needs to be established by two witnesses.[23] In this context our own spirit's consciousness constitutes one witness; but while this may be a true testimony, it needs to be established. Wonderfully the Spirit himself (the language is emphatic) adds his testimony to ours. The issue is settled.

This has probably never been more vividly expressed than it is by John Owen:

---

20 Rom. 8:15–17.
21 Gal. 4:6.
22 See Mark 14:36.
23 Deut. 17:6; 19:5.

The Spirit comes and bears witness in this case. An allusion it is to judicial proceedings in point of titles and evidences. The judge being set, the person concerned lays his claim, produceth his evidences, and pleads them; his adversaries endeavouring all that in them lies to invalidate them, and disannul his plea, and to cast him in his claim. In the midst of the trial, a person of known and approved integrity comes into the court, and gives testimony fully and directly on behalf of the claimer; which stops the mouths of all his adversaries, and fills the man that pleaded with joy and satisfaction. So is it in this case. The soul, by the power of its own conscience, is brought before the law of God. There a man puts in his plea,—that he is a child of God, that he belongs to God's family; and for this end produceth all his evidences, everything whereby faith gives him an interest in God. Satan, in the meantime, opposeth with all his might; sin and law assist him; many flaws are found in his evidences; the truth of them all is questioned; and the soul hangs in suspense as to the issue. In the midst of the plea and contest the Comforter comes, and by a word of promise or otherwise, overpowers the heart with a comfortable persuasion (and bears down all objections) that his plea is good, and that he is a child of God. And therefore it is said of him, Συμμαρτυρεῖ τῷ Πνεύματι ἡμῶν. When our spirits are pleading their right and title, he comes in and bears witness at our side; at the same time enabling us to put forth acts of filial obedience, kind and child-like; which is called "crying Abba, Father," Gal. iv. 6. Remember still the manner of the Spirit's working before mentioned,—that he doth it effectually, voluntarily, and freely. Hence sometimes the dispute hangs long,—the cause is pleading many years. The law seems sometimes to prevail, sin and Satan to rejoice; and the poor soul is filled with dread about its inheritance. Perhaps its own witness, from its faith, sanctification, former experience, keeps up the plea with some life and comfort; but the work is not done, the conquest is not fully obtained, until the Spirit, who worketh freely and effectually, when and how he will, comes in with his testimony also; clothing his power with a word of promise, he makes all parties concerned to attend unto him, and puts an end to the controversy.[24]

Yet the question remains an open one. The key issue is: In what way does the Spirit testify? In particular, in Romans 8:16 does Paul regard the Spirit's testimony as either (a) a testimony *to* our spirit or (b) a testimony *with* our spirit? Paul's verb, *summartureō* can be used in either sense.

In his commentary on Romans, C. E. B. Cranfield (now followed by others) argued forcefully that the testimony of the Spirit must be given *to* our spirits and not (along) *with* (the testimony of) our spirits. He asks: "What standing does our spirit have in *this* matter? Of itself it surely has no right to testify to our being sons of God."[25]

But there seem to be good reasons to reject this view, as follows.

1) Paul uses the verb *summartureō* elsewhere in Romans.[26] In both instances the idea seems to be that of a witness *with* rather than *to*. In addition, Romans 8 is replete with *sun* compound words. We are heirs *with* Christ (8:17); we suffer *with* Christ (v. 17); the creation groans *together* (v. 22); it travails *together* (v. 22); the Spirit helps us (*along with* us) in our weakness (v. 26); things work together *with* each other for our good (v. 28). This further suggests that the *sun* compound verb *summartureō* also carries the sense of "witness along with" rather than "witness to."

2) Contrary to Cranfield's contention, it is of considerable importance to stress that we do in fact bear witness to our standing

[24] John Owen, *Works*, 2:241–42.

[25] C. E. B. Cranfield, *A Critical and Exegetical Commentary on The Epistle to the Romans*, 2 vols. (Edinburgh: T & T Clark, 1979), 1:403. Cranfield is followed in this particular argument by Leon Morris, *The Epistle to the Romans* (Grand Rapids, MI: Eerdmans, 1998), 317. Apart from this specific argument, commentators in favor of the view that the Spirit bears witness "to" rather than "with" our spirits include Luther, Calvin, and Charles Hodge. Although unstated at this point in his commentary, in my own view the manner in which Cranfield's question is asked betrays a perspective heavily influenced by his undergirding indebtedness to the thought of Karl Barth, for whom a priori man's testimony in divine things is to be discounted. His question assumes the answer without giving biblical reasons. Does not a child have "the right" to testify to his or her being a child? If God has given us "the right to become children of God" (John 1:12) then surely as children we have the implied right to testify that this is what we are. The apostle John certainly thought so (1 John 3:1–2)!

[26] Rom. 2:15; 9:1.

before God. While in Galatians Paul says that "God has sent the Spirit of his Son into our hearts, crying, 'Abba! Father!,'"[27] in Romans it is the believer who cries, "Abba! Father!" thus expressing his or her own consciousness of being a son of God and therefore a joint heir with Christ.[28] In this context then the witness of the Spirit must, in some sense, be additional to that of our own spirit.

Cranfield asks a proper question: "What place does the witness of our spirits play in this matter of being assured we are children of God?" But the answer is not: "No part." Rather, Paul's point is that it is precisely in the weakness of our consciousness of our new identity, and the fragility that may attend our sense of assurance, that the Spirit bears his joint testimony. Thus the question of our status is confirmed by two witnesses. In essence Cranfield's interpretation makes the Spirit the sole witness.

This view is confirmed by the parallel, but not identical, statement Paul makes in Galatians 4:6. While in Romans 8 it is we who cry, "Abba! Father," in Galatians 4 it is the Spirit who utters this cry.

How are we to correlate these passages?

Here Paul's statement that it is only through the Spirit that a person can say, "Jesus is Lord," may provide a key.[29] It is the believer who bears witness thus to Christ; but it is only through the ministry of the Spirit in his life that this can take place. In the same way, it is the believer who cries, "Abba! Father!" but we can do this only as the Spirit bears his joint testimony with our spirit. The testimony of the Spirit of sonship is therefore not something existentially distinguishable from this testimony of our own spirits.

---

[27] Gal. 4:6.

[28] The point of the language of adopted *sons* in this context (as readers or viewers of such English classics as *Pride and Prejudice*, or for that matter *Downton Abbey*, will know) is that until relatively recently in a family it was sons who inherited. Paul is not here passing comment on the social structures of the first century (in a society in which marriage was normative, a woman was expected to share in her husband's inheritance, and in this way balance was anticipated). Rather, he is using the only term that will make sense of his theological point about our spiritual inheritance in Christ. It is worth noting in this context that Old Testament law wonderfully contrasts with Roman law and its derivatives by its specific inclusion of daughters in the line of inheritance, thanks to the daughters of Zelophehad in Numbers 27:1–11.

[29] 1 Cor. 12:3.

It is distinct from it, but it cannot be distinguished by an introspective analysis of our consciousness—any more than we can directly detect the work of the Spirit when we say, "Jesus is Lord!" B. B. Warfield finely expresses the balance here when he writes:

> Distinct in source, it is yet delivered confluently with the testimony of our own consciousness.[30]

Why Is the Witness of the Spirit So Special?

Paul speaks of the believer *crying*, "Abba! Father!" His verb, *krazō*, normally indicates a loud or needy cry. The verb is used in the Septuagint version[31] of the Old Testament in this sense.[32] It is found in the Gospels of the blind beggar crying out for help,[33] and of the crowd crying out, "Crucify him!"[34] and in Revelation of a woman in childbirth.[35]

The verb itself is onomatopoeic—its sound expresses the sharpness of the cry. Paul therefore seems to have in mind a loud cry that issues from a situation of great need. "Abba! Father!" is not a restful whisper of contentment and security. It is the cry of a child who has stumbled, tripped, and fallen, and is crying out for his or her father to come to help. It is the deepest instinct of the child in need.

This is precisely why the cry, "Abba! Father," is so significant. It expresses, at a point of intense need, an instinct that is absent from the unbeliever's consciousness. At best such a person may (and often does) cry out, "O God!" but not instinctively, "O Father!" That cry is the fruit of the ministry of the Spirit; it is his co-testimony with our spirit; even in the hour of darkness the believer

---

[30] B. B. Warfield, *Faith and Life* (New York: Longmans, Green, 1916), 184. Boston speaks of the Spirit's witness as being "with" our spirits, but also "to" us, without further explication. *Works*, 2:17. The impression given is that the "to" takes place in the context of and is existentially indistinguishable from the "with."

[31] The Greek translation of the Old Testament with which Paul was familiar.

[32] For example, in Ps. 141: "O Lord, I call upon you; hasten to me! Give ear to my voice when I call to you!" (v. 1).

[33] Luke 18:40.

[34] Matt. 20:30; Mark 15:13.

[35] Rev. 12:2.

possesses an instinct, a testimony: he or she knows him- or herself to be a child of God!

The one who confesses, "Jesus is Lord," by the Spirit is also the one who cries out in time of need, "Abba! Father!" by the same Spirit. John Murray was therefore right to affirm that even at its lowest ebb the believer's consciousness differs by a whole diameter from that of the unbeliever.

Notice what this means. Gospel assurance is not withheld from God's children even when they have not shown themselves to be strong. What good father would want his children's assurance of his love to be possible only when they have sufficient accomplishments in life to merit it? Shame on such a father! Yet how sad that we impute such an attitude to our heavenly Father.

It should be noted, however, that while the witness of the Spirit is not the same as the fruit of the Spirit, Paul does not present it as a kind of "Route B" to assurance for those whose lives are empty of that fruit. The witness of the Spirit goes hand in glove with the fruit of the Spirit, for Paul has been describing the believer as a person who walks according to the Spirit, not according to the flesh, who lives by putting to death the misdeeds of the body. So the Spirit's testimony with our spirits that we are God's sons does not exist in isolation from the family characteristics that the Spirit produces in our lives. His witness is a joint witness with our spirits and takes place within the complexity of our own consciousness of our sonship (however subliminal that may be). It is therefore not independent of the marks of God's grace in our lives. Paul had already made this clear in Romans 8:12–14 in relating the mortification of sin to the ongoing leading of the Spirit,[36] who bears witness with our spirits that we are sons of God.

B. B. Warfield once again well expresses the balance here when he says that the witness of the Spirit

[36] In this context it is noteworthy that the one reference in the New Testament to "the leading of the Spirit" is related not to "guidance" in general but to holiness in particular.

> is, in a word, not a substitute for the proper evidence of our childship; but a divine enhancement of that evidence. A man who has none of the marks of a Christian is not entitled to believe himself to be a Christian; only those who are being led by the Spirit of God are children of God. But a man who has all the marks of being a Christian may fall short of his privilege of assurance. It is to such that the witness of the Spirit is superadded, not to take the place of the evidence of "signs" but to enhance their effect and raise it to a higher plane; not to produce an irrational, unjustified, conviction, but to produce a higher and more stable conviction than he would be, all unaided, able to draw; not to supply the lack of evidence, but to cure a disease of the mind which will not profit fully by the evidence. . . . The Spirit . . . does not operate by producing conviction without reason; an unreasonable conclusion. Nor yet apart from the reason; equally unreasonable. Nor by producing more reasons for the conclusion. But by giving their true weight and validity to the reasons which exist and so leading to the true conclusion, with Divine assurance.
>
> The function of the witness of the Spirit of God is, therefore, to give to our halting conclusions the weight of His Divine certitude.[37]

Thus there are different strands of influences that together make up the complex harmony that is Christian assurance. Actual assurance has a psychological as well as a theological dimension. Precisely for this reason, even when we have developed a clear doctrine of assurance, our actual experience of it may be prevented by numerous obstacles. To some of these we must now turn.

---

[37] Warfield, *Faith and Life*, 187, 191.

11

"HINDRANCES STREW ALL THE WAY"

The New Testament regards the enjoyment of assurance of salvation as normal and healthy Christian experience. Ordinarily lack of assurance is a pathological condition, and this may be due to any one (or more) of a number of factors.[1] The diagnosis of the presence of these factors points us directly to the pastoral medicines Scripture provides in order to encourage assurance among God's people.

Rubble in the Foundation

Perhaps the single most subtle hindrance to assurance is also the most common, the tendency that has already been mentioned: confusing and compounding the foundation of salvation with the means by which assurance of salvation is confirmed and developed.

Thus, for example, fruitful Christian service will encourage assurance; we recognize the work of the Spirit creating new desires and dispositions. We ascribe that to him, and yet imperceptibly we begin to ground our assurance on the fruitfulness of our service rather than on the fact that by faith we have a great Savior. The foundation of our assurance does not lie in us, but in him.

[1] The title of this chapter is from verse 2 of Gerhard Tersteegen's hymn, "Thou hidden love of God," trans. John Wesley.

Abraham is a helpful biblical example for us here. He found assurance of God's promise that he and Sarah would have their own son not by focusing on his own or Sarah's body. These were the means, not the ultimate source, of God's blessing. Rather, he anchored his assurance on the promise of God, and thus he grew strong in faith as he gave glory to God.[2]

Another way to express this is to say that practical syllogisms have their place: assurance can be confirmed by the fruits of righteousness. Self-examination therefore also has its place: we are to examine ourselves to see whether we are in the faith.[3] But neither practical syllogism nor self-examination can encourage assurance of faith *apart from* the exercise of faith. We can never say: "Leaving trust in Christ to one side for the moment, let us see how assurance can be ours." This is the vital point Boston makes when he speaks about making sure we "run up unto faith" every evidence we see that we do indeed belong to Christ.[4] There is no assurance derived simply by examining our sanctification. We must never confuse the heart of assurance in faith with its confirmation in a life of service.

Inconsistency in Obedience

Inconsistent Christian living leads to lack of assurance. At least, it leads to a lack of true assurance (although, alas, not necessarily to a lack of self-assurance). Where there is no actual obedience to Christ, there will be no evidence of present love for him as Savior. Where salvation is not actualized, and a person has no consciousness of Christ's saving mercy, assurance will inevitably be hindered. Thus the Christian who has developed a pattern of disobedience in his or her life will lose assurance.

David's anguished cry of penitence in Psalm 51 illustrates this. As a consequence of his disobedience he confesses, "My sin is ever

[2] Rom. 4:18–21.
[3] 2 Cor. 13:5.
[4] Edward Fisher, *The Marrow of Modern Divinity* (Ross-shire, UK: Christian Focus, 2009), 197n.

before me."[5] His consciousness of forgiveness is clouded. He does not "hear joy and gladness."[6] He fears the complete loss of the Spirit's witness in his life. He loses all sense of the joy of salvation.[7] He has become like the double-minded man of whom James writes, full of doubt and unstable in all his ways.[8] Where consecration is in question, secret doubt must ultimately flourish and assurance wane. Such inconsistencies of life grieve the Holy Spirit and cause a loss of the sense that he dwells in us as the seal, the security of our redemption.[9]

The remedy? What is required here is an emetic labeled "Repentance."

Frowning Providence

Lack of assurance can also be related to misunderstanding the role of affliction in the Christian life. As William Cowper puts it, providence frowns, we see only "the clouds ye so much dread," and in response we "judge . . . the Lord by feeble sense."[10] It is a not-uncommon instinct among contemporary Christians to encounter difficulties and immediately conclude that they have fallen into divine disfavor.

We must always have the remedy to hand. We are not the best interpreters of divine providence. Nor is our conviction of the Father's love for us grounded in his providential ways with us. The fatal mistake here is to base our assurance of grace and salvation on the fact that "God is blessing my life." When we do so, we have no anchor if life turns sour. No, God anchors us to himself in Christ. He has *demonstrated* his love for us specifically in the cross—"God demonstrates his own love for us in this: While we were still sinners,

[5] Ps. 51:3.
[6] Ps. 51:8.
[7] Ps. 51:3, 8, 11, 12.
[8] James 1:8.
[9] Eph. 4:30.
[10] From Cowper's hymn entitled, "Light Shining Out of Darkness," better known by its first line, "God Moves in a Mysterious Way" (1774).

Christ died for us."[11] From the crucified Christ, now risen, ascended, and reigning, we must never allow our eyes to be diverted nor view providence except through cross-shaped lenses.

But, in addition, it is helpful for us to understand that affliction may have several different functions in the Christian life.

1) Afflictions may exercise a corrective function: "Before I was afflicted I went astray, but now I keep your word. . . . It is good for me that I was afflicted, that I might learn your statutes."[12] Chastened by pain and sorrow we return, prodigal-like, to our waiting Father's arms of love. "Yea," writes Samuel Rutherford, "when Christ in love giveth a blow it doth a soul good; and it is a kind of comfort and joy to it to get a cuff with the lovely, sweet, and soft hand of Jesus."[13]

2) Afflictions are also productive of character: tribulation produces patience, patience produces hope, says Paul.[14] Many of us think we are "relatively patient people." But it is a law of life that patience can be manifested, exercised, and strengthened only in circumstances that can create impatience! Thus afflictions become a divine investment in us as they build character.[15]

3) Afflictions also create the context in which our Lord reveals his grace and glory, to us and in and through us (all three dimensions are significant). Thus Paul's thorn in the flesh was the arena in which he discovered the sufficiency of grace and the strength of Christ made perfect in his weakness.[16] It was in his weakness that the power in his ministry was evidently God's and not his.[17] And it was through the comfort for his afflictions, which he found in God, that he was equipped to comfort others.[18] More than that,

[11] Rom. 5:8 (NIV).
[12] Ps. 119:67, 71.
[13] A. A. Bonar, ed., *The Letters of Samuel Rutherford* (London: Religious Tract Society, 1891), Letter 130, 255. A "cuff" is a blow to the head made by the hand.
[14] Rom. 5:3–4.
[15] Cf. Heb. 12:10–11.
[16] 2 Cor. 12:9.
[17] 1 Cor. 2:3–5.
[18] 2 Cor. 1:3–7.

had he asked the question "Lord, why are these things happening to me?" the chief answer would not have been found in Paul himself, but in others: "For we who live are always being given over to death for Jesus' sake, so that the life of Jesus also may be manifested in our mortal flesh. So death is at work in us, but life in you."[19]

Ultimately, of course, afflictions make us long for and prepare us for glory. Only when we have a sense of that glory's "eternal weight" do we see our afflictions in proper perspective as "light" and "momentary."[20]

What is vital is that we understand that these afflictions are controlled by the hand of our sovereign Father. Otherwise we do not see them in their true perspective, and our assurance of God's love will sink underneath them.

This is what happened to the author of Psalm 102. In his affliction he thought, "You have taken me up and thrown me down."[21] It was in this false light that he interpreted his sickness, his sense of isolation and desolation, and his difficult circumstances[22] as evidence that God had cruelly disposed of him. Only when his gaze was fixed again on who God really is did he begin to recover an assurance of God's sovereign purpose and covenant faithfulness. Then his sense of assurance revived to such an extent that he began to look forward to future blessings as well as present ones![23] The basic axiom here is that of Hebrews 12:5–6 (which is cited from the Greek version of Proverbs 3:11–12):

> My son, do not regard lightly the discipline of the Lord,
> nor be weary when reproved by him.
> For the Lord disciplines the one he loves,
> and chastises every son whom he receives.

[19] 2 Cor. 4:11–12.
[20] 2 Cor. 4:17.
[21] Ps. 102:10.
[22] Ps. 102:3–7.
[23] Ps. 102:25–28.

Sin's Guilt Removed, Dominion Ended, Presence Still Troubling

A fourth hindrance to assurance is a misunderstanding of how justification and regeneration change the Christian's relationship to sin. Younger Christians in particular can be misled by the dramatic transformation of the affections that takes place in regeneration—the joy of deliverance and the empowerment to obedience can be misunderstood as though sin's presence will rarely trouble them again. Subsequently any powerful reawakening of indwelling sin may lead to the (false) conclusion that perhaps, after all, their conversion was simply another passing phase and that they have never really become Christians at all.

This is where the New Testament theme of union with Christ is so important. Happily there has been a renaissance of writing on this theme in the first decade or so of the twenty-first century. Otherwise it would be a profound embarrassment to us as contemporary Christians with vast resources in books, seminars, conferences, podcasts, and the like to reflect on the fact that one eighteenth-century minister in a remote rural parish in the Borders of Scotland almost single-handedly introduced entire generations of Christians to the significance of their union with Christ. This was what Boston accomplished in his *Fourfold State*.[24]

But what are the implications of union with Christ? In essence this: through our union with him in his death we are set free from the penalty of our guilt, which he has paid for us; in union with him in his resurrection a complete, final, and irreversible righteousness is ours; in union with him in his death and resurrection we have been set free from the reign of sin. Yet we remain sinners in ourselves. Sin continues to indwell us; only when our regeneration comes to further flowering beyond this life will we be free from sin's presence.

These distinctions are vital. While guilt is gone and the reign of

[24]Thomas Boston, *Human Nature in Its Fourfold State* (London: Banner of Truth, 1964), 253–320 [*Works*, 8:177–231].

sin has ended, sin continues to indwell us and to beset us. It still has the potential to deceive us and to allure us. Once we understand this, we will not confuse the ongoing presence of sin with the absence of new life in us. Without that stability in our understanding, our assurance will be liable to ebb and flow.

No Theology without Psychology?

The great masters of "the cure of souls" have always recognized that natural temperament, whether forged by nature or nurture, can impact our enjoyment of assurance. This is not to deny that the Scriptures provide us with a clear doctrine of assurance. Nor is it to deny that assurance is Spirit given. But it is given to us and in us by the Spirit. As such it presses itself into our self-consciousness and self-awareness, and so how we think about the gospel impacts how we think about ourselves and who we are in relation to God.

Since assurance is a state of self-consciousness then, the truth of the gospel presses itself into the lives of individuals each with his or her own history, understanding of the gospel, life context, and psychological makeup. That being the case it may face greater obstacles in some Christians than it does in others. An individual may have quite strong faith, much grace, and rich evidence of fruitful service yet lack full assurance because of natural temperament. We are, after all, physico-psychical unities. A melancholic disposition de facto creates obstacles to the enjoyment of assurance—partly because it creates obstacles to the enjoyment of everything.

In this context, it is significant that the exhortation of the author of Hebrews to approach God in full assurance of faith (Heb. 10:22) is ultimately based on his exposition of the humanity of Christ as a merciful and sympathetic high priest, who has taken our frail flesh in a fallen world, shared our infirmities, experienced our temptations, and known what it is to pray with loud crying and tears.[25]

[25] Heb. 2:14; 4:14–16; 5:7–10.

Those who are of a melancholic spirit and are prone to doubt need to have their minds steeped in the assurances of divine grace that are to be found in such a Savior fully clothed in the garments of his gospel. Such believers often feel Christ to be distant, so what Hebrews does is bring him near.[26] The one whose penultimate recorded words in the frailty of pre-resurrection humanity began with an interrogative "My God, why?" is the God who is near enough to those who feel themselves distant from him to bring them into assurance of his grace. Christ, says Calvin, not only takes our flesh; he "is our flesh." Knowing that he knows us enables us to know our safety in him all the better.

An Enemy Has Done This[27]

Attacks of the Devil are also hindrances to assurance and often have this as their specific aim. Satan knows he cannot ultimately destroy those whom Christ saves. He is therefore determined to destroy our *enjoyment* of our new relationship to the Lord. The first satanic attack had this in view and sought to disrupt the first couple's confident assurance of God's benevolence: "Did God put you in this magnificent garden, and then mock you by forbidding you to eat from any of its trees?"[28]

This first temptation, as well as being historical, is surely also paradigmatic. Christians continue to experience what the Confession of Faith describes as having "the assurance of their salvation divers ways shaken, diminished, and intermitted . . . by some sudden or vehement temptation."[29]

These considerations appear to shed fresh light on the way Paul concludes his argument in Romans 8. His declaration of assurance in Romans 8:37–39 ("In all these things we are more than conquerors . . . [nothing] will be able to separate us from the

[26] 2:14ff.; 4:14ff.; 5:7ff.
[27] Matt. 13:28.
[28] Gen. 3:1.
[29] Westminster Confession of Faith, 18.4.

love of God in Christ Jesus our Lord") serves as the conclusion of a series of questions beginning in 8:31. Perhaps the most striking feature of these questions is the way in which each of them begins with the personal interrogative pronoun *who* and not the impersonal *what*.

Paul is not asking: "*What* can be against us? *What* charge can be brought against us? *What* can condemn us? *What* can separate us from the love of Christ?" Rather, his questions are: "*Who* . . . ? *Who* . . . ? *Who* . . . ? *Who* . . . ?" Satan, not circumstances, is in his crosshairs. It is in the face of all Satan's attempts to mar it that Paul enjoys the assurance that Christ keeps his people secure. As Samuel Rutherford again put it:

> If my inner side were turned out and all men saw my vileness, they would say to me "It is a shame for thee to stand still while Christ kiss thee and embrace thee." . . . But seeing Christ's love will shame me, I am content to be shamed.[30]

Paul's defense here is found in the fullness and finality of justification. Those who are as fully and permanently righteous before God as is his own Son, because united to him, may be certain that no thing and no one can ever separate them from the love of God in Jesus Christ.

"Let Not Conscience Make Thee Linger"[31]

It has long been an accepted principle: "Follow your conscience." But that cannot be the whole story for a Christian, for conscience can be unreliable. It can be misinformed. Indeed it needs to be reformed and recalibrated according to God's Word.

Interestingly, in this context the person who sees himself as having a "strong conscience" may rather fit into Paul's category of the

[30] Bonar, *Letters of Samuel Rutherford*, Letter 130, 256–57.
[31] From the hymn by Joseph Hart (1712–1768), "Come Ye Sinners, Poor and Needy."

"weak."[32] When that is the case, it is possible for our conscience to hinder assurance.[33] It may condemn us.

This seems to be the sense in which the apostle John speaks about our heart condemning us.[34] John also prescribes a general remedy: God is greater than our heart. He has provided a gracious salvation that our heart and conscience could not provide. This is good news if our conscience rightly condemns us.

But there is a further sense in which conscience may act as a hinderer of assurance: by restricting our liberty more narrowly than Scripture, and therefore God himself, does.

But how does this hinder assurance? Is this not really a matter of Christian liberty rather than assurance? Perhaps, but if conscience condemns us when God does not, we may so align conscience with God that we impute to him the restrictions that our own conscience has unbiblically placed upon our life.

When conscience draws lines of restriction around our life, permitting a narrower radius and smaller circumference in life than God's Word does, inevitably this distorts our view of God. The result? We view him (and, if we are preachers, we may also present him) in a restricted, less bountiful way. It is then not long before our disposition toward him is similar to that expressed by the elder brother in Jesus's parable. A spirit of bondage, rather than the enjoyment of assurance, is the end result. We have fallen prey to "the theology of Satan," for this is simply an echo of his insinuations to Adam and Eve in the garden of Eden.

Negligence

Loving and assured relationships require cultivation if they are to remain strong. God has provided us with important means to cul-

[32] As in Rom. 14:1–15:7, where the "weak" are actually those with "strong" consciences that will not permit them to eat certain foods and insist on the observance of certain days. Their consciences restrict them from the freedom the gospel provides.
[33] Notice how Paul speaks about "doubt" in Rom. 14:23.
[34] 1 John 3:19–20.

tivate the assurance we enjoy in our fellowship with Christ. But misuse or neglect of these ordinances of God (so-called means of grace[35]) may strangle assurance.

There are significant examples of this in Scripture. The downcast and disturbed spirit of Psalms 42 and 43 is related apparently to the fact that the author has been isolated from his previous sphere of worship, ministry, and fellowship. He used to go with the multitude and even lead the processions of praise. Now he is surrounded by unbelievers: "My bones suffer mortal agony as my foes taunt me, saying to me all day long, 'Where is your God?'"[36]

Hebrews is instructive again in this context. Its summons to draw near in full assurance of faith is coupled with the exhortation not to neglect worship and fellowship.[37] The ministry of God's Word; the mutual instruction believers give one another through singing psalms, hymns, and spiritual songs; the encouragement believers give each other as they stir one another up to love and good works—all these are, as divine ordinances, ways of promoting in us an increase of assurance that we really are Christ's, since we love him, we love his Word, and we love his people. The neglect of them correspondingly tends to hinder and diminish assurance.

Here the ministry of baptism and the Lord's Supper play important roles. Of course we do not get a different or a better Christ in the sacraments than we do in the Word, as Robert Bruce well said. But we may get the same Christ better, with a firmer grasp of his grace through seeing, touching, feeling, and tasting as well as hearing:

> Therefore I say, we get no other thing in the Sacrament than we get in the Word. Content yourself with this. But if this is so, the Sacrament is not superfluous.

[35] It will be clear by this point in our study that the expression "means of grace" carries certain liabilities, partly because of its medieval overtones, but also because of the way in which it objectivizes "grace" without specific reference to Christ.
[36] Ps. 42:4, 10 (NIV).
[37] Heb. 10:22–25.

> Would you understand, then, what new thing you get, what other things you get? I will tell you. Even if you get the same thing which you get in the Word, yet you get that same thing better. What is this "better"? You get a better grip of the same thing in the Sacrament than you got by the hearing of the Word. That same thing which you possess by the hearing of the Word, you now possess more fully. God has more room in your soul, through your receiving of the Sacrament, than he could otherwise have by your hearing of the Word only. What then, you ask, is the new thing we get? We get Christ better than we did before. We get the thing which we had more fully, that is, with a surer apprehension than we had before. We get a better grip of Christ now, for by the Sacrament my faith is nourished, the bounds of my soul are enlarged, and so where I had but a little grip of Christ before, as it were, between my finger and my thumb, now I get Him in my whole hand, and indeed the more my faith grows, the better grip I get of Christ Jesus. Thus the Sacrament is very necessary, if only for the reason that we get Christ better, and get a firmer grasp of Him by the Sacrament than we could have before.[38]

It is one of the wiles of the Devil to discourage the doubting believer from seeking fellowship, sitting under the Word, and coming to enjoy the gifts Christ has given to reassure us of his love for us. At such a time it is vital to remember that this, inter alia, is what the ministry of the Word and of baptism and the Supper are for. We ignore them to the peril of genuine assurance.

"The Clouds Ye So Much Dread"?[39]

The tradition in which the Marrow Brethren were nurtured believed that there was such a reality in the Christian life as:

[38] Robert Bruce, *The Mystery of the Lord's Supper*, trans. and ed. T. F. Torrance (London: James Clarke, 1958), 84–85. This Robert Bruce (1555–1631) was successor to John Knox and James Lawson as minister in St. Giles ("The High Kirk") Edinburgh. He is not to be confused with the earlier Scottish hero Robert the Bruce (1275–1329). His sermons on the sacraments, preached in St. Giles in 1589, belong to the blood stream of the Reformed view of the Lord's Supper.

[39] From the hymn by William Cowper (1731–1800), "God Moves in a Mysterious Way."

> God's withdrawing the light of his countenance, and suffering even such as fear him to walk in darkness and to have no light.[40]

It is not easy to trace in detail such spiritual withdrawals of the consciousness of assurance in the New Testament. There are hints. But this was clearly a reality in the post-Reformation church. In it Isaiah 51:10, which speaks of a child of light walking in the darkness, was often regarded as a key text urging resolute faith until the reality of salvation in Christ was accompanied by a sense of it. Here we need to bear in mind again that assurance is a psychological reality in the life of a person who is a psychosomatic unity, and in this context if such a sense of withdrawal becomes prolonged and there is never any relief, it is always wise to remember that we are bodies and not disembodied souls and consider the possibility of a physical cause. It is possible for a Christian to develop a lifestyle that induces lethargy of spirit, a melancholic disposition, and low levels of assurance. Some physical conditions have a similar effect on our spirits. All this should be borne in mind. Yet, at the end of the day, there is a promise given to us in Scripture from God himself: "Draw near to God, and he will draw near to you."[41] On that word the doubting soul may rest.

"The Hill of Zion Yields a Thousand Sacred Sweets"[42]

The Confession of Faith states that rather than produce antinomianism and license, assurance produces gracious fruits. In essence, it involves what the Westminster Divines describe as an enlarged heart:

> In peace and joy;
> In love and thankfulness;
> In strength and cheerfulness in duties.[43]

---

[40] Westminster Confession of Faith, 18.4.
[41] James 4:8.
[42] From the hymn by Isaac Watts (1674–1748), "Come We That Love the Lord."
[43] Westminster Confession of Faith, 18.3.

This conforms well to the joyful confidence of the New Testament church. There, assurance of salvation produced boldness in witness; eagerness and intimacy in prayer; poise in character in the face of trial, danger, and opposition; and joy in worship.

The lack of these is also evidence of a lack of the assurance that produces them, for rather than breed presumption or antinomianism, assurance produces true humility. Christian assurance is not self-assurance and self-confidence. It is the reverse: confidence in our Father, trust in Christ as our Savior, and joy in the Spirit as the Spirit of sonship, seal of grace, and earnest of our inheritance as sons and daughters of God. When these are the hallmarks of our lives, then the grace of the Lord Jesus Christ has come home to us in full measure.

And that, surely, is one of the great needs of our times.

CONCLUSION

These "Variations on Some Themes from the Marrow Controversy" have now reached a conclusion, ending not with a climactic crescendo but with the calmer notes of a deep and well-grounded assurance. The importance of the theme is by now, hopefully, clear. But what in essence is the message, and what implications does it carry?

At least for Thomas Boston, and for many since, the basic issues involved in this controversy have served as both a litmus test and a catalyst.

As *a litmus test* it increases our sensitivity to and unmasks the depths of the legal disposition that lingers, often hidden, in our hearts. "The human heart" wrote Calvin, "has so many crannies where vanity hides, so many holes where falsehood lurks, is so decked out with deceiving hypocrisy, that it often dupes itself."[1] The Marrow emphasis on the grace of God and on the God of grace, who in Christ is the gospel, functions as spiritual angiography—it injects a gospel dye into our spiritual heart arteries and reveals whether there has been any degree of gospel hardening.

As *a catalyst* it causes us to reflect on and wrestle with key theological and pastoral issues and thus leads us to a deeper appreciation of the nature of the gospel and how to live in it, preach

[1] John Calvin, *Institutes of the Christian Religion*, trans. F. L. Battles, ed. J. T. McNeill (Philadelphia: Westminster Press, 1960), 3.2.10.

it, and apply it. This not only affects us theologically, at the level of the understanding, but also acts on the affections and the will. It then begins to suffuse and transform Christian service—not least preaching. It creates the "tincture" that Thomas Boston said people began to notice in his ministry.

Boston was by no means unique in this respect. A century later, the same reality was noted in the life and ministry of Robert Murray M'Cheyne. It was perhaps most movingly expressed in a letter that lay unopened on his desk on the day he died at the age of twenty-nine. A correspondent writing to thank him for a sermon he had preached commented that it was not merely what he had said but *the manner in which he spoke* that had made an indelible impression.

Readers who have made their way thus far to the conclusion of *The Whole Christ* will be interested (and perhaps also amused) to learn that when the manuscript was first sent to the publisher it bore the title *Marrow for Modern Divines*. Any right-minded, twenty-first-century author knows that few if any self-respecting publishers today would publish a book under such a title. Presumably the *Marrow of Modern Divinity* would suffer the same fate. Marrows do not customarily fly off the shelf with the frequency a publisher desires! At the time it seemed worth putting the publishers to the test. In this case they passed! They renamed the book *The Whole Christ*.

You may have encountered that expression before in its time-honored Latin form, *Totus Christus*. It goes back at least as far as Augustine. It is echoed by John Calvin when he tells us that Christ does not consider himself to be complete apart from us. It is language that stresses that all our salvation comes to us from God the Father in Jesus Christ and through the Holy Spirit. This is salvation by grace alone, in Christ alone, through faith alone. It is Ephesians 1:3–14, Christ-centered, Trinity-honoring, eternity-rooted, redemption-providing, adoption-experiencing, holiness-producing, assurance-effecting, God-glorifying salvation. It was the fuller realization of this that created the "tincture" in Boston's life and ministry. In essence it involved his own heart being bathed in a new sense of God's graciousness in Christ. The result was that his preaching became an expression of Christ's preaching. To rework Paul's words in Ephesians 2:17, through Boston's ministry of the Word, Christ himself came to his first parish in Simprin, and later to Ettrick, and Christ himself preached peace.

Perhaps Paul had something like this in mind when he urged Timothy so to grow that in his ministry "all may see your progress."[2] For this is the essence of real growth in ministry. It is part of developing sanctification; in a word, it is Christlikeness. Perhaps it was the experience of—or at least the desire for—such ministry that led the Scottish forefathers to have a small brass plate fastened *inside* the pulpit of many churches, the words engraved on it being visible only to the preacher:

> Sir, we would see Jesus.[3]

For that to be true—whatever our gifts and calling—we who serve Christ and his people must first "see him more clearly, love him more dearly, and follow him more nearly."[4] If we do—no matter what our gifts are, or where our ministry may be—then the "tincture" of which Thomas Boston spoke will be seen again.

The prayer that this may be true again lies behind the writing of *The Whole Christ.*

---

[2] 1 Tim. 4:15.
[3] John 12:21 KJV.
[4] From a prayer of Richard of Chichester (c. 1197–1253).

Appendix

THOMAS BOSTON ON FAITH

Commenting on Paul's words to the Philippian jailer recorded in Acts 16:31, "Believe in the Lord Jesus, and you will be saved," the author of *The Marrow of Modern Divinity* wrote: ". . . that is, be verily persuaded in your heart that Jesus Christ is yours, and that you shall have life and salvation by him; that whatsover Christ did for the redemption of mankind, he did it for you." Thomas Boston adds the following extensive commentary in a note on the nature of faith.[1]

In this definition of saving faith, there is the general nature or kind of it, viz. a real persuasion, agreeing to all sorts of faith, divine and human—"Be verily persuaded"; the more special nature of it, an appropriating persuasion, or special application to oneself, agreeing to a convinced sinner's faith or belief of the law's curse (Gal. 3:10), as well as to it.—"Be verily persuaded in your hearts"; thus, "If thou shalt believe in thine heart that God . . . thou shalt be saved" (Rom. 10:9): and, finally, the most special nature of it, whereby it is distinguished from all other, namely, an appropriating persuasion of Christ being yours, &c. And as one's believing in one's heart, or appropriating persuasion of the dreadful tidings of the law, imports

[1] Edward Fisher, *The Marrow of Modern Divinity* (Ross-shire, UK: Christian Focus, 2009), 136–43.

not only an assent to them as true, but a horror of them as evil; so believing in the heart, or an appropriating persuasion of the glad tidings of the gospel, bears not only an assent to them as true, but a relish of them as good.

The parts of this appropriating persuasion, according to our author, are:

1. "That Jesus Christ is yours," viz. by the deed of gift and grant made to mankind lost, or (which is the same thing in other words) by the authentic gospel offer, in the Lord's own word; the which offer is the foundation of faith, and the ground and warrant of the ministerial offer, without which it could avail nothing.

That this is the meaning, appears from the answer to the question immediately following, touching the warrant to believe. By this offer or deed of gift and grant, Christ is ours before we believe; not that we have a saving interest in him, or are in a state of grace, but that we have a common interest in him, and the common salvation, which fallen angels have not (Jude 3); so that it is lawful and warrantable for us, not for them, to take possession of Christ and his salvation. Even as when one presents a piece of gold to a poor man saying, "Take it, it is yours"; the offer makes the piece really his in the sense and to the effect before declared; nevertheless, while the poor man does not accept or receive it; whether apprehending the offer too great to be real, or that he has no liking of the necessary consequents of the accepting; it is not his in possession, nor hath he the benefit of it; but, on the contrary, must starve for it all, and that so much the more miserably, that he hath slighted the offer and refused the gift.

So this act of faith is nothing else but to "believe God" (1 John 5:10); "to believe the Son" (John 3:36); "to believe the report" concerning Christ (Isa. 53:1); or "to believe the gospel" (Mark 1:15); not as devils believe the same, knowing Christ to be Jesus, a Saviour, but not their Saviour, but with an appropriating persuasion, or special application believing him to be our Saviour.

Now what this gospel report, record, or testimony of God, to be believed by all, is, the inspired penman expressly declares, "This is the record, that God hath given to us eternal life; and this life is in his Son" (1 John 5:11). The giving here mentioned, is not giving in possession in greater or lesser measure, but giving by way of grant, whereupon one may take possession. And the party to whom, is not the election only, but mankind lost. For this record is the gospel, the foundation of faith, and warrant to all, to believe in the Son of God, and lay hold on eternal life in him; but that God hath given eternal life to the elect, can be no such foundation nor warrant: for that a gift is made to certain select men, can never be a foundation or warrant for all men to accept and take it.

The great sin of unbelief lies in not believing this record or testimony, and so making God a liar: "He that believeth not God, hath made him a liar, because he believeth not the record that God gave of his Son. And this is the record," &c. (1 John 5:10–11). On the other hand, "He that hath received his testimony, hath set to his seal that God is true" (John 3:33). But the great sin of unbelief lies, not in not believing that God hath given eternal life to the elect; for the most desperate unbelievers, such as Judas and Spira,[2] believe that, and the belief of it adds to their anguish and torment of spirit; yet they do not set to their seal that God is true; but, on the contrary, they make God a liar, in not believing that to lost mankind, and to themselves in particular, God hath given eternal life in the way of grant, so as they, as well as others, are warranted and welcome to take possession of it, so fleeing in the face of God's record and testimony in the gospel (Isa. 9:6, John 3:16, Acts 4:12, Prov. 8:4, Rev. 22:17).

In believing of this, not in believing of the former, lies the dif-

[2] The name of Franciesco Spira (1502–1548) was a byword in the seventeenth and early eighteenth centuries for spiritual despair. Italian by birth, he had been influenced by the teaching of the Reformation but when arraigned had rejected his "errors." As a result, he felt his conscience inconsolably distressed because he had denied and rejected the truth. Despite the best efforts of many counselors he could not be comforted, and he died in despair later that same year. Nathaniel Bacon had published an English account of his death, *The Fearfulle estate of Francis Spira* (London, 1638). Many of the Puritans subsequently made reference to him, none more vividly than John Bunyan in his autobiography *Grace Abounding to the Chief of Sinners*. Bunyan's description of the Man in the Iron Cage whom Christian saw in Interpreter's house is clearly modeled on him.

ficulty, in the agonies of conscience; the which, nevertheless, till one do in greater or lesser measure surmount, one can never believe on Christ, receive and rest upon him for salvation. The truth is, the receiving of Christ doth necessarily presuppose this giving of him. There may, indeed, be a giving where there is no receiving, for a gift may be refused; and there may be a taking where there is no giving, the which is a presumptuous action without warrant; but there can be no place for receiving of Christ where there is not a giving of him before. "In the matter of faith (says Rollock, Lect. 10 on 2 Thess p. 126) there are two things: first there is a giver, and next there is a receiver. God gives, and the soul receives." The Scripture is express to this purpose: "A man can receive nothing, except it be given him from heaven" (John 3:27).

2. "And that you shall have life and salvation by him"; namely, a life of holiness, as well as of happiness—salvation from sin as well as from wrath—not in heaven only, but begun here and completed hereafter. That this is the author's notion of life and salvation agreeably to the Scripture, we have had sufficient evidence already, and will find more in our progress. Wherefore this persuasion of faith is inconsistent with an unwillingness to part with sin, a bent or purpose of heart to continue in sin, even as receiving and resting on Christ for salvation is.

One finds it expressed almost in so many words: "We believe that through the grace of the Lord Jesus Christ we shall be saved" (Acts 15:11). It is fitly placed after the former, for it cannot go before it, but follows upon it. The former is a believing of God, or believing the Son: this is a believing on the Son, and so is the same with receiving of Christ, as that receiving is explained; "But as many as received him, to them gave he power to become the sons of God, even to them that believe on his name" (John 1:12). It doth also evidently bear the soul's resting on Christ for salvation; for it is not possible to conceive a soul resting on Christ for salvation, without a persuasion that it shall have life and salvation by him;

namely, a persuasion which is of the same measure and degree as the resting is. And thus it appears, that there can be no saving faith without this persuasion in greater or lesser measure. But withal, it is to be remembered, as to what concerns the habit, actings, exercise, strength, weakness, and intermitting of the exercise of saving faith, the same is to be said of this persuasion in all points.

3. "That whatsoever Christ did for the redemption of mankind, he did it for you."—"I live by the faith of the Son of God, who loved me, and gave himself for me" (Gal. 2:20). This comes in the last place; and I think none will question, but whosoever believes in the manner before explained, may and ought to believe this, in this order. And it is believed, if not explicitly, yet virtually, by all who receive and rest on Christ for salvation.

From what is said, it appears that this definition of faith is the same, for substance and matter, though in different words, with that of the *Shorter Catechism*, which defines it, by "receiving and resting upon Christ alone for salvation, as he is offered to us in the gospel." In which, though the offer to us is mentioned last, yet it is evident it is to be believed first.

Objection: But the author's definition makes assurance to be of the essence of faith?

Answer: Be it so; however, he uses not the word assurance or assured in his definition; nor will anything contained in it amount to the idea now commonly affixed to that word, or to what is now in our days commonly understood by assurance. And—

(1.) he doth not here teach that assurance of faith whereby believers are certainly assured that they are in the state of grace, the which is founded upon the evidence of grace, of which kind of assurance the *Westminster Confession* expressly treats (18:1–3); but an assurance which is in faith, in the direct acts thereof, founded upon the word allenarly[3] (Mark 16:15–16, John 3:16); and this is nothing else but a fiducial appropriating persuasion.

[3] A Scottish word meaning "only" or "solely."

(2.) He doth not determine this assurance or persuasion to be full, or to exclude doubting: he says not, be fully persuaded, but, be verily persuaded, which speaks only the reality of the persuasion, and doth not at all concern the degree of it. And it is manifest, from his distinguishing between faith of adherence, and faith of evidence, that, according to him, saving faith may be without evidence. And so one may have this assurance or persuasion, and yet not know assuredly that he hath it, but need marks to discover it by; for though a man cannot but be conscious of an act of his own soul as to the substance of the act, yet he may be in the dark as to the specifical nature of it, than which nothing is more ordinary among serious Christians. And thus, as a real saint is conscious of his own heart's moving in affection towards God, yet sometimes doth not assuredly know it to be the true love of God in him, but fears it to be an hypocritical flash of affection; so he may be conscious of his persuasion, and yet doubt if it is the true persuasion of faith, and not that of the hypocrite.

This notion of assurance, or persuasion in faith, is so agreeable to the nature of the thing called believing, and to the style of the holy Scripture, that sometimes where the original text reads faith or believing, we read, assurance, according to the genuine sense of the original phrase; "Whereof he hath given assurance" (Acts 17:31); orig. "faith," as is noted in the margin of our Bibles. "Thou shalt have none assurance of thy life" (Deut. 28:66); orig. "Thou shalt not believe in thy life." This observation shows, that to believe, in the style of the holy Scripture, as well as in the common usage of mankind in all other matters, is to be assured or persuaded, namely, according to the measure of one's believing.

And the doctrine of assurance, or an appropriating persuasion in saving faith, as it is the doctrine of the holy Scripture (Rom. 10:9; Acts 15:11; Gal 2:20), so it is a Protestant doctrine, taught by Protestant Divines against the Papists, and sealed with the blood of martyrs in Popish flames; it is the doctrine of Reformed churches abroad, and the doctrine of the Church of Scotland.

The nature of this work will not allow multiplying of testimonies on all these heads. Upon the first, it shall suffice to adduce the testimony of Essenius, in his *Compendium Theologiae*, the system of divinity taught the students in the College of Edinburgh, by Professor Campbell.

"There is, therefore," says he, "in saving faith, a special application of gospel benefits. This is proved against the Papists

(1.) From the profession of believers (Gal. 2:20), "I live by that faith of the Son of God, who loved me, and gave himself for me."—(Ps. 23:1), "The Lord is my shepherd, I shall not want; in cotes of budding grass he makes me to lie down, &c. Though I walk through the valley of the shadow of death, I will not fear evil; for thou art with me," &c. And Job 19:25; Philippians 1:21–23; Romans 8:33–39, 10:9, 10; 2 Corinthians 5:1–6, with 2 Corinthians 4:13, &c." Essen. Comp. Theol. chap. 2, sect. 12.

And speaking of the method of faith, he says, it is '4. That according to the promises of the gospel, out of that spiritual desire, the Holy Spirit also bearing witness in us, we acknowledge Christ to be our Saviour, and so receive and apply him, every one to ourselves, apprehending him again, who first apprehended us (2 Cor. 4:13, Rom. 8:16, John 1:12, 2 Tim 1:12, Gal 2:20, Phil 3:12). The which is the formal act of saving faith. 5. Furthermore, that we acknowledge ourselves to be in communion with Christ, partakers of all and every one of his benefits. The which is the latter act of saving faith, yet also a proper and elicit act of it.—7. [sic] That we observe all these acts above mentioned, and the sincerity of them in us; and THENCE gather, that we are true believers, brought into the state of grace,' &c. Ibid. sect. 21. Observe here the two kinds of assurance before distinguished.

Peter Brulie, burnt at Tournay, anno 1545, when he was sent for out of prison to be examined, the friars interrogating him before the magistrate, he answered—"How it is faith that bringeth unto us salvation; that is, when we trust unto God's promises, and believe steadfastly, that for Christ his son's sake our sins are forgiven us" (Sleid. Comment. in English book 16,. 217).

Mr Patrick Hamilton, burnt at St. Andrews about the year 1527. "Faith," says he, "is a sureness; faith is a sure confidence of things which are hoped for, and a certainty of things which are not seen. The faith of Christ is to believe in him, that is, to believe in his word, and to believe that he will help thee in all thy need, and deliver thee from all evil" (Mr Patrick's Articles, *Knox's History*, p. 9).

For the doctrine of foreign churches on this point, I shall instance only in that of the Church of Holland, and the Reformed Church of France:

> Q. What is a sincere faith?
>
> A. It is a sure knowledge of God and his promises revealed to us in the gospel, and a hearty confidence that all my sins are forgiven me for Christ's sake (Dutch Brief Compend. of Christian Religion, Vra. 19, bound up with the Dutch Bible).
>
> *Minister*. Since we have the foundation upon which the faith is grounded, can we rightly from thence conclude what the true faith is?
>
> *Child*. Yea; namely, a certain and steady knowledge of the love of God towards us, according as, by his gospel, he declares himself to be our Father and Saviour, by the means of Jesus Christ (*Catechism of the Reformed Church of France*, bound up with the French Bible, Dimanche 18).

To obviate a common prejudice, whereby this is taken for an easy effort of fancy and imagination, it will not be amiss to subjoin the question immediately following there.

> M. Can we have it of ourselves, or cometh it from God?
>
> C. The Scripture teacheth us that it is a singular gift of the Holy Spirit, and experience also showeth it (Ibid.).

Follows the doctrine of the Church of Scotland on this head.

> "Regeneration is wrought by the power of the Holy Ghost, working in the hearts of the elect of God an assured faith in the promise of God, revealed to us in his word; by which faith we apprehend Christ Jesus, with the graces and benefits promised in him" (*Old Confess*. art. 3).

> "This our faith, and the assurance of the same, proceeds not from flesh and blood, that is to say, from no natural powers within us, but is the inspiration of the Holy Ghost" (Ibid. art. 12).

For the better understanding of this, take the words of that eminent servant of Christ, Mr John Davidson, minister of Salt-Preston, alias Preston-Pans (of whom see the fulfilling of the Scripture, p. 361), in his Catechism, p. 20, as follows:

> "And certain it is, that both the enlightening of the mind to acknowledge the truth of the promise of salvation to us in Christ, and the sealing up of the certainty thereof in our hearts and minds (of the which two parts, as it were, faith consists), are the works and effects of the Spirit of God, and neither of nature nor art."

The Old Confession above mentioned is, "The Confession of Faith, professed and believed by the Protestants within the realm of Scotland, published by them in Parliament, and by the estates thereof ratified and approved, as wholesome and sound doctrine, grounded upon the infallible truth of God" (Knox's Hist. lib. 3. p. 263). It was ratified at Edinburgh, July 17, 1560, Ibid. p. 279. And this is the Confession of our Faith, mentioned and sworn to in the national covenant, framed about twenty years after it.

In the same national covenant, with relation to this particular head of doctrine, we have these words following, viz. "We detest and refuse the usurped authority of that Roman antichrist—his general and doubtsome faith." However the general and doubtsome faith of the Papists may be clouded, one may, without much ado, draw these two plain conclusions from these words:

> '1. That since the Popish faith abjured is a doubtsome faith, the Protestant faith, sworn to be maintained, is an assured faith, as we heard before from the Old Confession, to which the covenant refers.
>
> '2. That since the Popish faith is a general one, the Protestant faith must needs be an appropriating persuasion, or a faith of special application, which, we heard already from Essenius, the Papists do deny. As for a belief and persuasion of the mercy of God in Christ, and of Christ's ability and willingness to save all that come unto him, as it is altogether general, and hath nothing of appropriation or special application in it, so I doubt if the Papists will refuse it. Sure, the Council of Trent, which fixed and established the abominations of Popery, affirms that no pious man ought to doubt of the mercy of God, of the merit of Christ, nor of the virtue and efficacy of the sacraments' (*Concil. Trid.* cap. 9).

I hope none will think the council allows impious men to doubt of these; but withal they tell us, "It is not to be affirmed, that no man is absolved from sin and justified, but he who assuredly believes, that he himself is absolved and justified." Here they overturn the assurance and appropriation, or special application of saving faith maintained by the Protestants; and they thunder their anathemas against those who hold these in opposition to their general and doubtsome faith. "If any shall say, that justifying faith is nothing else but a confidence of the mercy of God pardoning sins for Christ's sake, or that confidence is it alone by which they are justified, let him be accursed" (Ibid. cap. 13, can. 12). "If any shall say, that a man is absolved from sin, and justified by that, that he assuredly believes himself to be absolved and justified, let him be accursed" (Ibid. can. 14).

Moreover, in the national covenant, as it was renewed in the years 1638 and 1639, mention is made of public catechisms, in which the true religion is expressed in the Confession of Faith (there) above written, (i.e., the national covenant, otherwise called the Confession of Faith), and former Large Confession (viz. the Old Confession), is said to be set down. The doctrine on this head, contained in these catechisms, is here subjoined.

M. Which is the first point?
C. To put our whole confidence in God.
M. How may that be?
C. When we have assured knowledge that he is almighty, and perfectly good.
M. And is that sufficient?
C. No.
M. What is then further required?
C. That every one of us be fully assured in his conscience, that he is beloved of God, and that he will be both his Father and Saviour (*Calvin's Cat.* used by the Kirk of Scotland, and approved by the *First Book of Discipline*, quest. 8–12).

This is the catechism of the Reformed Church of France, mentioned before:

M. Since we have the foundation whereupon our faith is builded, we may well gather hereof what is the right faith?
C. Yea, verily; that is to say, it is a sure persuasion and steadfast knowledge of God's tender love towards us, according as he hath plainly uttered in his gospel, that he will be both a Father and a Saviour unto us, through the means of Jesus Christ (Ibid. quest. 111).
M. By what means may we attain unto him there?
C. By faith, which God's Spirit worketh in our hearts, assuring us of God's promises made to us in his holy Gospel. (The manner to examine children before they be admitted to the supper

of the Lord, quest. 16. This is called the Little Catechism, Assembly 1592, sess. 10).

Q. What is true faith?
A. It is not only a knowledge, by which I do steadfastly assent to all things which God hath revealed unto us in his word; but also an assured affiance, kindled in my heart by the Holy Ghost, by which I rest upon God, making sure account, that forgiveness of sins, everlasting righteousness, and life, are bestowed, not only upon others, but also upon me, and that freely by the mercy of God, for the merit and desert of Christ alone. (*The Palatine Catechism*, printed by public authority, for the use of Scotland.)

This famous Catechism is used in most of the Reformed Churches and schools; particularly in the Reformed Churches of the Netherlands, and is bound up with the Dutch Bible. "As for the Church of Scotland, the Palatine Catechism," says Mr Wodrow, in the dedication to his History, "was adopted by us, till we had the happiness to join with the venerable Assembly at Westminster. Then indeed it gave place to the *Larger* and *Shorter Catechisms* in the Church: nevertheless it continued to be taught in grammar schools."

Q. What thing is faith in Christ?
A. A sure persuasion that he is the only Saviour of the world, but OURS in special, who believe in him. (*Craig's Catechism*, approved by the General Assembly, 1592.)

To these may be added the three following testimonies:

Q. What is faith?
A. When I am persuaded that God loves me and all his saints, and freely giveth us Christ, with all his benefits. (*Summula Catechismi*, still annexed to the Rudiments of the Latin tongue, and taught in grammar schools to this day, [1726,] since the Reformation.)

What is thy faith?
My sure belief that God both may and will save me in the blood of Jesus Christ, because he is almighty, and has promised so to do. (Mr James Melvil's Catechism, in his *Propine of a Pastor to his People*, p. 44, published in the year 1598.)

Q. What is this faith, that is the only instrument of this strait conjunction between Christ crucified and us?
A. It is the sure persuasion of the heart, that Christ by his death and resurrection hath taken away our sins, and, clothing us with his own righteousness, has thoroughly restored us to the favour of God *(Mr John Davidson's Catechism,* p. 46).

In the same national covenant, as it was renewed, 1638 and 1639, is expressed an agreement and resolution to labour to recover the purity of the gospel as it was established and professed before the [there] foresaid novations; the which, in the time of Prelacy, then cast out, had been corrupted by a set of men in Scotland addicted to the faction of Laud, Archbishop of Canterbury. In the year 1640, Mr Robert Baily, then minister of Kilwinning, afterwards one of the Commissioners from Scotland to the Westminster Assembly, wrote against that faction, proving them guilty of Popery, Arminianism, &c.: and on the head of Popery, thus represents their doctrine concerning the nature of faith, viz. "That faith is only a bare assent, and requires no application, no personal confidence; and that that personal application is mere presumption, and the fiction of a crazy brain" (Hist. Motuum in Regno Scotia, p. 517).

Thus, as above declared, stood the doctrine of the Church of Scotland, in this point, in her confessions, and in public catechisms, confirmed by the renewing of the national covenant, when, in the year 1643, it was anew confirmed by the first article of the Solemn League and Covenant, binding to (not the Reformation, but) the preservation of the Reformed Religion in the Church of Scotland, in doctrine, &c., and that before the *Westminster Confession, Larger and Shorter Catechisms*, were in being.

When the *Westminster Confession* was received, anno 1647, and the *Larger and Shorter Catechisms*, anno 1648, the General Assembly did, in their three acts, respectively approving them, expressly declare them to be in nothing contrary to the received doctrine of this Kirk. And put the case they were contrary thereto in any point, they could not in that point be reckoned the judgment of the Church of Scotland, since they were received by her, as in nothing contrary to previous standards of doctrine, to which she stands bound by the covenants aforesaid. But the truth is, the doctrine is the same in them all.

> "This faith is different in degrees, weak or strong; growing in many to the attainment of a full assurance." (*WCF* 14:3). Now, how faith can grow in any to a full assurance, if there be no assurance in the nature of it, I cannot comprehend.

> "Faith justifies a sinner—only as it is an instrument, by which he receiveth and applieth Christ and his righteousness" (*WLC* 73).

> "By faith they receive and apply unto themselves Christ crucified, and all the benefits of his death" (*WLC* 170).

> Q. When do we by faith receive and apply to ourselves the body of Christ crucified?
> A. While we are persuaded, that the death and crucifixion of Christ do no less belong to us, than if we ourselves had been crucified for our own sins; now this persuasion is that of true faith (*Sum. Catech.*).

> "Faith in Jesus Christ is a saving grace, whereby we receive and rest upon him alone for salvation, as he is offered to us in the gospel" (*WSC*).

Now, to perceive the entire harmony betwixt this and the old definitions of faith, compare with it, as to the receiving therein mentioned, the definition above cited from the Old Confession, art. 3. viz. "An assured faith in the promise by which they apprehend Christ," &c. Mr John Davidson joins them thus:

> Q. What is faith?
> A. It is an hearty assurance, that our sins are freely forgiven us in Christ. Or after this manner: It is the hearty receiving of Christ offered in the preaching of the word and sacraments, by the working of the Holy Spirit, for the remission of sins, whereby he becomes one with us, and we one with him, he our head, and we his members (Mr John Davidson's Catechism, p. 24).

As to the resting mentioned in the Westminster definition, compare the definition above cited from the *Palatine Catechism*, viz. "A sure confidence whereby I rest in God, assuredly concluding, that to me is given forgiveness," &c. (quest. 21). See also *Larger Catechism*, quest. last:

> "We by faith are emboldened to plead with him that he would, and quietly to rely upon him that he will, fulfil our request; and to testify this our desire and assurance, we say, Amen."

In which words, it is manifest, that quietly to rely upon him that he will, &c. (the same with resting on him for, &c.) is assurance in the sense of the Westminster Divines.

GENERAL INDEX

SCRIPTURE INDEX